THE OCHRE ROBE

Worüber man nicht sprechen kann,
darüber muss man schweigen

WITTGENSTEIN, *Tractatus Logico-Philosophicus*

Whereof one cannot speak,
thereof one must be silent

MISS ANSCOMBE's translation

AGEHANANDA BHARATI

THE OCHRE ROBE

AN AUTOBIOGRAPHY

DOUBLEDAY & COMPANY, INC.
GARDEN CITY, NEW YORK
1970

The Ochre Robe was first published by George Allen and Unwin Ltd., London, in 1962. Doubleday edition is published by arrangement with The University of Washington Press.

Allen and Unwin Ltd

Also by Agehananda Bharati:

THE TANTRIC TRADITION

TO THE MEMORY OF

BERTRAND RUSSELL

CONTENTS

INTRODUCTION

Samkarācārya, the illustrious founder of my order, reportedly died at the age of thirty-three, having embraced the monastic life at eight. At the time of his death he had traversed India several times on foot, founded the most prestigious order of Hindu India, and ordained four learned and active disciples who were to create its four monastic headquarters in the four corners of India. He wrote at least five important commentaries and treatises, though well over eighty are ascribed to him. He had restored the brahmanic tradition which had been virtually absorbed in a popular mixture of Hindu and Buddhist elements and safely established himself as the leading scholastic philosopher of his day.

My intentions match those of my master of twelve hundred years ago, at least in part. I, too, desire to uphold, preserve, interpret, and further the brahmanical Hindu tradition, to defend it against falseness and mediocrity, against the shallow neo-eclectic and other infinitely more sinister foes than the ones encountered by Samkarācārya. His opponents were limited regionally, linguistically, and ideologically. I, on the other hand, have had to tackle the religious establishment in India and the wide-eyed, well-intended, but ill-informed admirers of India's wisdom in the West.

The Hindu monastic ordination bestows a character *indelebilis* like that of the Catholic priest; it cannot be refuted or rescinded except by marriage or death. The first of the two for me is quite unlikely; the latter is not, considering travel hazards, pollution, cholesterol, the rat race, departmental and committee meetings, and the more general mortality afflicting men. I have been given some beautiful land by devotees in Kerala, the extreme South-west of India, amid a high, cool, tropical forest overlooking the Arabian Sea from a steep promontory. I plan to build a monastery there of my design; it will be a new house within the Sannyasi Order, but one with a library stocked with modern philosophical, anthropological, and other critical literature in addition to the corpus of the obligatory Sanskrit classics. It will have pleasant living quarters for monks and novices, perhaps even a guest house at some distance for visiting laymen and for women who, of course, cannot enter the monastic premises proper. The monks will be trained both in the Hindu monastic lore and in the modern liberal arts, which are a totally Western creation. Before that I have about another twenty years as professor of anthropology. If I live that long I shall presumably write and lecture. After that I shall return to India and to my cloister.

The chief object I had in mind when I wrote this book was to offer my very personal, irrefutably unique experiences as the basis for a way of life which presents a valid, powerful, viable, and no longer utopian alternative to the good life in the American sense, or to its milder alternatives in Europe. Let me state now that I am indeed making a plea for the monastic life. I think I am illustrating here a definitive answer to the young and not-so-young Euro-American seeker of a non-establishmentarian alternative. I think this autobiography carries a message for the neo-mystic, just as it does for the sensitive critic and for a wide range of people somehow clustered within and around the counter-culture brilliantly presented and analyzed by Theodore Roszak.[1] I hope to present what a good many modern people have been looking for, people who are willing to love and explode, but are unable to find their equilibrium in an increasingly love- and ecstasyless universe.

First of all, I am trying to develop a new kind of human-

---

[1]Theodore Roszak, *The Making of a Counter Culture* (New York, 1969).

ism, one that values *men* but denies that the value of *mankind* is something beyond and above men. I want to show that while humanism can be universal, it must be fastidious, selective, and exclusive in a manner which will be grasped as this book is read. A humanist, as I see him, does not seek out human beings as such, but only certain human beings, namely people with whom he can and does establish an encounter, one of love or passion, or of confrontation, or both; that is, people who can be helped by him, whom he can be helped by, and who want this possibility of mutual help and fascination to begin and to last, or to cease when it becomes dull. The humanist, then, seeks out people with whom voluntary, intensive communication is possible, and desired by him. The others are just neighbors, fellow human beings in the best scriptural tradition, and my humanist looks upon them as human beings like himself, less interesting perhaps, but beings who must not be harmed. He ignores people with whom he cannot communicate, but he does hope that others can.

In spite of, or rather as a result of these structural strictures, the humanism which I propose is universal in that any man of good will can pursue it. It is tough, fastidious; it chooses its partners and desires to be chosen by them. The pathetic wish to be loved by everyone, pathological in many cases but well nigh universal with middle-class Euro-Americans is something very different from my humanist's desire to be chosen; he wants to be chosen by the people he wants to choose.

Communication means courtship, successful courtship; it must be a two-way affair. It generates a deliberate mutual relationship. It does not take mutual communication for granted, even when it has been established. There are dozens of refined methods for the winning of souls; the most important paradigm, of course, is the wooing between men and women, with the orgasmic core at its center. We have in orgasm an overlap between mystical, humanistic experience and ordinary people's experience.

To the non-initiate this must remain a paradox: that to the mystic and the lecher the erotic segment of life is far more important than it is to most people in most societies.

The monastic life which I recommend accordingly is very different indeed from that of the Christian. Anyone familiar with the non-Christian, Asian religious orders will understand my idea of the monastic life better than those who hold monasticism synonymous with chastity in the medieval sense. The Christian tradition does share some vows with non-Christian Indian traditions which preceeded and informed it. The implications for the individual choosing between the two traditions are radically different. I could no doubt explain the difference in theory, but I hope that this report will make it clearer by its concrete statement of concrete events; there is some discursive speculation interspersed in my report, commentary as it were on my peregrinations through India and other lands. My view of monasticism derives its inspiration from the Hindu tradition, but some modern Hindus repudiate it and prove to be more shocked than equally sophisticated Westerners when I propound my monastic doctrines, reinterpreting the concept of *brahmacarya.*

It is important to understand before the book is read that the monasticism which I practised in India was not typical of the monastic life appreciated by modern Hindu society. On the contrary, I actively challenge ordinary monasticism in India, as represented by some five million people who have taken some sort of monastic ordination. I present a monastic alternative which has its roots in a somewhat obscure, yet well rooted segment of Indian monasticism. In the seventh chapter I shall describe these roots which are truly embedded in Indian monasticism but which lie hidden deep in a dark, unexplored, partly inaccessible niche of the Indian lore. If recognized at all, the tantric tradition has been viewed with hostility and almost total incomprehension even in India. My own thinking, and the trouble and travail which I experienced have reinforced my conviction that my idea of a monastic alternative reflects more accurately the essence of the spiritual tradition of India than that which modern Hindus consider proper.

Ethical humanism has become a substitute for organized religion to many, as witness the numerous humanistic organizations and publications which insist that humanism replaces religion or that if there must be such a thing as religion, it must be ethical humanism. The implication is that the specifically religious experience should be eschewed. This is nonsense. I certainly grant that if we wish to be autonomous individuals in the coming century, humanism is by far preferable to any dogmatic, ecclesiastic religion. However I do not believe that people, including intellectuals in the strictest sense, can find the total wealth of spirit without authentic ecstatic religious experience; and by this I mean mysticism and the mystical practice. I do not believe that even the most consummate communication between man and woman provides a recipe for complete fulfillment. Such fulfillment is generated by a combination of personal communication *and* mystical practice. I wish to propound a humanistic mysticism, wherein two different kinds of experimentation may generate genuine interpersonal relations between people who choose each other by consent, as well as the mystical union of the solitary individual with the cosmic matrix where nothing whatever, no person, and no army can harm him, a state of complete immunity – not that of the old-time escetic who is, as the Indian text says, 'like unto a stone', but immune and living with warmth, communication, and potential ecstasy – not joy, if you please, for joy is a stale pulpit word of little avail.

Humanistic mysticism rests squarely on an undogmatic, experimentally open, yet tradition-reinforced meditative practice. What do I mean by 'undogmatic'? We cannot fall back on Christianity. In this post-Christian era, silence is the only thing which makes sense – the mystical way recaptures the ecstasy which early saints experienced. The difference is that the mystic doesn't talk about it. Even

Eastern cults are no longer dishes that can be devoured by sheer hunger; uncritical man is not the religious man of the future. With all their differences and with all their trivial similarities, the official teachings of the West and of India have one thing in common, they are opposed to humanism. They demand and enjoin attitudes which reject man in the final analysis as an individual, or at least put him very low in their hierarchies. They regard the empirical human being either with condescension and contempt or with downright hate; if a person tries to enumerate the slurs and the insults the prophets, teachers, and priests have hurled against themselves, each other, and man in general, one will get a sickening taxonomy – man is polluted, frail, sinful, wicked, deviant, unholy, ignorant. True, some of the great religions say proper things about man, but only by dint of his being God's creature.

I reject any set of values, Hindu, Buddhist, Judaeo-Christian, Islamic or whatever which does not put all human beings on the same shelf in the cosmic household. All men have the same dignity; this is quite fundamental. But it does not mean, of course, that all men are or ought to be interesting to all men. I experienced a union within myself where I found the mystical traditions of India, yoga, vedānta, and tantra highly congenial; yet any other contemplative tradition can provide a starting point. What I am really after is something new: a consummate syncretism of intellectual, mystical, *and* sensuous elements, each perfectly matched with the other. Hitherto the three were *de jure* exclusive of one another. True, well-read mystics claimed to be intellectuals, but the sort of discursive efforts they made and suggested for emulation were curtailed by implicit rules of exclusion; read books, yes, if they do not deflect you from the spirit; make love, yes, but only if it doesn't weaken you; get involved, yes, but only for the purpose of proving your strength to withdraw. There was very little radical risk in traditional mysticism, it alone was to be taken seriously; forays into the world were permitted only if retreat to the eternal citadel was guaranteed. I visualize a radical syncretism, with no compromise between the mystical and the intellectual. I am convinced that meditation and intellectual humanism together can generate a unique combination which will eclipse the lopsided, arid, 'scientific', non-involved scientism prevalent at Western academies until the late fifties, before the campus revolt began to bother administrators. It will also avoid the equally slanted, anti-intellectual mysticism of much older date based on the mistaken ascription of ontological status to subjective experience, or on some sort of revelation which happened to provide a historical matrix for the old-time mystic.

I must emphasize the parallel nature of these two discrete ventures, that of the intellectual life and that of the mystical, since they cannot operate with harmony in one human being unless he grasps their fundamental discreteness in the first place. In India today there are dozens if not hundreds of schools, sects, and *ashramas* constituting the Hindu Renaissance, which this book will discuss. No one so far has dealt with the actual mystical practitioner in India today; the orientalists have kept their noses in the Sanskrit texts, the anthropologists still keep charting kinship systems, and the modern Hindu who wants to extol Hinduism often encourages intellectually dishonest proponents of it. Now I think it is exceedingly important that the critics, the young and not so young in or marginal to our new counter-culture, the very people Theodore Roszak writes about, get better acquainted with the Indian scene precisely because India has become a sort of catch-all refuge for the seekers. If I exposed some clay feet on which the Indian edifice stands today, let me assure my readers that some of the feet are of flesh and gold as well; they need to be extricated from the morass of the false which abounds in India as elsewhere.

The time has come to realize that the religions and moralities of the world teach very, very different things indeed in both essence and accident. This we will discover if we take the trouble to penetrate behind the smooth facade of sermonistic pleasantry from all pulpits, Hindu, Buddhist, Judaeo-Christian. Humanitarian smugness is the style of many mystics and of other good men. Each of us had to choose his own meditation, his own religion. The brighter younger generation is not really very worried about lack of communication with parents or peers; they want to know what is inside themselves as individuals, as new persons, perhaps as potential mystics and philosophers, and this is something fresh and unique in this generation.

One person may consummate his mystical ambition through strict, unsexed asceticism; another will find it through the passionate love for a theologically defined godhead; another again may reach it through spending his days in selfless action, surrendering the fruits thereof to divinity; another will succeed by the maximization of his cognitive potential; yet another, under the guidance of an experienced master, will find it through the arcane physical consummation in the embrace of a mystically trained partner. When all has been said we shall have found that mysticism, like the love of the *Sufi* poets and the troubadours, has something illicit about it; society does not permit the mystic to advertise his goods except under cover and under the guise of conformity, through a language that has passed the censorship of the religious establishment, its priests, doctors, teachers, legislators. The intimacy of the mystical union is as tabu to the institutionally religious as is the intimacy of the sexual act and the euphoria of the psychedelic scene. Such choice of a contemplative method is impossible for the serious devotee of a gospel which permits only one way and which makes the experience of one founder of one single faith universally valid and binding. The fact remains that the humanistic mysticism which I want to convey using my own career as a paradigm, cannot be practised by the orthodox Christian, Muslim, or Jew, if orthodoxy is to be identified with the consensus of sacerdotal and ecclesiastic opinion.

Imagine two automechanics, one an eager, voting Republican, the other an equally eager, voting Democrat. Both of them do equally good jobs on equally good cars. Now the Republican mechanic thinks and tells his neighbours that he is a good mechanic because he is a Republican and because the Republican creed, discipline, etc. inspire him. The Democrat makes the same assertions for himself; he does his job as well because he is inspired by the thoughts and actions of the Democratic Party. Both are wrong; they are good mechanics because they have learned their trade well. Humanism is an attitude like being a Democrat or a Republican. Mysticism is a set of skilled actions as well as the training leading up to them and to their ecstatic consummation; it is like being a mechanic. I maintain that mysticism, *yoga,* is a skill involving the body with its senses; it is your body that *does* mysticism. This body includes what traditions have split into the hostile two, the flesh and the soul. If a person perpetuates this dichotomy, he may find it hard to be a humanist; he will find it impossible to be a mystic.

India is not any more mysterious than the West, nor is it more profound. With contemporary India's puritanism, the strait-laced actions and counsel of its saints, it in no way matches the complexity of the American metropolis or hinterland with its new communes of seekers added to it. When faced occasionally by the manifestations of today's occidental counter-culture, the Hindu saints recoil with a mixture of non-understanding and disgust. When the Westerner reminds them of the erotic sculpture on Hindu shrines, of the *Kamasutra,* and other objects there is unchanging response; they prudishly refuse to accept them as part of their heritage. India, too, is hard to comprehend, not on account of its soul and spirit, but because Sanskrit, a complex language with many grammatical rules and exceptions, has an enormous literature which is hard to learn. Among the better informed in the West there is now some vague idea of the extreme discursiveness and the extraordinary aridity of much of the Asian religious tradition embracing paradox and contradictions which may scare away the puzzled Occidental, but complexity is not mystery.

The many books which are published each year about Indian matters fall roughly into two categories. One consists of a specialized genre, steadily improving, but of use to full-time scholars only. These books are now published by important houses and are accessible to everyone. The second category contains that wide literature which popularized India by showing what its authors want it to be for the West. There is considerable, albeit steadily decreasing, value in this brand of publication, mainly because it is promotional and has encouraged some people on the fence to jump over and learn about the real India; I do not mean the hundreds of poor forlorn American youths whom I have seen at Indian railway stations or in the Khatmaṇdu bazaar looking wistfully at U.S. travel posters, empty as yet of India's recondite wisdom but full of amoebic dysentery. Indian wisdom is hard to find, as its agents don't speak English and initiation requires more than benign smiles and mystical osmosis. The historical background of the counter-culture generation's quest for the East lies in the odd presentation of miracles and wonders and the constant high-pitched amazement at everything allegedly flowing from the East which began during the late Romantic period in Europe. When Heinrich Heine, more sarcastic than his fellow poets, wrote "beautiful silent people kneeling before lotus flowers" he could not have been aware of the unlikelihood of such an event at any time in India since nobody ever knelt for worship or meditation, but neither could he have anticipated that this sort of nostalgic rambling would provide the ideological nucleus for incipient revolutionary moods in later days.

I am not a spoilsport; in playing down the miraculous element I am trying to show that there is indeed profound wisdom and beauty in India without the farfetched and the bizarre.

THE OCHRE ROBE

CHAPTER I

VIENNA YOUTH

In Conspectu Timentium Deum

'VOTA *Mea Reddam in Conspectu Timentium Deum*', thus the full inscription on the architrave of the baroque Karlskirche in Vienna. The Emperor who built it had promised to do so in thanksgiving if only the plague would cease. The Karlskirche was to become an important symbol in my life. One of its priests baptized me, not in the church itself, that would have been too lowbrow, but about five minutes walk away in the Wohllebengasse, situated in 'the only district you can live in'.

My father was a retired cavalry captain, who had served with the hussars in the first years of the First World War and then towards its end in the newly-formed air force. He was a great sportsman, and when peace broke out he took to polo and became one of the best known trainers in Central Europe. On mother's side we were in sugar. Nothing to do with diabetes: my maternal grandparents were sugar manufacturers in Moravia. During the school holidays my brother Hans (who is now a successful painter, married to a Swedish doctor of philosophy) and I used to stay at the family manor house in Hungarian-Ostrau near Brünn. I did not know why it was called Hungarian-Ostrau, because it was in Czechoslovakia, and I do not know even now, but like so many other things in childhood that was quite unimportant. In the very large grounds there was a railed-off enclosure with a deer affectionately called Lottie, but she was so shy and she ran so fast she was rarely seen. And then there was a glass house with four crocodiles in it. A bit odd perhaps, but then, my uncle Felix who lived there was an oddity himself: he was a mathematician, who always went bare-footed. He never married, and he would explain this omission by saying that he preferred real crocodiles.

Later on, when things began to look disagreeable in Europe, he emigrated to Morocco, and from there he went to Monrovia, the capital of Liberia, still bare-footed. Finally came an official intimation that he had died of malaria. Rumours reached us that disgruntled witch doctors had had something to do with it, so my mother travelled all the way to Liberia to see what was what, but without result. Uncle Felix was gone.

I suppose this is the point at which I ought to tell you whether my childhood was happy or not, but the fact is that I do not know. I had 'everything', from a Noah's ark full of animals that was the envy of all the children of the neighbourhood to steam engines, wireless, building bricks, a gramophone, and a full Indian brave rig-out made to measure with a magnificent feathered Sioux headdress to match. My chief interest was, as far as I can remember, eating; and it had to be good and a lot of it, including generous helpings of the world-famous 'Sachertorte'. Not surprisingly therefore, I was overweight. In fact the only reproaches my father ever made me during my childhood were on that score. He thrashed me only once, and that was for something quite different; one year on the morning of Christmas Eve, before the already decorated Christmas Tree officially existed for children, I crept up to the drawing-room, gently opened the door and took a look at it—and got caught. He gave it to me hot and strong, and I bear him a grudge for it to this day. He also had a hangover that morning.

For her class and her generation my mother was quite a well-read woman, though her outlook was limited and her interests one-sided. For example, she knew the full genealogy of the European royal houses by heart, and she was deeply interested in mediaeval art.

There was always a rather tense atmosphere at home, and my mother had a scathing tongue. But the house was too big for us to hear much of it, because Hans and I each had our own room, and the drawing-room was out of earshot, so my father had it all to himself. There was certainly no sort of communication between my parents, and that affected us children. Father was away playing polo, and when he was at home he would often go out in the evening to post a letter—and not come back to the early hours. But neither Hans nor I ever missed him.

However, there was one devoted soul in the house and that was Frau Blümel, She was there when I arrived, and she did everything for me that is done in poorer houses by a mother.

She loved me dearly, but she did not care much for mother. She shared in the ingratitude shown by my family to all its servants for at least three generations.

When I began to grow up, my fellow Viennese, Sigmund Freud, was all the rage, and this fashion produced the most extraordinary neuroses in families like ours. As far as I was concerned it just made me want to get away from it all. I once had my bag packed for that very purpose, but Frau Blümel caught me, and that was the end of that. I do not suppose my mother had really read Freud seriously, one or two of his popular writings perhaps, but he was the source of her pedagogic ideas. One of her principles was that you must not be 'repressed' and 'inhibited'. I do not know quite what she meant by that, but in general it was taken to mean indulgence in sexual intercourse as often as you got the chance. According to her, if you did not live your life to the full you went mad, or else you turned to masturbation and became perverse. In any case, your fate was pitiable.

When I look back over those years I feel almost certain that it was largely that facile jargon which revolted me and tended to send me in the opposite direction. Similarly it was probably more the fanatical jargon of the Catholic catechists that put me off rather than the intolerant doctrine of the Church and its claim to universal validity, turning me into an early and precocious apostate.

My father disliked books, feeling quite rightly that any time spent on them meant less for the things he regarded as of greater importance. However, the 'Freudian spirit' did not leave even him untouched, though it certainly did not affect him in any pedagogic sense; he happened to be a very robust and healthy extravert, a man of the world of the old school. Neither of my parents bothered very much when our school reports were not all they might have been, and that was certainly very sensible of them. But they were both too much under the influence of the Freudian 'Zeitgeist' to pay any attention to the specific qualities of my character, though it should have been obvious enough even to them that I was very different from other children. My father once gave me a glass of whisky, and I emptied it under the impression that it was a soft drink. The result was that I never touched whisky again, though as a child I was always very fond of wine, and in particular champagne, and I drank quite a lot of it on the quiet. My mother's enlightenment as to the urgent necessity of 'living one's life to the full' for fear of dire consequences—which cannot have been easy to impart to me at the age of fifteen, since we had always lived what used to be called 'a sheltered life'—had a somewhat similar effect, making me take a private vow never to have anything to do with a woman at all. That was at a time when I was still a staunch Catholic and knew nothing about Hinduism and Buddhism. This vow (though it remained in abeyance from time to time later on) may have had something to do, if only unconsciously, with later decisions.

What I have just said about my father and mother may sound ungrateful, but you cannot *make* people love or be thankful, a fact that neither the Christian nor the Brahmin-Buddhist tradition recognizes, since both in their various ways impose an obligation on children to feel grateful to their parents. No, contrary to the generally accepted opinion (both occidental and Indian), religion and ethics have nothing to do with each other: but they have been running in double harness so long that their respective teachers arrogate judgements to themselves which they are not entitled to make. 'Thanks' and 'thankfulness' are psychological phenomena and therefore as such not attached to any scale of values, but if you want to value them then they belong to ethics, to philosophy; and only a philosopher free of all theological prejudices is in a position to pass judgement on them. The Fourth Christian Commandment says: 'Honour thy father and thy mother', and it seems to me that this entails love and gratitude. The subsequent clause which promises consequential reward would strike the Hindu as nothing less than immoral; but then the command is not an ethical but a theological one. There are, in fact, no ethical commandments, but only descriptions. 'This is a good deed' is an ethical sentence. But 'do this deed because it is pleasing to God' is a theological sentence, a command (and in all theologies, including the Brahminist there are sentences and commands) because it says something about God, but nothing about the deed itself. Nor is it an ethical sentence when people say: 'This is good; do it therefore because it is good for human society'; which is a sociological sentence. 'This is bad, therefore don't do it because it is against nature' is also not an ethical sentence, but an axiom of natural science.

Quite apart from these in themselves quite important ethical considerations, this short and negative description of my family life was absolutely necessary for an understanding of my subsequent development, since if my home had been one which sought to understand and to communicate, I might never have wanted to 'get away'; and this 'getting away' was an important factor at a time when I began to free myself from the tradition into which I had been born. I have said that at home there was no communication between us at all, because communication means to realize the judgements of the other, or at least to try to, and not merely to share the other's interests, because even deadly enemies can do that. The gradual arrival at human communication, to which I attach more value than to anything else, is first of all to want to understand, then to learn to understand, and finally the full intuitive and intellectual recognition of the other's scale of values. This does not mean that you have to share that scale of values—if you do then that is fortuitous, a happy chance. The particular finesse and profundity of communication reside in the fact that each partner is completely free to seek and further his own scale. Amongst my friends (by 'friend' I always mean someone with whom I have successfully entered into communication; that is to say, someone whose scales of values I know and recognize, and who knows and recognizes mine) is a Catholic missionary in India, yet he knows perfectly well that in my scale of values few things are lower and more contemptible than to try to convert anyone from or to some belief.

When I was nine years old I became a choir-boy in the Karlskirche. I know perfectly well what attracted me: it was the ritual. Otherwise I just 'went to church' like all the other children did. My parents rarely went, and they were, in the truest sense of the word, 'irreligious'. They were 'Catholics' because it was the thing to be in Vienna, otherwise they were not in the least interested in the Catholic Church, though they saw to it—for the same reason—that Hans and I went to church with Frau Blümel. I had made my first communion, and I enjoyed it, on account of the long candles, the sentimental pictures of Jesus, and all the to-do, particularly the group photograph afterward in Schwarzenberg Park. Incidentally, I never got as far as confirmation; by that time I was practically a pagan.

I went to the Academic Gymnasium; a sort of grammar school and nothing to do with gymnastics, except perhaps where the involvements of Latin syntax were concerned, and these were taught with almost mediaeval severity. But apart from this the school existed to hammer a particularly aggressive form of Catholicism into its pupils (though about half of them were Jews) and this made my schooldays into one of the decisive stages in my subsequent apostasy. It is not easy, and often quite impossible, in looking back on such an important phase to make any one person or persons 'responsible' for it, but at least there was one master (a priest) who unconsciously did his best to make the practice of Catholicism obnoxious to me. He took us for religious instruction, and he was quite generally unpopular because of his pedantry, his frequent fits of anger and his violence. Religious instruction was the only subject which seemed to require hard blows and knocks. Our catechists were more irritable and showed less self-control in their behaviour towards us than any of the other masters, and they shouted at us even more loudly than the notorious Latin master Professor Backenlacher, whose bawling could be heard out in the street when some unfortunate boy did not know an irregular perfect. Perhaps on its own all this would not have had quite such an effect, for you get over disagreeable experiences in school, but suddenly my specific relationship with this master worsened.

At the age of about thirteen I joined the Indian Club in Vienna—I was already keen on India and everything Indian, and I sought every opportunity of talking with Indian students, both male and female (most of them were studying medicine) about my proud attempts at Sanskrit and Hindi, languages my fellow pupils had never even heard of before I mentioned them, but which then caused them to regard me with awed respect. Naturally I was also much impressed by the gods and goddesses and the pious wise men of India. My religious mentor got to hear of this, but instead of summoning me and discussing it reasonably he reacted by doing his best to make my life a misery; and during religious instruction he would thunder angrily against the 'sinful, foolish, wicked heathen', and praise to the skies the splendid work being done, at great risk and sacrifice, by the Catholic missionaries in India. At the same time he would exhort the boys to pray for the poor Indian heathen children and collect silver paper for them. We all wondered what they wanted silver paper for, but no one dared ask.

One day I decided to take the bull by the horns so I went

direct to the sacristy where this particular cleric could usually be found in the breaks. I was not yet fourteen, and with me I took a Latin missal which I had been given as a present, in the hope of using it as some sort of bridge to what I wanted to say and did not know how to. And now something happened that made a deep impression on me, so deep that I have never forgotten it. He looked at me with the expressionless eyes of a salamander and at the same time he began to scratch his back voluptuously, and at every movement his cassock moved ludicrously up and down his back. He probably did not realize that he was doing it; he did it so often that it had become a habit. At the same time he said slowly, and again and again without pausing, as though it were a litany: 'Yes, yes, Fischer. Work hard. Work hard.'

That was all, but it had a distinct traumatic effect on me. It was perhaps at that moment that my aesthetic sensibility in religious matters was awakened. From that time on it was no longer easy for me to avoid the feeling that Christian saintliness was concomitant with not taking a bath. Much later on when I became acquainted with mediaeval religious literature and found saintly writers recommending dirt as holy and condemning taking baths as a trap set by Satan for the downfall of Christian souls, my own feelings were corroborated. I had already heard vaguely that in some of the boarding schools run by nuns girls were not allowed to take a bath. Twenty years later, as a monastic pilgrim through the villages of India, I discovered that in fact Christian communities attached far less importance to physical cleanliness than the Hindus did, particularly those Christian communities which had been established within the past century. The so-called Syrian Christians of Malabar ('Syrian' refers solely to their liturgical language, these Christians being of the same Dravidian origin as their neighbours) live in all respects like their Hindu neighbours, having the same caste system, and paying the same attention to physical cleanliness. But their Christianity is almost two thousand years old.

Christian theologians regard the abandonment of physical ritual as progressive, as against the Jews; so did Protestant reform movements in the Middle Ages. I have never been able to share this view, regarding it as a form of aggressive primitivism whose phychological roots lie much deeper than in a mere aversion to empty ritual. For Hinduism bathing is a part of religious devotion, and belongs to religious ritual; and every Hindu holy place has or is a bathing place. It is utterly out of the question for any Hindu, no matter what his social status, to perform his religious devotions, or to enter a temple, without having bathed immediately beforehand. In this book I shall frequently have occasion to stress the great importance of the aesthetic factor in all things relating to meditation and religious practice, and to indicate to what an amazing extent aesthetic feeling is central in the emergent phenomena.

I think I am right in saying that if my stern religious mentor in Vienna had been merely religiously intolerant and fanatical, and had not at the same time been an offence to the eye and the nose, I might never have fallen away from the one true source of all Grace, the Catholic Church. At the very least it would have happened much later. I would have clashed with him, put up with some of his heaviest clouts, and perhaps revenged myself like any other good Catholic boy by putting a stink bomb in his desk. But that might have been all. Instead of that I remained resentfully silent and gradually drifted away.

In fact, this trivial and somewhat morbid episode is of importance, because at that time it could not be said that my apostasy and my Hinduism had any, or at least any exclusively, rational and intellectual basis. I am reporting this development chronologically, and therefore I must record that what strikes me today as the argument against Christian teaching was not in my mind then. I also regard it as important to show the effect of compulsory catechism and enforced religious observances on a sensitive child. Just one last word about this religious mentor. It was at a time when Mahatma Gandhi was my hero, and his picture hung over my bed where formerly the crucifix had been. A trifle provocatively I asked the good Father where he thought the soul of the Mahatma would go after his death, and he replied: 'Straight to Hell, of course. Where else?'

How did it happen that I went to India? It is a question I have been asked again and again by Indians and by Westerners, by priests, monks and laymen—with a variety of motives, but always with concern. What caused the development which led the son of a well-to-do Vienna family to throw overboard the traditions of his own world, to abandon the shores of the blue Danube for the shores of the greyish Ganges, and to wander along the dusty roads of India as a mendicant monk? I can report very little about the beginnings of the process, and I do not propose to suggest anything mystical, since I can remember nothing of the sort in my childhood. Others may have seen it, but the people in my environment were not particularly observant. However, my Uncle Harry did tell me much later that once when I had measles I started up in bed and announced in a clear voice to my mother: 'You see, mother; you come and you go; you come and you go; you come again and you go again—and one day it's all over.' My mother could not remember anything about it, and, in any case, you can interpret the alleged words as you like: as a disconnected fever fantasy, as an indication of some metempsychotic experience, as an eruption of some slumbering knowledge, or as sheer nonsense. Whatever interpretation you choose will make no difference, nor will it be of any help. A Hindu would, of course, regard the words as a formulation of the doctrine of reincarnation, but I had the measles long before I had even heard of India.

The first time I really learned anything about India was in a penny blood; the sort of thing we boys were not allowed to read, and therefore read with avidity. There were bejewelled Maharajas, magic crystals, supernatural happenings and veiled ladies. My youthful fancy was greatly taken and that was the first time that I decided I would go to India. Somewhat later, when I was about eleven, I got hold of one of my mother's books. It was a novel by Rabindranath Tagore (a rather melancholy and beautiful story, but not easy for me to read) about nineteenth century Bengal—not exactly a woman's book, but almost. I did not understand much of it, but more than my mother suspected—not gnostically (I was too young for that) but with a kind of what Levy-Brühl would call 'participation mystique'.

Not long after that Uday Shankar and his company of musicians and dancers came to Vienna; and I sat in the front row of the Konzerthaussaal. This was the first time I saw Śiva and Pārvatī, Rādhā and Kṛṣṇa, and heard Kṛṣṇa's flute. Those performances were undoubtedly amongst the first impulses which sent me on my way. A few years ago I met Uday Shankar again, he is now well over fifty and the highly respected director of the State Dance Academy in Calcutta. I told him that I regarded him as largely responsible for my presence in India and for my wearing of the ochre robe. He laughed politely and obviously did not take me seriously, thinking perhaps that I was merely trying to be agreeable.

When we were still quite young Hans and I started to learn English—we started several times in fact, and a string of Misses came to teach us. We neither of us learnt very much, but perhaps in my case the basis of a good articulation was laid. Uday Shankar's visit brought me back to English and I decided to learn it again—properly this time—but from an Indian. There were quite a lot of Indians in Vienna, and Uday Shankar's evenings brought them into the concert hall in masses, so that it was not difficult to find one. I got to know a young student from southern India named Balakrishna Sarma, who was in Vienna studying chemistry, and I persuaded him to teach me. I was very lucky, because the English accent of even educated Indians is usually far from perfect; for example, they tend to pronounce their 'd's' and their 't's' as though they were identical with certain phonemes in their own language, whereas they are really quite different. But Balakrishna had learnt his English when quite young from English-speaking people, and at the age of nineteen he had gone to live in England for a while, so his English really was impeccable. I plunged into my new task enthusiastically, and within three months we were reading Dickens, and three months later Shakespeare. I made no attempt to learn any Indian language from him, because his mother tongue was Telugu and not Hindi, and I already knew from my first tentative studies of India that Hindi would be the most important language for me, whereas Telugu is one of the five South-Indian Dravidian languages, and as different from Hindi as Italian is from Finnish.

Balakrishna was not very impressed by my enthusiasm for classical, Hinduist India, and in him I met for the first time a type which is very common amongst Indians who have had a Western education: he was what is called forward-looking; he wanted to see India playing her part in the technical and scientific world; and, what was more, he wanted non-Indians to regard her in that light too. Indians of Balakrishna's type find the natural admiration and respect of occidental lovers of India for her religious, aesthetic and philosophical traditions rather embarrassing, and they do not as yet share the misgiving of the non-technical Westerner towards scientific achievements and scientific progress. But you can also meet the other extreme amongst Indians with a Western education, the type which contemptuously dismisses all culture other than Indian and regards India as the one source of human cultural inspiration.

After some hesitation Balakrishna agreed to take me to the Indian Club, which was styled the Hindustan Academical Association and had been founded by two famous Indians. One was Vitthalbai Patel, the brother of the first Minister of the Interior of Free India, a prominent jurist who played a leading role in the inner circle of the Indian movement for independence. The other was the Indian national hero Subhas Chandra Bose, about whom opinions are very divided. The Association was founded in 1933, and at first its rooms were in the Hôtel de France on the Schottenring, but later it moved to a house of its own near the Vienna General Hospital—about 90 per cent of the Indian members were doctors, students or patients, who had been drawn to Vienna by the high reputation of the Viennese clinics.

I was 13 years old when I became a member of the club—its youngest, and its most enthusiastic. The Indian men and women I got to know took to me and I served them as a willing and unpaid guide and interpreter, and also as a typical example of the effect of Indian culture on the intelligent West. In their company I got to know India about as well as an Indian child. I read all the Indian newspapers kept at the Club, and I read all the books in the club library. In fact, I spent all my free time there, and in particular I was keenly interested in what the club had to offer me philologically and religiously—although I was about the only one interested in these aspects of the scene.

First of all philologically: the young Indian students of medicine had to learn German very quickly as without it they could not study, but the intensive courses held at the University were not suited to everyone, and they cost money. I therefore seized the opportunity to teach them German, and in return they taught me Indian languages. I say 'Indian languages', because I started to learn four simultaneously: classical Sanskrit from a young pandit who was studying occidental music; Hindi from a doctor from Allahabad who was specializing in tuberculosis; Urdu from a Mohamedan Indian from Lahore, who was studying medicine; and Bengali from a delightful young Indian lady from Calcutta who was studying music, without a great deal of success, under the famous pianist

Sauer. She was twenty and I was close on fourteen. She had been educated in Tagore's University in Santiniketan, a delightful rural setting about four hours by train from Calcutta. In the fashion inspired by the Indian poet-prince she was a pious Hindu girl; her piety being of a quite specific type in which the aesthetic element excludes all harshness and all religious zealotrey. According to the Brahmin-Hindu tradition God is truth, goodness and beauty, which is reminiscent of the ancient Greek *καλοκ'αγαθια*. Now every Hindu can, and must, choose which suits him best, laying the stress on that particular element of the axiom that pleases him. In this way the great poet and his followers chose beauty as the chief manifestation of the divinity; and this atmosphere prevails in Santiniketan as nowhere else in the world. The classes are held in the open air under trees, and the two sexes really are educated together, whereas in other Indian Universities which officially practice co-education social contacts between the sexes are reduced to a minimum in a rather ludicrous fashion.

The name of my attractive Bengali teacher was Suchitra, which means 'very colourful'. Bengali is perhaps the most mellow amongst the modern Indian tongues, and its literature is quite the richest amongst the thirteen languages of modern India with their nine different alphabets. Bengali has succeeded in bringing about a unique synthesis between the traditional poetic forms of India and the literature of the West.

The Hindu is not a missionary—at least he was not until 1947. However, the intelligent Hindu is certainly agreeably moved when someone shows a real interest in his religion; and in my case there was the added interest of my extreme youth, I was still not yet fifteen, though by that time I had completed my inner secession to Hinduism. My emotions were still those of a child, but they were deep and sincere, and all my Indian friends: Suchitra, Doctor Kesarbani, Chaudhuri and the others I had got to know in the Hôtel de France realized this. Without trying to deprive Christianity of a soul, since this would have been completely against Hindu tradition, which teaches an unconditional *suum cuique* in all religious matters, they did assist the transformation, but probably more unconsciously than deliberately.

Two episodes are deeply ingrained in my memory, and in the memory of those who witnessed them, which I know since I met a number of them afterwards in India. Doctor Chauduri was a very capable Indian doctor from Benares, and for a number of years he was President of the All-India Medical Association. He had come to Vienna for an operation, which at that time was performed only there, by one of Vienna's leading surgeons. He was in the Auersperg sanatorium and I went to visit him every day. In the same room with him was a highly educated Mohammedan from Northern India. On one occasion, to the great delight of Chaudhuri, I praised the tolerance of Hinduism and compared it favourably with the intolerance of the religion in which I had been brought up. However, the Mohammedan interrupted me and defended Christianity against my attacks.

Now the chief charge of Mohammedanism against Hinduism is that it has many gods and idols, whereas the Mohammedan does not regard the Christian as '*kāfir*', as a heathen, even though the doctrine of the Trinity strikes him as suspect. But for Mohammedans, particularly if they are Indian, the Hindus are the quintessence of the heathenism condemned by the Prophet. The truth is, of course, that Hinduism is no more polytheistic than Islam, and the charge of ignorant Moslems and Christians is just baseless. The many idols, gods and other heavenly creatures which populate the Hindu pantheon fulfil a function, though infinitely richer and wider, similar to that fulfilled by the saints of the Catholic Church. The fanatical Mohammedan is therefore often inclined to regard Catholicism, and in particular Catholicism in the Latin countries, as idolatrous, a prejudice he shares with a good many Protestant Christians.

The truth about Hinduism is that every Hindu, whether he belongs to a monist, a pluralist, a scholastic-absolutist or a theistic-emotional school of Hinduism, believes in the last resort in one, absolute, neutral, impersonal God, the *Brahman*, as the highest principle. This knowledge of God is a gnostic act, and 'love of God' is not really the right expression to describe this devotion to, meditation on or impersonal veneration of this highest, neutral principle. In order to make use of the emotional-human side of religious observance the Hindu postulates a multiplicity of divine manifestations which are intentionally anthropomorphic, and the worship of these manifestations, which are amenable to human longing and supplication, constitutes what one might call 'the love of God'. Each Hindu chooses the particular manifestation of the impersonal, absolute *Brahman* which accords with his own psychological and emotional make-up. For example, one Hindu may chose the flute-playing shepherd-god Krishna as his *iṣṭam*, as his 'chosen, beloved and divine ideal'. Another may choose the dark goddess Kālī. A third may prefer the ascetic god Śiva.

In short, the one impersonal God presents Himself in many manifestations and many functions. Just as one man plays the role of father to his sons, husband to his wife, friend to his friends, and master to his servants, so God is father to the one, lord and master to the other, a friend to the third, and so on. And as this supreme God is first of all a neutral omnipresent principle, it can manifest itself in either a male or a female form. It can manifest itself as the lover or the beloved, or as a much loved and cossetted child. Now both the Mohammedan and the Christian, who know no better, and who, unfortunately, often do not want to know any better, regard this multiplicity of forms and expressions as representing so many different gods. But a man is not five men because he is at one and the same time a father, a son, an uncle, a master and, say, a poet. On the other hand, the weightiest objection of the Hindu and the Buddhist to the Mediterranean religions, Judaism, Christianity and Islam, is psychological: no two men are the same in all things, and it is therefore impossible for all men to venerate God in one form or one function alone; for example, solely as a father, or solely as a just judge. Since then, what would those men do who desire neither fatherhood nor judgeship?

But our Mohammedan patient in the sanatorium Auersperg defended that philosophically weak but—for Mohammedans—emotionally very powerful principle that 'there can be only one truth'. I replied, on the basis of what I know now as I knew then, that, first of all, we cannot know whether there is only one truth or not, unless indeed, we let a particular faith simply state the matter for us; and secondly, even if there is only one truth there are many ways which lead to it. This is laid down very clearly in the canonical literature of Hinduism, and the Upanishad declares: *ekaṃ sadviprā bahudhā vadanti*—'There is only one truth, but Wise Men call it by many names'. I quoted this passage to my two Indian friends who lay in the same sick-room but thought so differently in these fundamental matters. The Mohammedan fell silent, and from the expression on Doctor Chadhuri's face I could see that he thought I had won a victory for Hinduism.

The second episode which took place in the same period was

the birthday celebration for Mahatma Gandhi on October 2nd 1937. A number of prominent people had been invited, including the Rector of Vienna University, and many famous doctors, since the Indians in Vienna were particularly associated with the medical profession. Dr Kesarbani, who taught me Sanskrit, was unavoidably absent in Rome, and before leaving he had delegated to me the honour of reading the second chapter of the Bhagavadgita in Sanskrit, because there was no one amongst the Indian students who was sufficiently sure of his Sanskrit to undertake it. So I stood on a dais in the Hôtel de France and read out the old text in clear Sanskrit before 350 invited guests from the Viennese *haute volée*. And it went off very well. Unknown to me, my Latin and Greek professor at the Academic Gymnasium was in the audience, and the next day the school was full of it and there were even notices in the *Neue Freie Presse* and the *Tagblatt*, the leading newspapers in Vienna. That was the moment when I decided to become an Indologist. I was fourteen years old at the time.

Somehow I managed to obtain permission from Professor Frauwallner to sit in on his Indological and Sanskrit classes at the Oriental Institute of the Vienna University. His audience—as is the case in all the universities of Europe and America—consisted of an average of three oddities, thus increased by another.

In 1938 Pandit Jawaharlal Nehru visited Vienna and stayed for a few days at the Hôtel de France. At the invitation of the President of the Indian Club I rushed round to the hôtel, with my heart in my mouth. The good Viennese had already heard something about Gandhi as a faster, but very few of them had heard of Nehru, so the worthy hall porter was much astonished to find so much interest being shown in the exotic guest. Nehru was in Room No. 114 with friends, and when I came in he offered me a chair near him. They had probably told him about the strange lad who was so interested in Indian affairs. In addition, he is fond of children, and I was a child then. He does not care so much for monks. He expressed surprise at how good my Urdu was and he asked me whether I had read his latest book, and what I thought about it, adding that if I found anything unclear I shouldn't hesitate to ask him about it. What I did ask him was what he thought were the best Indian newspapers; and in reply he gave me a little lecture on the Indian press.

The Nazi period which had now opened at school might well have done harm to my mind, but this was prevented by my devotion to music, which comforted and consoled me. I was in the gallery of the Vienna Opera House almost every evening—people like me had what was called 'standing seats'. Even so, tickets for the greater performances were very difficult to get, and most of the seats were reserved for the Nazi Party and the Army—and therefore, together with others of a like mind I would start queuing at the box-office at nine o'clock in the evening before the performance on the following evening; and there we would wait until 9 a.m. the next morning when advance booking began. It was not so bad in warm weather, but on cold nights it was purgatory, and I think it was whilst waiting in that queue that my horror of cold first developed. Only the thought of Tristan, Parsifal and Wotan kept me alive. If Furtwängler happened to be conducting there were already hundreds of enthusiasts in the queue by ten o'clock.

In the meantime life was more difficult than ever at school. I was no longer troubled with religious instruction, since with the advent of the Nazis it had become facultative, and hardly anyone took it; but as against that there was 'Germ. Lit.' taken by the Rector himself, Doctor Schmidt. And what Germ. Lit. it was! 'The speeches of the Führer Adolf Hitler are the culminating genius of the German language'—at least according to Doctor Schmidt they were; and we went through them with a fine-tooth comb, analysing them, listening to their praises, and comparing them with—Doctor Schmidt compared them to—Goethe's prose; though from the Nazi point of view even Goethe was a bit off centre, and *Faust* Part Two in particular remained a closed book, charged with slight senility.

But at least I managed to dodge the Hitler Youth. For one thing it turned out that we were Czechs by nationality, though how that came about I really do not know. In any case, it made us 'Protected Persons' second-class citizens, and so I was not under an obligation to join. And secondly it seemed that there was something wrong with one of my grandmothers. Of course, in those days there were lawyers who specialized in the provision of non-kosher forbears, and we could easily have bought ourselves another one, but we preferred to save our money—and as far as I was concerned that was another reason why I wasn't allowed in the Hitler Youth. Thank goodness for whichever grandmother it was!

I am well aware of the fundamental difference, the diametrical philosophical, ideological and human antithesis, between a Catholic education and a totalitarian-political education. But as both forms of education affected me and influenced my life in a way which the supporters of neither could possibly have wished, and to such an extent that I became a political and religious apostate, I feel entitled to pass this harsh judgement: the fact is that Catholic religious education and Nazi political education produced identical results in me, the same traumatic conditions, the same spiritual nausea. And the direct representatives of the two, my religious mentor, and 'Party-Comrade' Doctor Hans Schmidt, were equally manifestations of a daemonism which insists: 'You must, because someone else wants you to!' A charisma was created around the person of Hitler which was little different from the old Catholic dogmatic charisma. I am using the word 'charisma' here in a special sense to denote that numinous personality image deliberately infused into the victim.

In this connection I remember a scene which is even more gruesome and horrible to me now than the memory of those scenes in Vienna in 1938 when 'Aryan' servant girls were encouraged to drive their Jewish mistresses on to the street to wash down the pavement, surrounded by an insulting mob of gratified onlookers. One warm April evening in that fateful year I was crossing the Rathausplatz, which had already been re-named Adolf-Hitler Platz. A huge portrait of the Führer had been fixed to the façade of the Town Hall. It was decorated with flowers, and candles were burning in front of it as though it were an altar. A large crowd stood there devoutly. No one dared to speak, as though they were present at the elevation of the Host. An old woman who had been standing there turned to go, and as she did so she made the sign of the cross—and immediately looked shocked and horrified, but the deed was already done. I subsequently told this little story to a Jesuit missionary I met in India, and his immediate reaction was: 'The brave old woman! She wanted to exorcise the Devil!' I made no comment, perhaps because I was tired; but in fact my Jesuit friend's interpretation was quite wrong, unless he was being facetious. What had obviously happened—and only someone who had stood there with resentment in his heart and witnessed the incident could be quite certain—was that the charismatic situation had automatically produced the intended effect, even though it was not a picture of Christ, but of Anti-Christ.

With both teachings, the Nazi and the Catholic, I experienced the same thing: the prohibition of interest on the one hand, and the imposition of interest on the other. The Nazis did not want me to learn Sanskrit and go to the opera; the Catholics did not want me to learn Sanskrit and go to the opera. In each case the reason was the same: they did not want me to escape from their sole source of grace. Superficially, of course, their reasons were different: the Nazis wanted me to become a heroic follower of Hitler; the Catholics wanted me to become a heroic soldier of Christ. I am quite sure—and my pastoral experience has repeatedly confirmed it—that in an increasingly complex world the forms and methods of a teaching or a pedagogic ideology, are more important than its content. What is taught to the pupil is a matter of complete indifference so far as his capacity to learn is concerned. He will learn to like Rock 'n Roll just as easily as he will learn to like the Brandenburg Concertos provided the form of the teaching suits him.

I must therefore stress one thing in particular: nothing is more evil than to prohibit interest on the one hand, and to impose it on the other. A father does not really know what is 'good' for his son, because to know that he would have to be his own son and not himself. In former times perhaps it was different when the family was a stronger unit than it is to-day. But in this age we are developing away from the group (whether family, town, nation or 'humanity') towards the human being; towards the individual freely communicating with other individuals—not because the other individual belongs to the same or a similar group, but because as an individual he possesses the highest value. Because the father is a lawyer that is no reason why the son should become a lawyer; that would be an imposition of interest. Or if the father, to his permanent regret, has never succeeded in becoming a lawyer, the son should become a lawyer to provide a vicarious satisfaction for the father; that too is an 'imposition of interest'. Because the father is a Catholic that is no reason for the children to be Catholics, because it is 'good' for them, when all they knew about the baptismal water was that it was cold. The situation is even worse—and here is the qualitative difference between religious and political totalitarianism—when a young man is compelled to conform within a political or nationalistic framework because his conformity is 'good' for the 'community' in question.

It would be wrong at this point for me to list all the reasons which led me to become an apostate from Christianity as I now see them. From what has already been said the reader will have some idea of the atmosphere in which my final falling away became inevitable; an atmosphere—as I frequently stress—in which anyone would have to become an apostate who was similarly affected by it. It would have been a sin for me to remain a Christian—and sin to my mind is of one kind only: the sin against the spirit; or, to put it in less archaic terminology, intellectual dishonesty: a compromise with what reason recognizes as correct and what emotion rejects as false.

I should like to make a proposal here which could be of advantage to the education of human beings in so far as it is carried on institutionally: instead of reacting in bitterness against confessional education with all its stupidities and excesses by abolishing religious teaching altogether—which is the tendency in our time wherever there are schools—it should be possible to give schoolchildren a humanistic, tolerant, intelligent catechism; even if only for the sake of their general education, because religion belongs to the cultural values of the world, quite apart from its intellectual and spiritual value or lack of it; and even if only as an inherent part of the art and literature of the world.

I have experimented in this direction with children both in India and, latterly, in the United States, and I think in time it might meet with real success. As the confessional catechism leads inevitably to de-humanization, stupidity, or, at least, thoughtless intolerance, and only very rarely to real seeking after truth (and that, as in my case, frequently by way of contradiction) the educators of the world could get together to produce a non-confessional catechism. This would be all the easier today because the myths, legends, teachings and philosophies of all religions have already been translated into almost all languages, so that European and American children can easily be made acquainted in a suitable fashion with the Indian epics, the Mahābhārata and the Rāmāyana; or Hindu children with Christian teachings and legends; and the teachers would not need to know Sanskrit, Greek or Aramaic, since both Christian and Brahmin literature is readily available in English and in all Indian languages. According to my idea, therefore, schoolchildren would be given simple but authentic anthologies made up of all the religious traditions of the world in the appropriate legendary form. For example, instead of teaching Protestant children in England and America only from the Bible, they would be given a sort of universal bible with extracts from the literature of Christianity, Buddhism, Islam, Taoism, Confucianism, Hinduism, and so on.

To maintain authenticity and preserve freedom from indoctrination with regard to such a universal anthology, there would have to be a control committee consisting not of priests of the various religions but of scholars who have studied comparative religion, and they too must of course come from various traditions. Every specific confessional interest would have to be kept away from this new-style catechism, and, of course, it would have to be taught by laymen, whereby the stress would be on the literary and not the religious aspect. Only in this way would the individual pupil find his way to the numinous and to genuine religious interest which is the implication of all religious literature. Thus a child would learn to think for himself and, finally, to make his own choice. By his own decision he would then be a Christian, a Moslem, a Hindu, a Buddhist, or an agnostic. No such decision should be influenced by ideological suggestion. The very extent of the conflict of ideas and the multiplicity of religious ideals would stimulate the mind to choose between the many forms of quietist-pietistic religions and the pragmatic-activist ones.

I am, of course, quite aware that in the present situation such a proposal is utopian, because this form of religious instruction would become an instrument to bring about the final dissolution of those outlooks and ideologies which I regard as the fundamental evil of modern humanity, but which are held up to emulation as cardinal virtues by teachers in most countries: patriotism and nationalism, or rather chauvinism, marxist internationalism in its many aspects, and claims to confessional universality. This, that, or the other religion is the only true religion and must apply to everyone!

The modern Indian idea of secular education comes closest to my proposal: secularism implies the definite freedom of religious observances. And I should like to add that this 'definite freedom' should also imply an equally definite acquaintance with all religions. The anthology I suggest, and the education which would be based on it, would, in due course, lead to this. I am not proposing one universal bible for use in all countries indiscriminately; on the contrary, I propose that many different books should be prepared so that all the various regional and cultural peculiarities can be taken into account. Children should not be taught *what* they must know, but *how* they can know. The adult and mature individual must seek for the content of his knowledge himself. A great variety in these universal religious textbooks is necessary above all because if only one were produced then, no matter how wide its scope, it would inevitably grow supercilious—superciliousness being the result of over-simplification.

In religious instruction one thing is particularly important: to show what teachings are being taught, and how religious thought arises, but not to teach which religion is the right one. Every kind of teaching which sets out to demonstrate the correctness of one teaching in particular is prejudice and inevitably inculcates prejudice. Perhaps 'prejudice' has been best defined by Mendelssohn when he wrote: 'prejudice is to believe to have the truth, *se credere habere veritatem*'.

And now for a short, chronological account of my final apostasy. I have already spoken of the revolt which conditioned it. The forcing on to me of, first, the Catholic Catechism, and then the Nazi Catechism, was, so to speak, the negative preliminary condition for my falling away from Christianity. The Nazi education did actually to some extent attain what it set out to attain, but not with the desired sequels, since, in fact, it turned me away from all forms of dogmatism, from all forms of axioms which begin: this, that, or the other is true because so and so says it is true. For this, that and the other, and so and so, you can insert what you like: the Christian Bible, *Mein Kampf*, the Veda, Immanuel Kant, and many other things. The positive preliminary condition was my loving contact with the India shown to me by her best, youthful and earnest representatives in the Hindustan Academical Association in Vienna, and in my own, similarly youthful and equally earnest Indological studies.

On my sixteenth birthday, April 20th 1939, which was also Hitler's birthday and therefore a school holiday, I performed two ritual acts in the Indian Club. The one was before the rather sentimentalized oleographs of the Indian nationalist leaders which hung on the walls. Before them I swore that I would fight for India's freedom. In my excuse I plead my tender years; it was another ten before I realized the ridiculousness of any form of nationalism. It was 8 a.m. and I was alone in the club. At eleven o'clock Bhai Sachidanand arrived. He was a Hindu preacher who happened to be travelling around Europe at the time making propaganda on behalf of his beliefs. Unfortunately this type of Hindu has increased in numbers in recent years. A few days previously I had asked him to accept me into Hinduism. According to 90 per cent of orthodox Hindu opinion, anything of this sort is impossible—you have to be born a Hindu. However, according to the sect to which Bhai Sachidanand belonged, anyone could become a Hindu who was prepared to recognize the authority of the Veda, and ceremoniously take into himself 'The Five Things of the Cow', namely milk, buttermilk, butter, urine and dung—the last two incidentally in a very diluted form. At the same time you must solemnly renounce 'The Sixth Thing of the Cow', namely its flesh, and take a vow never to eat it. I was given the Hindu name of Ramachandra, later often shortened to Chandra. Bhai Sachidanand chose this name—which is about as common in India as Tom, Dick or Harry in England—because I had demonstrated my knowledge and my great love of the deeds of the hero god Rama, which have been preserved for subsequent generations in the national epic 'Rāmāyana'. I must confess that in the course of time my attitude to Rama was to change quite considerably.

I did not formally leave the Catholic Church at that time—too many others were doing it for reasons I didn't approve—and I did so only in 1947 when I returned from a prisoner-of-war camp to Vienna and there was no longer a Hitler to embarrass me.

CHAPTER II

THE INDIAN LEGION

Para Bellum

In hundreds of small and large temples throughout India, and in most households from the Himalayas to Cape Comorin, but particularly in the eastern provinces, in Bengal, and, above all, in Calcutta, the capital of Bengal, you see pictures, statues, or some other kind of effigy of a man in glasses, and often in uniform. In at least half-a-dozen places I have seen his figure in small shrines—in the same uniform with an elephant's head. This is the head of the God of All Things Favourable, the God of Success, the Leveller of all Obstacles, Ganeśa, the son of Śiva and Pārvatī, which two godheads represent the most essentially native aspect of the Hindu idea of god. The man thus identified with Ganeśa is Subhas Chandra Bose.

He was born in a well-known and highly-respected Bengali family and brought up to enter the Civil Service. Sent to England, he passed the Civil Service Examination with marks that laid open for him the highest ranks of the Indian Civil Service. But Bose created a sensation by returning his diploma and joining the Indian Congress Movement instead. It soon became clear that he was made of very different stuff from most of the other leaders of the Indian Congress movement, who came, like himself, from well-to-do-families. Bose was an extreme radical and before long the breach between him and the Mahatma and the other moderate Congress leaders became final. But his ardour fired the enthusiasm of young nationalists throughout India, and on a number of occasions—long before the day of liberation dawned for India—it looked as though he would seize the undisputed leadership of the Indian nationalist movement; indeed, it was only the great personal influence of the Mahatma himself which succeeded in preventing this. Bose founded his own political group of young radical nationalists, the so-called Forward Bloc, and he and his party sympathized with every radical movement in Europe—with Communist and Nazis alike. The Mahatma and Nehru strictly rejected all totalitarian movements and doctrines.

Not unnaturally Bose soon found himself in prison, and as his health suffered in consequence, the British authorities allowed him to go to Europe to recuperate. He came to Vienna, where he was treated by the famous lung specialist, Professor Neumann, but on his return to India he was immediately re-arrested. It was whilst he was in Vienna in 1933 that he founded the Indian Club there—and he also met a young Viennese girl named Mimi Schenkl, who stood loyally by him and helped him in the production of his only book *India's Struggle for Freedom*, which was to become a sort of Indian nationalist bible. They married towards the end of the war, and she still lives in Vienna with her daughter Anita.

In 1942 the Indian nationalist leaders launched the 'Quit India!' movement, and all of them were put into gaol, including Bose. Then one day it was reported that he had escaped. He had not been in prison but under a sort of house arrest, owing to his poor state of health. The next report was that he was dead, and this was accepted as a fact both by the British authorities and by the other imprisoned nationalist leaders, including the Mahatma himself. Incidentally, the report also appeared in the Nazi *Voelkischer Beobachter*.

One day towards the end of the year I received a somewhat mysterious telegram asking me to report as soon as possible to O. Mazzotta, 7, Sophien Strasse, Berlin. I did not know what to make of it, and the name was completely unknown to me. However, about an hour later Doctor Raghulal, an Indian doctor at the Vienna General Hospital, rang me up and told me he was going to Berlin; it appeared that he had received a similar telegram but even more urgent. In the end, in the company of a young Eurasian whose mother was a Viennese, and who had also received a telegram, I set off for Berlin, and we reported to the Sophien Strasse as requested. Number seven turned out to be a magnificent house—before the war it had been the headquarters of the British Press Attaché. We waited in some excitement and a servant in livery, *rara avis* in those days, brought us real coffee and chocolate. That was occasion for comparatively mild surprise only, but then the doors were opened, and we stood before the man we had all believed dead—Subhas Chandra Bose.

How Bose got from the house in Elgin Road (now renamed Netaji Subhas Road, *netājī* meaning respected leader) to Berlin is likely to remain a mystery. He often promised to tell us 'after the final victory', which was an expression we were familiar with from elsewhere, but he never had the opportunity. The accounts I have heard are contradictory; in fact I do not think I have heard the same story twice. But roughly speaking it must have been somewhat as follows: Whilst under arrest Bose let his beard grow; then, disguised as a Moslem traveller, he escaped from Calcutta and with the help of friends and followers reached Kabul. He was obviously making for Moscow, where he thought he could work for India's freedom—though how he expected to do that is rather unclear to everyone, and was perhaps not at all clear to him. He seems to have expected a call to Moscow and he waited around in Kabul for a while in hopes. But in the meantime the men in the Kremlin had—for obvious reasons—lost their interest in Bose as a stirrer up of trouble for the British in India. Bose therefore did what he considered to be 'the next best thing'—he made his way to Berlin, where he got into touch with Hitler, and presumably the whole Nazi hierarchy. They quartered him in the Sophienstrasse—with diplomatic status. In his spare time the liveried flunkey who waited on him was, of course, an agent of the Gestapo. Mimi Schenkl was now called from Vienna to be Bose's secretary.

He established the Free India Committee in the Liechtensteinallee, and most of those Indians who happened to be in Germany and Austria at the outbreak of the war, or in the territories subsequently occupied by the Germans, rallied to him. His aim was to set up both a civilian propaganda apparatus and a military fighting body. Azad Hind Radio (Free India Radio) operated from the Reich's Sport Arena, broadcasting its programme on short-wave to India and South-East Asia in English and in all Indian languages. Bose had Indians from all parts of India on his staff, and there is no doubt that this part of his plan met with a good deal of success, particularly amongst the Indian troops under British command. Although he was never in a position to exercise any direct strategic influence on British India there is no doubt that his broadcasting caused a good deal of confusion. One broadcasting station was supposed to be located in the North-West Province, now Pakistan. Faked instructions were broadcast, including phoney messages referring to the alleged dropping of parachutists; and this activity undoubtedly caused the British one or two headaches, and flung the administration into confusion.

Bose was tremendously impressed by the German Army, and he took an intensive course of training, and was subsequently very fond of wearing uniform. In North Africa Rommel had about 17,000 Indian troops from General Alexander's Fourth Division among his prisoners. They were brought to Europe and distributed amongst a number of prisoner-of-war camps. Bose now negotiated with the German High Command and was given facilities for setting up an Indian Unit. With one or two assistants from his civilian staff he visited these camps in order to recruit men for the 'National Army of Liberation'. The formula was quite simple: 'Out of poverty and lack of national honour, which Britain had robbed us of during the past one hundred and fifty years, you took service in the army of the oppressors of your Motherland and helped to oppress your brothers and sisters. But now your chance had come to make good. Join the fighters for freedom, help to liberate your country, and return in triumph to your families—not as slaves of the foreign oppressor, but as free men. You have been told that Hitler and the Germans are our enemies. That is not true; they are our friends. Let us fight shoulder to shoulder with them in our own interests, and be their allies instead of their prisoners.'

Incidentally, all this did not sound so trivial in the languages of India. In fact it is rather astonishing that out of those 17,000 men only about a quarter did join him; and of those who did, only the first five hundred volunteered spontaneously. It is no business of mine to go into details about the recruiting methods adopted, but it is quite certain that the majority of the volunteers—who were ultimately sufficient in number to make up an under-strength regiment—did not volunteer exclusively for patriotic reasons. Life in the Nazi prisoner-of-war camps was hard and the food poor; and in order to encourage Bose's recruiting, Indian prisoners of war were now deprived of almost all the rights guaranteed to them by the Geneva Convention, including the right to receive food parcels from home. On the other hand, if an Indian prisoner-of-war volunteered for Bose's army he was immediately vastly better off. Despite this, and despite force and threats, only about 3,000 men came forward.

The other 14,000 preferred the hard, and now dangerous life of prisoners-of-war.

It is difficult to say just why this was so, but perhaps the strong and very real loyalty of the Indian soldier to the British Indian Army was the decisive factor. And, in fact, most of the 'volunteers' were men who had belonged to non-combatant units: cooks, batmen, drivers, and so on. Not one single commissioned officer volunteered. The 'Free India Legion', as Bose's men were called, took the new oath to Bose and Hitler at a parade on the big army training ground at Königsbrück near Dresden and Bose took the salute. On one occasion Hitler himself addressed these men, and in a short speech, which was subsequently translated into Urdu, he declared: 'I am the leader of 80,000,000 Germans. Bose is the leader of 360,000,000 Indians. He will lead you to freedom.'

Bose remained in Germany until the beginning of 1943, and we do not know exactly how his relationship to Hitler developed towards the end of his stay. I have my own ideas on the subject, but I do not feel called upon to express them here. A good deal has been said by Indians, and there has been a good deal of speculation, some of it quite false, but so far no objective account in a historically acceptable form has been available.

The members of the Legion did not know that Netājī (as everyone in India, including Pandit Nehru himself, now refers to him) had left Germany, though some months after his departure we did hear that he was in Singapore, which was by that time occupied by the Japanese, and that he was on his way to Tokio. He had set out in a German submarine in the company of two officers of the Legion. Off the Cape of Good Hope he had been transferred with them to a Japanese submarine, in which he continued his journey to Singapore. Now millions of Indians have lived in South-East Asia for many generations. Some of them occupied high positions in the Burmese and Malayan civil services. Indian businessmen controlled trade and export in Indo-China, Malaya, and in Singapore and Hong-kong. Other Indians were just rickshaw coolies and suchlike lowly workers in all these and many neighbouring countries.

It was amongst these people that Bose very quickly found the following he needed as a national hero. He was a consummate demagogue, and he knew how to sway masses and make them subject to his will. Now the sinews of war are money, and Bose was waging war. Fortunately for him he was also a genius at raising money. Where Rash Behari Bose (no relation) might with great difficulty and after many long speeches raise a million or two, Bose could raise a hundred million after a short talk. Of course, it is also true to say that the Japanese High Command showed a very much greater understanding and sympathy for Bose's efforts than the German High Command had ever done; for one thing the Japanese were very keen on mobilizing allies for their particular war in South-East Asia.

In less than a year an Indian National Army was raised. Formally it was on a basis of equality with the Japanese forces, but actually its tactical status was not much different from that of the Indian Legion in Germany. The exact strength of this Indian National Army is not known even today, but I do know that it consisted of at least two fully equipped divisions, a tremendous difference to the 3,000 men of the Legion in Germany. The Indian Legion in Germany wore the uniform of the German Afrika Korps with a shield-shaped flash on the right arm showing a tiger about to spring, against a background of the Indian national colours, saffron, white and green, surmounted by the words 'Free India'. The men of the Indian National Army wore a uniform of their own, different from either the Japanese or the German army uniforms. Whereas the men of the Legion in Germany were not generally fighting soldiers, there were quite a number of such men in the Indian National Army in East Asia; there were both officers and men who had served under the British flag, including field officers and even one or two General Staff officers. However, the bulk of the recruits came from the local populations of the South-East Asian countries which were all at that time occupied by the Japanese.

It was during the two and a half years from his arrival in Singapore on board a Japanese submarine up to the dropping of the atom bombs on Hiroshima and Nagasaki that Bose became a national hero. He still is in India to-day, and is likely to remain so. In India his name is uttered with charismatic pathos, more so than that of the Mahatma himself. His name fascinates the mythically oriented fantasy of four hundred million people in search of a hero. But Bose was not honoured only by Indians, but by all those Asiatics who came into contact with him. For example, speaking to thousands of Indians and Siamese, the Siamese Premier Pibul Songram once declared:

'If there is a man to-day who is like Buddha and worthy of emulation for all time, a full human being, a complete teacher, it is Netājī Bose'.

Bose's mysterious disappearance heightened the charismatic effect of his personal image. Official reports contradict each other as much as the popular mythological legends. The plane in which he was flying from Saigon to Formosa, a Japanese machine, is said to have crashed and burst into flames, and he is said to have died of his burns. This sober and banal account naturally does not satisfy the Indian sentiment, and you can constantly hear both in India and South-East Asia that in reality Bose is living somewhere in retirement until the time is ripe for him to re-appear. He is said to be living as an ascetic in the Himalayas—or in China, or Russia. . . . I think this myth will become even more firmly rooted as the years go by. After all, Indian mythology has quite a number of Barbarossas: the *ciranjīvīs*, or the 'eternal occupants of the body', such as the ape-prince Hanuman, sanctified on account of the services he rendered to the divine pair Rāma and Sītā; or the divine singer Nārada, who wanders through heaven and earth with his lute and is recognized only by the initiated. It is quite possible that Bose will enter into Indian mythology in some similar guise; more so perhaps than even the Mahatma himself, who is already regarded by many Hindus as an 'avatāra', or a human manifestation of the world god.

However, the heroic in mythology is perhaps closer to the Hindu masses than even the ascetic element, even though the latter is officially and theologically the superior. The two great Brahmin epics tell a hundred times of seers and ascetics to whom the heroes themselves go for advice and whom they serve —the Avatār Rāma and his divine wife Sītā, who were not born of an earthly mother, but by Mother Earth herself, and who was found by King Janaka whilst ploughing; in fact, Sītā means 'ploughed furrow'. All Hindus bow to the mild wisdom of Vasiṣṭha, the quintessence of wisdom, renunciation, and all that is worthy of veneration. Nevertheless Rāma is the main focus of Indian veneration today as in the past, together with Kṛṣṇa, the next Avatar of the World God. Kṛṣṇa, too, is another hero of arms and not of contemplation, even though in the Bhagavadgītā he teaches meditation. Gandhi's last words were 'O Rāma!' And when his murderers were being led to the gallows they read the Bhagavadgītā, Kṛṣṇa's words. In my opinion this popular hero worship is a master-key to the understanding of the modern India which is now emerging.

I was called up in February 1943, and hoped that on account of my special knowledge I should be seconded to the Indian Legion at once, particularly as I had put in an application to that effect, mentioning Bose. But I was wrong. My Colonel looked me up and down and then said drily: 'You'll stay with us until we've made a soldier of you, Fischer'. But by the following November I'd managed it. At that time the Indian Legion was posted between Arcachon and Hourtin in the Gironde, not far from Bordeaux, as part of the forces defending the Atlantic Wall. Almost until the uncomfortable end I managed to overlook the military side of the affair fairly successfully, and to regard my comradeship with the Indian soldiers and my assimilation into a very representative sample of the population of India as the main feature of those years. Philologically speaking, the time I spent in the Legion was of enormous importance to me, for I was not yet twenty and my articulation had not yet had time to become too rigid. On top of my very thorough theoretical knowledge, gained from my studies and from my period of apprenticeship in the Indian Club in Vienna, the unique opportunity now came of constantly hearing the Indian languages spoken and constantly using them myself. My one ambition was to be regarded by my Indian comrades as a fellow Indian. They knew me only as 'Ramchandra', and although they, of course, also knew that racially I belonged to Europe, they gradually began to regard me as one of themselves. In order to bring about this acceptance I had to learn something which applies to anyone who, for whatever reason, wishes to identify himself with a different ethnic group, namely the purely phonetic identification with the language, in this case, a completely Indian pronunciation.

This point may seem trivial to the non-linguist, but in my experience it is an inescapable fact that throughout the world no one will be regarded as belonging to any particular people unless he is complete master of its language; and that not merely, or even necessarily, grammatically, but above all phonetically. Apart from myself there were three other non-Indians in the Legion who had a good knowledge of Urdu or Hindi: Father Bannert, a leading oriental philologist and language teacher, who is now a professor at the Oriental

Institute of the University of Vienna, and the author of an Urdu grammar; Thieme, Professor of Indology at the University of Leipzig, who is now at Yale University teaching Sanskrit and Indology; and, finally, a young German student who had learnt Urdu in an interpreters' course. Professors Bannert and Thieme were, of course, much greater scholars than I was at the age of twenty, and they certainly had a much greater vocabulary of Urdu and Hindi words than I had, but nevertheless they were never regarded by the Indian soldiers as anything but 'German professors', whereas from the beginning I was addressed, and regarded as '*bhāī sāhib*', 'Mr Brother' and a companion in arms. Unfortunately, the German commandant did not regard this relationship favourably, and in consequence there was friction. At the same time there were some Indians who regarded me with suspicion and thought I was probably up to no good. But that was because suspicion on principle is a feature of primitive souls, and we had lots of them in the Legion—and they weren't all Indians.

Veltheim-Ostrau's 'undividedly-open life' unfortunately also has a good deal of this primitive mistrustfulness; and I have met with it amongst many Indian holy men: although gentle, good and wise they are not above suspecting their colleagues in holiness of ignoble motives. Those members of the Indian Legion who were ill-disposed towards me solely on account of this primitive mistrust seem to have argued something like this: this fellow Ramchandra, whom the Germans call Fischer, pretends to be an Indian. In fact he does speak as we do; joins in our prayers and ostentatiously avoids mixing with the Germans. On the other hand, he also speaks excellent English, better even than his German and his Indian. In all probability therefore he is really a British spy who is pretending to be one of us whilst in reality awaiting an opportunity to betray us. But he might well be a German officer who has been given the job of living amongst us as an ordinary Legionary in order to report all we say and do to the Germans. One way or the other, he's one of those clever, cunning, dangerous fellows you have to be on your guard against.

I was not unaware of the existence of this attitude, but I ignored it as well as I could, particularly as the men concerned were usually simple, and often illiterate. How could they possibly understand my somewhat farfetched motives? Later I was to learn that this was a baseless consolation; and, in fact, throughout the whole of that Asia which is belatedly awakening to nationalism there is an element of deep and permanent suspicion, if not xenophobia; and it is possibly worse in India than elsewhere.

For the moment I was more troubled by the attitude of the German personnel attached to the Legion. All the staff officers, and even the company commanders were Germans. All the administrative personnel too. And of them all, the only man who was more or less up to his ticklish job was the regimental commander, Colonel Krappe. Bose himself had proposed his name as commander. Krappe had served in the German African colonies, and he was a calm and tactful man—which was a help with us, but not at the end of the war when he fell into French hands and was treated very harshly. I don't know what considerations governed the appointment of the others; probably it was merely that they could speak a little English. In any case, as human material they were totally unsuited for their jobs. In less than two years they succeeded in completely alienating the Indian volunteers serving under them, with the result that they achieved the reverse of what they had desired. The Legionaries were not slow in comparing their new masters with their old, and the British came off better in this rating, because although they were oppressors by definition, British officers had at least been tactful in their relations with Indian troops, whereas the attitude of the Germans was tactless and overbearing, as a few instances will illustrate.

When I was finally posted to the Legion I came to the Eleventh Company at Grand Piquey, a delightful little village near the sea. Our company commander was a Hamburger, and excessively proud of it. He was also frankly a Nazi, a fact which there was no need to play down with the Indians to the same extent as in the purely German units, in which it would automatically have aroused the disapproval of his brother officers and meant social ostracism. Two of his platoon commanders were as thorough Bavarians as he was a thorough Hamburger. The other two platoon commanders were Indians, who held the rank of lieutenant. The German personnel had their own mess —from company commander to batmen—and so had the Indians: a perfect commensural apartheid. As I was unpigmented, I at first ate in this superior mess amongst the *Herrenvolk*. At first my pro-Indian attitude and my complete identification with the Indians were the subject of ribaldry, but after a while the amusement gave way to frowns and disapproval; and in the end, under somewhat disagreeable circumstances, I no longer ate in the German mess, but with the Indians; something for which I was truly thankful.

It was in December, I had gone to my room—all the Germans had rooms of their own, whereas the Indians slept with their non-commissioned officers in dormitories of between twenty and thirty bunks. My room had no window and it was in one of the evacuated houses taken over for the Legion. I took off my uniform, wrapped myself in the white cotton garment which had been presented to me by my pandit in Vienna together with my name, Ramachandra, and began my evening meditation. Suddenly I heard loud voices outside, and I recognized that of our company commander amongst the others. Then there was a thumping on my door and shouts of 'Open up, Fischer. Enemy attacking!' At least that was true enough. I hurriedly put on my greatcoat, did up the belt and opened the door. A bucket of ice-cold water hit me. Then they all burst into my room and began to throw my few belongings around, kicking over the small altar I had set up, and knocking the Bhagavad-gītā and one or two other canonical books on to the floor. After which they doused the whole room with buckets of water.

'Is your rifle loaded, Fischer?' demanded my company commander. Wordlessly I handed it to him. I could see by this time that they were all very drunk. He snatched the rifle, released the safety catch and fired two shots through the ceiling. Three of the others then seized me and marched me out. 'Don't get excited, Fischer', one of them whispered in my ear. 'It's just a joke'.

They marched me into the next house, where there were two pretty French girls on a sofa. One of them looked no more than fifteen. Someone gave me a bottle of schnaps. 'Have a drink.' I replied as calmly as I could that, since I had embraced Hinduism, I did not drink alcohol. 'Drink!' bawled my company commander. 'And that's an order, Fischer'. But it wasn't a lawful order, and so I shrugged my shoulders and put the bottle on the table. 'Take your coat off!' Now that might be construed as a lawful order, so I obeyed. 'Up on that wardrobe!' So might that—physical exercise; so up I clambered, though with some difficulty, and there I crouched; the ceiling was so low that crouch was all I could do. After that there was a volley of whispering and giggling between the two girls and one of them poured out a glass of wine and threw the wine up at me. It made me think of the wine bath in the Decameron, except that the present circumstances were far less congenial. Down below the men grouped themselves around and sang bawdy songs. Their repertoire wasn't very great, but they kept it up tirelessly. My relative indifference seemed to annoy them, and my company commander shouted at the girls: 'Now go and show us what he's got.'

That was too much, and without more ado I clambered down, despite furious orders to stay where I was. Then I addressed the company commander calmly but firmly: 'In my opinion you are exceeding your authority. But I don't care whether you are or not; I'm not putting up with this any longer. You can have me court-martialled if you like. But it so happens that I'm under orders you don't know anything about'.

'Clap the fellow in the cells,' he bawled furiously, and I was carted off. But not before I had heard one of them whisper anxiously to him: 'be careful, sir, he's obstinate. He'll go through with it.' The door of the cell, a small, dark, musty-smelling room closed behind me and I stretched myself in relief on the wooden bench it contained. It was probably about three in the morning. I lay there and thought—I had made thinking my profession, and here was a good opportunity to practice it. Of course, at the time my thinking was not meditatively trained; it was too discursive, and directed outwards to things instead of inwards to the source which we represent. The pandit in Vienna who had made me into the Hindu boy Ramachandra had told me I must learn to meditate; the books of Swami Vivekananda had given me a vague idea of what meditation meant; and in the daily *pūjā*, or ritualist contemplation, which I had practised since then, I had perhaps occasionally approached the meditative state, but what was meant from the primeval beginnings of Indian meditational exercise dawned on me for the first time in that cell. As I lay there, calm but very exhausted, and yet with a gentle feeling of happiness in my heart, something happened that I had been seeking for years. Quite suddenly I was no longer Rifleman Leopold Ramachandra Fischer, no longer the student of Sanskrit, no longer the opera-haunting Viennese student, and no longer the young man who had sworn before the oleographs of the Indian nationalist leaders in the Vienna Indian Club to fight for India's independence. I was suddenly everything, the All, and I surveyed everything that was. For a moment, or for an hour—I no longer know which—I was that which is proclaimed in the four great axioms of Upanishad wisdom: *Ahaṃ brahmasmi*—I am the Absolute; *tattvamasi*—Thou art that; *prajñātma brahma*—the conscious self is the Absolute; *sarvaṃ khalvidam brahma*—everything that is is truly the Brahman. Only now had I become a real apostate, because I had fulfilled the original heresy in me—that mystical pantheism against which early Christianity fought so hard, and with final success. I am God—that is the supreme wisdom; I—not the unimportant, physical bodied I, not the wishing I, not the intellectual I—but the all one impersonal I which alone exists. I experienced all this in that blessed moment for which I had not directly striven. And after that it took over ten years of hard monastic asceticism before I was and even then only momentarily, able to recover that intuition.

Then in the middle of my meditation the door was flung open and one of the platoon commanders appeared: 'Get up, Fischer,' he said, and there was a very uncertain quality about his voice. 'Nothing's happened. Just forget it. And go to bed now.'

'Go to bed now'. But my room was devastated and everything was soaked, including my bed. Corporal Rattan Singh, a tall powerfully-built Sikh looked into my room in horror, and told me that all the Indians knew what had happened, adding that I could have his bed if I cared. I accepted his offer gladly. I heard no more about my 'insubordination', and to my great relief I was removed from the mess of the Herrenvolk and three days later was transferred to one of the bunkers in which the men of the Legion were quartered. These bunkers were at the southern end of the Atlantic Wall, and they were not strongly manned. If the Allied troops had happened to land between two bunkers no one would have noticed.

From now on I lived as a legionary amongst the legionaries. There were no Germans around, and I was happy. The glorious Atlantic Ocean; the clear, warm, bracing air; the sound of Indian voices; the prayers of the Hindus and the Sikhs in the evening—I loved it all, and in my heart I felt I wouldn't mind waging this sort of war for quite a long time. But a few weeks later I heard from John Narbo, a Chinese born in Calcutta, who was serving as a cook in the Legion, that I was to be removed from the Legion. He had overheard this whilst serving in the German mess. I immediately wrote a letter to Colonel

Krappe, the commander of the Legion, reminding him of our first meeting together with Bose in Berlin, describing what had happened to me in the Eleventh Company and asked for his support.

Three days later I got my transfer to the regimental staff, signals Section, in Lacanau, a lovely place on a lake which runs into the sea. I reported to the Lieutenant in charge, a handsome, fair-haired brute of unsympathetic appearance. 'Keep your nose clean and you'll be all right here,' he said coldly. 'If you make trouble you'll find I can deal with you.' It looked as though my previous commander had passed on a disobliging word or two about me.

However, life was quite tolerable at Lacanau, and I made it more so by keeping out of the way of the minatory lieutenant and his German non-coms. It was perhaps at Lacanau that I really became an Indian Legionary. My duties at the teleprinter were neither long nor arduous and I had plenty of time for study and communication with my fellow legionaries. It was here that I learnt Punjabi and Bengali in addition to Hindi and Urdu, for my new comrades came from all parts of India. I also learned something of the spiritual troubles of these young Indians, who were not only far away from their homeland but also cut off from all connection with it. They were wearing a strange uniform and a good many of them were not at all sure why they were there. At the parade in Königsbrück Bose had promised them that they were to fight on Indian territory for the freedom of India, but instead of that, after a short training under German officers and N.C.O's, here they were, forming part of the German occupation army in France. They were treated either condescendingly or harshly by the German personnel of the Legion, and Germans enjoyed privileges which were not given to Indians of equal rank. As my fellow legionaries often told me, their old British officers would at least always listen to their complaints, but the German officers and non-coms had only one word for them if they attempted to lodge a formal complaint: '*Raus!*' It was a word they could all pronounce perfectly; they had heard it so often. It meant: 'Get out!'

I spent my next leave in Vienna, where I had a chance of kissing my old girl friends again, and I strutted around in the uniform of the Indian Legion—complete with turban, which wasn't obligatory, but allowed. Whilst I was there I saw the last performance in the old Opera House, significantly enough, it was *Götterdämmerung*. Soon after that the Opera House was hit by bombs and gutted by fire. I was glad to get back to warm Lacanau and the Indians. I sent and received secret messages concerning such varied subjects as army bread, and the increasing drunkenness amongst both Indian and German N.C.O's. And in some of my spare time I sat on a tree trunk outside the bunker and played Indian melodies on the recorder. On one occasion quite a sizeable snake slithered up and I was delighted to think that I might have charmed it into appearance by my playing.

My comrade on phone duty was Corporal Pritam Singh of Ludhiana. One evening he came rushing in to me with the excited information that 'they' were opening a flower garden for us. *Phūlwārī* is flower garden, but in Mogul camp-followers argot it also means brothel. The opening of the 'flower garden' was simple and agreeable and there was lots to drink. The active personnel consisted of eight girls, two of them were really beautiful, including an Italian who practised her ancient profession in Bordeaux in the process of naturalization. The 'flower garden' was for legionaries only; the ordinary German soldiers had their own establishment. The policy of apartheid extended to sexual matters too. For fourteen days I was Duty N.C.O. at the 'flower garden', together with the inevitable Medical Corps orderly. It was lively and amusing, and I never noticed any of the revolting coarseness and vulgarity inseparable from a German military brothel. The practice of the art of love in India is as old as that of religion or the dance, and the classic erotic tradition of India seemed to have extended somehow even to simple soldiers. From time to time I had an opportunity of chatting with Nina, the Italian girl, and she told me with surprise and appreciation—complete with biological details, which sounded very convincing—how much better and how much more affectionate the 'soldats Hindous' were than the Germans and Italians, for whose needs she had previously catered.

But it wasn't long before this peaceful, pleasant and instructive intermezzo came to an end. The Allied forces were inconsiderate enough to land successfully in Normandy, and the German First Army under General von der Chevallerie, to which the Indian Legion belonged, began to retire towards Germany. The four weeks retreat through France were hard and bitter for me—not because of the retreat itself (all soldiers like retreats provided they aren't too hard pressed), but because my enthusiasm for everything Indian received its first hard knock. The reason for this was that some of the legionaries behaved like beasts. Only a small minority did, it is true, but a drop of ink in a glass of water is enough to discolour the whole; and because of their abominable behaviour the whole Legion got a bad name. To my knowledge there were five cases of rape during the retreat, and all the victims were young girls under twenty. One of our fellows named Ghulam Jilani, from the Fifth Company, openly boasted that he had raped a twelve-year old girl. A week later a bullet got him.

And during this depressing period I was making my way through some of the most beautiful parts of France: Angoulême, St Pierre de Tours, Poitiers, Nevers, Dijon, and Remirmont, until at last we reached Kolmar in Alsace. From Kolmar we marched through Strassburg to Hagenau, where we were quartered in the military camp Oberhofen. This was a benumbing period for the Legion. Everyone knew that the war was lost. Allied forces had already crossed the Rhine at Remagen, and it could obviously not be long before our area was in the fighting line. Incidentally about a hundred of our men had deserted again—back to the British—and the Supreme Command, or what was left of it by this time, was well aware that the Legion was useless for fighting purposes.

At Oberhofen the religious element began to bulk larger amonst the legionaries. Up to then only the Sikhs had practised their religion regularly, and they had their *Gurdvāra*, a sort of temple on wheels looked after by Sergeant-Major Randhyr Singh and an N.C.O. named Nazar Singh. They also had a full-sized edition of the *Guru Granth Sāhib*, the Holy Book of the Sikhs, with them. I took part in their religious observances almost daily.

The Sikhs are the warrior race of North-West India, and in British service these big bearded men won a disproportionately large percentage of the total number of Victoria Crosses awarded for gallantry—in both World Wars. The leading Indian soldiers are usually Sikhs, and this is still the case now that India is free. 'Sikh' means 'initiated' or 'learned', and this refers to the initiation into their religion, which was founded in the fifteenth century at a time when Mohammedan Mogul rule threatened to wipe out Hinduism in Northern India altogether. The founder of the Sikh religion was Guru Nānak, a simple, pious man and a true mystic, though certainly no scholar or scholastic. He preached a simple, almost naive, monotheistic religion which took its style from Hinduism, but which nevertheless, particularly in its uncompromising patriarchal monotheism, had a good deal in common with Islam, which it opposed; just as every ideology which finds itself in rivalry with another ideology tends to use the terminology of the latter. Guru Nānak was followed by a line of nine other Gurus, the last of whom was Govind Singh, an outstanding aristocratic personality of considerable scholarly ability.

The ritual of the Sikhs is simple and very impressive. As in ordinary Hindu ritual the '*kīrtan*', or litany, plays a great role. Instead of an effigy or idol, the *Guru Granth Sāhib*, the Holy Book of the Sikhs, lies open on the altar under a canopy. The officiating priest makes passes over the open book with a fan, a service normally administered to kings and princes. Incidentally, almost the whole Indian ritual is—at least in its exoteric part—analogous to the ritual honour due to kings. The symbolic divinity is treated in the same way as a venerated king. It is bathed, offered sustenance, and carried to the palace—the South-Indian temple processions of the Hindus are a direct representation of this analogy. The language of the '*kīrtan*' is Punjabi, and the verses are taken from the *Guru Granth Sāhib*, which is a record of the words and poems of the Guru, together with those of various other holy men who travelled throughout mediaeval India and were at home, not in palaces, but in the villages and places of pilgrimage, because by that time the feudal, scholastic, aesthetic Hindu culture was practically at an end. It is said that the great Pandit Tulsī Dās composed his verses in honour of Rāma, the seventh incarnation of the world god Viṣṇu, in Sanskrit, because this was the only language of the gods, and no pandit might use any more ordinary language on pain of blasphemy. But then the god-hero appeared to him and ordered him to speak and write in his own mother tongue forthwith. In accordance with this command Tulsī Dās wrote the popular version of the epic of Rāmāyana, and in so doing founded the Hindi language, which in the course of centuries has developed into the national language of contemporary India.

The Sikhs had set up their *Gurdvāra* in one of the barracks of the military centre of Oberhofen and the weekends were devoted to religious observances. The two great Sikh religious celebrations are the birthdays of the first and last Gurus. It was at the celebration of the birthday of Guru Nānak that I was first carried away by the impressiveness of the Sikh ritual. We watched for two nights in succession, the litany was chanted, and pious sermons were delivered. I preached my first sermon, in Urdu, the language of the Indian soldier. Urdu is closely related to Punjabi, which is the mother tongue of the Sikhs.

Rifleman Sohan Singh of the Third Company was invariably addressed by all the Sikhs as *Jnānī-jī*, or 'Wise Sir'. The three Sikh lieutenants, Indar Singh, Gurumukh Singh and Gurbachan Singh, were always very smart and disciplined on duty, but they all three came into the *Gurdvara* bare footed and prostrated before the *Guru Granth Sāhib*, touching the ground with their foreheads; after which each one of them would rise and bow to Rifleman Sohan Singh, 'Wise Sir'.

Generally speaking, a wise or holy man is very clearly distinguishable both amongst the Sikhs and also amongst less scholastically affected Hindus. He is a man who performs his religious observances daily, reciting certain verses from the *Guru Granth Sāhib*, and meditating on them—and who, in addition, does his everyday duties conscientiously. The Sikh religion is soldierly, and its ideal is the *sant-sipāhī*, the soldier saint. In this respect Jnānī Rifleman Sohan Singh was a very suitable candidate. He delivered three speeches, each time with exactly the same content—every sermon in the *Gurdvara* begins with the greeting: '*Vāhi Guru Khalsā Śrī Vāhiguru dī fateh.* (Pure community, observe the Guru! May he be victorious!) Then Sohan Singh instructed the assembly: the Guru is God Himself. This a view which is accepted by all Indian religious teaching, and it was taken over by the Sikhs from their inception. The Hindus speak of *avatāras*, the divine incarnations; of Viṣṇu as a fish, as a tortoise, as a boar, as a lion man, as a dwarf; of Rāma with the axe, Ramacandra, Kṛṣṇa, Buddha and Kālki. But all great teachers are the incarnation of the One God. The great Gurus Nānak and Govind Singh both had the classic characteristics of *avatāras*. Their word is Veda, which is authoritative knowledge every bit as much as the Veda of the Hindus, the Qur'an of the Mohammedans, and the Bible of the Christians.

Those religious services of the Sikhs in Oberhofen were very important for me, because they saturated me with Indian ritual at a most impressionable age, though later on my preliminary awed admiration of the Sikh religion was not maintained. In fact, to-day the orthodox Sikhs in India stand for almost everything of which in the depths of my heart I fundamentally disapprove: fanatical monotheism and a naive claim to universal validity. There are some Sikh preachers who solemnly believe that the Sikh religion must one day become the religion of the whole world, if the world is not to go under. No religion indigenous in India was ever as naive until the Sikh religion was founded. In addition, their un- and anti-aesthetic puritanism is even worse than that of those followers of Gandhi who take his teachings literally. Unfortunately the modern English-educated Hindu and Sikh has taken on a good deal of the terminology of the Christian missionary.

On one occasion a famous Sikh doctor in Calcutta told me with glee that the Goddess with the Fiery Tongue (Jvālamukhī) venerated for thousands of years by the Hindus in the Punjab had now been exposed as a fraud. Government surveyors had discovered that underground oil deposits were responsible for the flames which had caused the superstitious awe of the Hindus all those years. The worthy doctor thought it very amusing; and together with many other modernistic Indians he was quite certain that this geological discovery would mean the end of the superstitious veneration of Jvālamukhī, and that, for the educated Hindu, she would no longer exist.

The doctor's attitude was typical of modern Indian symbol-blindness. Is there any reason why the All-Goddess should not appear in the form of petrol flames—even if they ultimately served the purpose of a thermo-dynamic station? If there is any reason why she should not, then, of course, the ancient cult was mere superstition. The scholastically-trained, mystical Hindu or Buddhist sees no such reason, but the modern Indian, whether he is a Sikh or a Hindu, lacks such subtlety.

We were on short commons in Oberhofen. The war was approaching its end. The allies were driving into Germany over the Rhine bridge at Remagen, and in the west the skies were constantly aglow. Rations were small and spirits were low. Finally the Legion crossed the Rhine from Oberhofen. For many days we marched through peaceful German villages and lovely German valleys. The smaller towns were very little damaged, and apart from the rumble of artillery in the distance everything was very quiet. In an ice-cold night just before Christmas 1944 the Legion occupied its last fixed quarters, the barracks on the

Heuberg. The Swabian Jura is the coldest part of Germany, and it was not a very happy thought to send the Indian Legion there. But fortunately, it was a well-built barracks and we had plenty of coal for heating—allegedly due to a special order from Berlin.

Until then only the Sikhs had conducted formally organized religious services, but now, as practically my last act as a member of the Legion, I set up a Hindu temple. Every Saturday night, in an empty room made available for the purpose, the vessels and the images were set up; the latter were fabricated out of the paper in which the Indian Red Cross wrapped its gifts of rice and tea—the members of the Legion were given Indian Red Cross packages intended for Indian prisoners of war. With the assistance of two pious comrades I prepared the *prasād* with potato flour paste, bread dough and a little milk and sugar. At about three o'clock in the morning the Hindu soldiers began to come into the room and sit on the floor. I read to them out of the Purāṇas and the Bhagavadgītā, and then preached a sermon, whilst Corporal Hardyal Singh from Rohtak read out the Hindi-Rāmāyaṇa of Tulsī Dās. Hardyal Singh now runs a small sugar factory at home in India. You may perhaps find it odd that I became the *purohita*, or priest of the Legion, but the reason for this was very simple: there was no one else who knew Sanskrit; the Hindu legionaries did not have much of a scholastic background.

It was at this time that I determined to become a Hindu monk.

Towards the end of February the Legion set out on its last march, the most melancholy, hopeless and senseless of my life. It was senseless because we might just as well have stayed where we were in the warm barracks at Heuberg, to await the arrival of the Allied troops, since there was no point in resistance, and no effective possibility anyway. We all knew that perfectly well. As we marched off a lieutenant of the renegade Vlassov 'army' billetted on the Heuberg with us, gave me a sad *dos-yvidania*. 'We soon all dead,' he said in broken German. 'You perhaps dead too, but perhaps live'. In his opinion we had a chance; they had none. And he was right. The Vlassov men were taken prisoner by the Americans, but a couple of months later they were all handed over to the Russians, and are reported to have been shot out of hand. Vlassov himself was tried and hanged as a foregone conclusion.

My platoon was led by Sergeant-Major Randhyr Singh. We all stood there, Sikhs, Madrassis, Gurkhas and the tall Mohammedans from the Afghan frontier, trembling with the cold. It was midnight and we had little food in our bellies. We were travelling light: packs, ground sheets, gas masks and rifles. '*Caukas ho! Bandūq ūpar! Dahine muṛo! Barābar qadam-calo!* (Attention! Slope arms! By the right! Quick march!)' The orders came smartly from Randhyr Singh—'Lion Patient in Battle'. It was raining and we plodded off. We did about eighteen miles that night and crossed the Danube bridge at Sigmaringen. There we piled into a train, a most unexpected happening, because the general dissolution was taking place on foot. The train moved slowly through the countryside. With us there were about a score of very dismal looking Frenchmen. Apparently they were members of the ex-Vichy Government, so they had every reason for looking down in the mouth.

We detrained at a place called Steisslingen, and started to march again, day and night with little rest. On April 30th we arrived at a little place called Rupermandlitz, and then there was a sudden shout of alarm: 'Tanks!' We broke ranks and threw away our rifles: we knew that there was no organized command in charge of us. The tanks were French. Randhyr Singh managed to get hold of a more or less white piece of sheet. It was fastened onto a branch and with our resigned sergeant-major at our head we approached the de Gaulle troops and gave ourselves up. After that we set off back the way we had come, passing through the same German villages, whose inhabitants looked at us with the same depressed indifference. Our German officers had long since disappeared, and the only two officers left were Indians, Lieutenants Gurumukh Singh and Indar Singh. We arrived in Lindau on Lake Constance and were drawn up on the market square where we were belatedly given something to eat, which was very welcome. After that our French guards were relieved by a group of Senegalese, who, in addition to their rifles, carried disagreeable looking clubs. They poked us with them now and again, but they did not hit us.

In Lindau we were put on a train and sent to Tuttlingen, where, it appeared, the biggest prisoner-of war camp under French command had been set up; and there we joined Germans, Poles, Czechs, anything in uniform that had been mopped up in the neighbourhood. There were probably about 25,000 of us in all, and there were no tents or huts; we were in the open all the time. At night it was bitterly cold, and during the day the sun beat down on us and it was very hot. There was only one latrine, a long trench with a couple of tree trunks fixed at a not too suitable height. To find your way to it at night and not fall in was something of a feat. We were fed once every three days: a lump of white bread and a piece of tuna fish. It was good though—the sort of thing one had forgotten the look of in Germany during the war. There was a certain amount of brutality and ill-treatment at Tuttlingen, but fortunately it was not systematic.

Then one evening a jeep drove up and an Indian and a British officer got out. Although our future was highly doubtful we were pleased to see them. There were about a thousand of us and we were collected by the French guards and presented to our visitors. The Indian officer ordered us to sit down and then he began to address us: 'You deserted the flag,' he said sternly. 'You betrayed your country. You joked, danced and laughed with the Nazis. Now you must weep with them.' And so on in the same vein—in a deliberate English accent but in fluent Hindustani. That elegant young Indian officer spoke Hindustani as his mother tongue, but for official purposes he spoke it with the Sandhurst accent the Indian Army Command adopted. The aim of his minatory speech was obviously to put us in the right frame of mind for interrogation, and he certainly succeeded.

The situation was a bit awkward for me, and I started to play a sort of blind man's buff. Now that the war was over I had only one wish: to get to India. As I was regarded as an Indian I thought I stood a good chance. On the other hand, none of us had any idea what the British intended to do with us. They might well charge the whole Legion with high treason, and then my fate would be unenviable. On the other hand, if I said who I was then I should be sent away from my comrades of the Legion to an ordinary prisoner-of-war camp for Germans, and ultimately I should land in Vienna—with very little chance of getting to India. I decided to take the risk with my Indian comrades, whom I had already urged to say nothing about the fact that I was not an Indian.

When it was my turn to be interrogated I spoke only Hindustani, or English with a deliberately Hindustani accent. My light-coloured skin did not arouse any suspicion, because in Kashmir and other parts of North-West India there are

Indian tribes with brown hair, blue eyes and a light skin—and even in the Punjab you find Indians with red faces. For my interrogators I was obviously what I said I was, a Brahmin from Kashmir. I was the Legionary Ramchandra Sharma, and I had studied in Germany. Without scruple I invented a Brahmin father and a Brahmin mother to suit my book. In any case, the interrogating authorities could not readily check up on the family details of about a thousand men. Finally the two drove off in their jeep; and after about a week of semi-starvation we were all loaded into lorries and driven off westward to Kehl near Strassburg, where we were handed out U.S. rations. Then we were loaded into twenty open railroad trucks and sent off to Toulon. Each wagon was guarded by two French soldiers wearing the de Gaulle armlet. They had heard that we had been stationed in the South of France, and it did not make them amiably inclined towards us.

It took us five days to reach Toulon, and in the meantime we had forgotten our hunger because of the tortures of thirst. We were given nothing to drink at all, though whether that was deliberate or just bad organization I don't know. From time to time our train was drawn into a siding, where it would stay for hours. We had a four-hour wait to the south of Lyons, and by this time the pangs of thirst was growing intolerable——heightened by the fact that within sight there was a tap which was actually dripping, and the water we all desperately needed was running away into the ground. It was too much, so despite the constant shouts of '*asseyez! asseyez!*' I got up and began to clamber over the side of the wagon. A sentry immediately raised his rifle and ordered me sharply to sit down, but I turned to him and said calmly that he could shoot me if he wanted to; it would be better than dying in agony of thirst. At that he became embarrassed and indicated with his head that I could go and get a drink. But I had overestimated my remaining strength and I fell from the side of the wagon to the ground. Two Frenchmen now came up and gave me a drink from their own water bottles. This incident had not gone unperceived, and now one after the other my fellow Legionaries climbed over the sides of their wagons and flopped down on to the ground. I had never seen so many fainting fits in one spot. The sentries were now partly-embarrassed, partly-amused, and they let everyone go to the tap and drink. I took off my German jackboot and filled it with water, and all the others followed my example. Such a receptacle will hold a good deal of water, but I drank the lot—a feat I have never emulated since, or tried to.

After that we were able to appreciate the beautiful countryside through which we were travelling, and two days later we arrived in Toulon, where we were mobbed by shrieking crowds, who seemed to think we were devils incarnate and demonstrated their belief by pelting us with bottles and anything else that came to hand. Two days later we were liberated from the French and a smartly uniformed British Captain in shorts addressed us not disagreeably in good Urdu. 'From now on you are under British command again, men. Pull yourselves together and show a little soldierly discipline. To-morrow morning you will be taken to Marseilles and from there you will be shipped back to India.'

Before we finally escaped from French hands I got a nasty whip lash from a French sergeant, followed immediately by an apology from a French lieutenant who rushed up and dressed the sergeant down indignantly. The journey from Toulon to Marseilles is very beautiful, and in our more peaceful mood we enjoyed it, though the circumstances of the trip were hardly more reassuring than before. When they unloaded us in Marseilles, U.S. army lorries were waiting for us, and we supposed that we were being taken to some more distant camp. However, the camp was quite close and we could easily have walked there. When we tumbled out the American in charge of us saluted to a group of British officers—including the one who had first looked us over in Tuttlingen—and handed us over to them. The amiable Captain who had talked to us in Toulon now addressed us again, in very good army Hindustani:

'Your uniforms are dirty—physically and morally. Take them off—everything, including the boots—and they'll be burnt. When you've had a bath you will put on the uniform you wore before you deserted.'

Before we were led off to divest ourselves of our German uniforms and have a bath the officer beckoned me up to him, and looking at me with obvious curiosity he addressed me by name and told me that I was to act as quartermaster. At that an Indian N.C.O. of the British Indian Army led me off into a supply tent; and there before my eyes were things the existence of which I could remember only theoretically: butter, milk, rice, *dāl*, (Indian pulse), spices, tinned meat, and vegetables of all kinds. 'Help yourself,' said my escort with a grin, 'but don't invite all the others. Quartermaster's privilege.' Needless to say, I tucked in and ate solidly until I could hardly move. An hour later, when I was sleeping off the effects of this gargantuan meal a bugle sounded the cookhouse call! This time there was food for all—hot food! Succulent curries for everyone, and everything the Indian Army soldier gets. The last time I had eaten such food was with Bŏse in Berlin—since then we had all been on shorter and shorter commons, and latterly things had been very bad indeed.

One of our non-coms, Sardul Singh Gill, had spent almost all his life in Berlin and had gone to school there. His mother tongue was practically German. We often talked the matter over, but he could never make up his mind whether I was an Indian or not; or perhaps part, and if so which part. Then he and I were called to the camp commandant and told to get ready to leave in ten minutes—by plane. 'Home to India?' we asked. 'Yes.' For some reason we two were apparently to precede the others. By plane to India, straight away! That exceeded my rosiest expectations. We got into a jeep, waved goodbye to our comrades and were driven off. In my mind's eye I could already see maidens with long black glossy hair, almond-shaped eyes, wearing garlands of flowers round their necks—and the Mahatma himself smiling at me and saying, 'Very good, Ramchandra!'

When we boarded the American plane our names were read out: 'Private Gill', 'Private Sharma'. Amongst the passengers were the two British intelligence officers. Their faces betrayed nothing. 'Fasten your belts!' came the order, and then we were airborne. Sardul Singh began to speculate as to our first stop. Cairo? Or perhaps Cyprus. But then the steward announced: 'In an hour and a half we shall be in Paris—city of glamour!' He was a U.S. sergeant and it was a U.S. Air Force plane.

That was something of a shock. Paris was all very well, but it wasn't on the way to India. I looked round at the two intelligence officers. They were both invisible behind large British newspapers. The plane landed at Orly, and we were driven off in an old-fashioned high-bodied taxi. The journey went through the most beautiful parts of Paris, but I was too worried to enjoy it. We stopped before a house near the Bois de Boulogne. The two intelligence officers got out and we followed them. They spoke to a group of French officers. Heavens! were we to be turned out of the British paradise into the French hell again? Without a word to us, or even a glance at us, the two British officers now departed and left us in charge of the French. It seemed only too true!

Two French sergeants, homely looking family men with embarrassed smiles on their faces took us into the house and then I spotted a notice, 'Allied Detention Centre'. We were put into a small room; there was not much furniture in it, but it was pleasant enough and it overlooked a garden. We discovered that particularly suspect types were detained here; Frenchmen suspected of collaboration, Americans suspected of heaven knows what, and so on. Our high hopes had come to nothing, and the outlook did not seem very bright.

We spent six weeks here with repeated interrogations—oh! all very decent, no harsh words, and cigarettes to boot!—in which I was asked questions about Bose, about the movements of the Legion, about our losses in action, and about our treatment, first by the Germans and then by the French. A British Colonel, a British Captain and an Indian Captain conducted the interrogations—two hours a day regularly. And all the time not one of them seemed to have the slightest suspicion that I was anything but what I wanted to be. That was a deep source of inner satisfaction to me; I had certainly studied well. Then one day a cheerful British sergeant blew into my cell, and in authentic Cockney he told me to get ready to leave. 'Where to?' I demanded. 'Just a bit nearer home, chum' was all I could get out of him. Sardul Singh and I packed our few things in the one British pack we had between us and we were ready. Outside, waiting for us, there was a lorry and a jeep, and two young soldiers. Before we clambered in the sergeant had a friendly word of warning for us: 'Now, lads, behave yourselves; and whatever you do, don't try to bunk, because if you do these boys have orders to shoot.' There was no threat about it, apart from the conditional one, and it was said in the greatest good humour, just as a matter of duty.

The following day we went on our way and near Aachen crossed the frontier into Germany. There was a good deal of bomb damage now, and the streets were full of Allied traffic. We had our midday meal in Cologne and then we began to race along the autobahn northwards. On the way two girls thumbed us, and we drew up: 'Cigarettes and a lift' they demanded. 'Don't fraternize!' was still a strict military order at the time, though from the beginning it was totally ineffective, and soon afterwards it was withdrawn. The sergeant and his two men went off into the bushes with the two girls, but before doing so the sergeant gave me his machine pistol; one of the other soldiers gave his rifle to Sardul Singh, and the third man put his down on the driving seat. 'We're just going to show the girls the scenery', the sergeant said. 'Shan't be long'. 'If anyone comes up and starts being funny let him have a burst or two of this. I suppose you can use it?' I told him I could. In fact it was a German weapon, but in any case there wasn't anything that fired or anything that went on wheels I couldn't use by that time.

And there Sardul Singh and I sat in British uniforms, armed to the teeth, and with a lorry and a jeep with full tanks at our disposal. We looked at each other and laughed. It was a lovely day. There was a pleasant breeze and the birds were singing in the trees. Now and again a car raced by, but no one took any notice of us. We did not have to wait long and then the Sergeant and his men returned with the two girls, who climbed into the back, and off we went. 'All right?' asked the Sergeant. I grinned. 'Quite all right', I said, 'but tell me, Sergeant: *ought* you to have fraternized with those girls?' 'We didn't fraternize,' he replied drily. 'We only . . . 'em'. He used a word the great O.E.D. lacks the courage to print so I suppose I must not use it here. But the British Army does—very frequently.

After many months imprisonment, internment, or whatever you like to call it, in various camps I was put into a car and taken to Herford juvenile gaol—or rather taken back; I had been there a few months before. This time I was kept there for three months in solitary confinement. Don't ask me why; I don't know; perhaps they forgot me; in any case no interrogators turned up at all. I even exercised on my own. The food was poor, and I gradually lost weight until finally, after an examination, the prison doctor ordered that I was to have an extra slice of bread with butter every day. The best day of the week—the food was always the same, and you knew exactly what each day was going to bring forth—was Wednesday, on which there was bean soup; and sometimes I got a bit extra. But at least the warders who knew I was a 'special prisoner', were all very decent to me.

When I realized that I was to stay for a while I organized my day systematically, using the shadow on the opposite wall as my clock. For a couple of yards I sang: the arias of Cavaradossi, Radames, Othello and Rodolfo, with one or two songs for make weight. For the third yard I meditated, sitting cross-legged on my bed. At three and a half yards the midday meal arrived. After that I slept for a couple of yards (on the other side of the building this time, as the sun had swung round gradually). Then I was taken out for exercise. For about half a yard I read, and then the evening meal—which isn't the right word, but it will have to do—arrived, together with the extra prophylactic slice of bread, with butter. After that it grew dark and the light was switched on. Then I read. The prison had a small library, with the obligatory Goethe, and I read the lot, making up for lost time. When the light was switched off I meditated for about an hour and a half, and then I went to sleep.

One day, without the slightest warning, I was put into an army car and driven for a long time along the Reich's autobahn. This time the accompanying officer was an R.A.F. man. He seemed disinclined for conversation, and I had long ago learned to ask no questions. It was a long journey, and finally we came into a lovely part of the country—it was Sauerland. After a while we pulled up in Iserlohn before a group of buildings guarded by many armed sentries. Three men with fixed bayonets escorted me through the gate and into a very nice and well-kept garden. We ended up in a low-roofed building where I was ordered to undress. 'Everything!' An R.A.F. sergeant then searched me from top to bottom—and when I say bottom I mean bottom. In the end he was satisfied: I don't know what he'd been looking for but apparently he didn't find it. 'Right, get dressed.'

I was then taken into the next room, where three R.A.F. officers were sitting at a table, looking very solemn and drumming on the table-top and doodling with pencils. One of them addressed me in fluent German. My name? I answered, of course, 'Ramchandra Sharma' as usual, and began to give further information in English. But the officer cut me short: 'Speak German from now on,' he said. 'You needn't bother to keep up the Ramchandra pretence. Your name's Fischer.' So that was it! Obviously during the past three months of my solitary confinement they had been making a few inquiries about me. I wondered how they had found out; and for a moment or two my confidence in my accent-free Hindustani was shaken.

However—and my confidence was restored—it turned out during my interrogation by a good-natured but not brilliant Staff Sergeant that one of my companions had let the cat out of the bag—perhaps through indiscretion; perhaps even because he thought it was a shame that I should be held unnecessarily instead of being sent home to mother. It must have shaken the Intelligence chaps a bit; but after that, of course, it was all quite simple. A few inquiries in Vienna, and they knew everything about me.

For once M.I.5 seems to have mislaid its famous efficaciousness—as a fantastic interlude whilst I was held in Senne camp indicates. One day a friendly British Colonel appeared, took Sardul Singh and me away and flew us to London. I much enjoyed the taxi drive through the streets of the West End out to Roehampton, where we ended up in a rest centre for Indian Army men. For two days we were treated like lords and fed like fighting cocks. And then the Colonel turned up again, looking a bit grumpy, and silently took us back to Senne. As we subsequently discovered, there was a special department charged with picking up Indian Army men who had somehow lost touch with their units—the sort of thing that does happen quite innocently in the hurly-burly of war. This department got wind of the fact that two Indian soldiers were languishing in a prison camp for Nazis—and promptly flew to their aid. Hence our two wonderful days in London!

After Iserlohn I was sent to a much bigger, but very nice camp at Hemer, where they kept me for a month and then suddenly discharged me. That was an accident, of course; and I was re-arrested again almost immediately, though I did manage to get as far as Arnsberg. Someone had to take me back to Hemer, and the only officer available was just going off to play tennis. He didn't bother to change, so I had an escort in shorts and sweater, and complete with tennis racket and a bag of balls. He was cheerful and friendly and even invited me to a game, but unfortunately there was no opportunity. Two weeks later I was finally released from political imprisonment and sent to Münster as an ordinary prisoner of war. It had taken them a long time, but at last they had discovered that although I was an interesting case, I was not dangerous. Just before my departure the prisoners at Hemer, whose level of education and intelligence was unusually high, gave a performance of the *Magic Flute*. I sang the part of Tamino, but at the last moment the bass felt ill and I had to sing Sarastro too. It went off very well, though the Queen of the Night was a bit difficult—they imitated her with a violin. Afterwards each singer had an extra portion for supper, and by common consent I was given two extra portions—after all, I had sung two parts.

And then finally I was released for good and all. I arrived in Vienna on January 27, 1947. The house was cold because there was a fuel shortage, and the family was assembled. 'You're looking very well,' they said, and then they started to tell me how they had suffered. I went to the University and put down my name for Indology again and philosphy as well. I also wrote five letters to India to friends I had made in the Indian Club who were now well on the way to high honour and position as the British were preparing to pull out. I also wrote in Sanskrit to three monastic orders and asked for admission, adumbrating my background and my purpose.

I took up singing again. I had started taking lessons in 1939—from an uncle. Owing to family squabbles I hadn't made his acquaintance before, though he lived quite near us. He was a sound engineer at the Vienna State Opera House, and in his spare time he taught singing—for nothing. He was altogether an unusual character; for one thing he was completely in sympathy with what the rest of the family referred to rather contemptuously as 'your Indian lark'. For years he had experimented with the human voice, and had come to some very unusual conclusions. According to him everyone *has* a latent singing voice; it only needs to be brought out properly. For that you needed long and careful study under a properly experienced master—as all his other pupils called him 'Maestro' so did I. Before I came to him I had rumbled bass now and again, but he came to the astonishing conclusion that my voice was really tenor in character. After a certain amount of falsetto I really did begin to develop a tenor voice. In fact I got so keen on the whole business that even India seemed to recede into the background for a while—but then came the war and the Indian Legion and altered all that. Now the situation was the other way round; I was too interested in India, and I no longer had the same enthusiasm for singing, so after a while it had to take a back seat. The same was true even of two girls with whom I was in love at the time. I subsumed their love in the monistic experience of Hindu philosophy, and they went along as best they could. A man whose interest is centred on becoming a monk may technically be a good lover, but his heart and soul are not really in it—if they were he could not be a monk.

I spent almost two years in Europe after the war before I finally left for good. Shortly before Christmas 1948 a registered letter arrived from the Indian Embassy in Berne informing me that my application for a visa to enter India had been granted. I told everyone that I had arranged to leave on the 26th, and there was to be a farewell party at the Maestro's on Christmas Day, but actually, in order to avoid all the formal leave-taking, good advice, and possible tears, I left on Christmas Day. My friend Gretl of Ottakring spent the afternoon with me; and it was an exultant, sad, and beautiful afternoon. In the evening we set off to the South Station—by tram (only black-marketeers could afford taxis). I had just one case, quite light and easy to carry; my portable typewriter, a small camera and one or two books. In those days the South Station consisted of one or two lines surrounded by ruins. Only two other friends were present: another Gretl and a Gerti. To send me off they sang my favourite piece: the tercet from the *Magic Flute*. And the train steamed slowly out of the station.

The following evening I was walking in the Piazza di San Marco in Venice. And the evening after that I boarded the S.S. *Taurinia* in Genoa. T. S. Eliot says: 'Home is where you come from'. This probably sounds banal to anyone who regards *The Cocktail Party* merely as a good play and not as a powerful cosmic allegory. But it really isn't as simple as that. For me that saying is elliptic: home is where you go away from—and where you don't go back to. I often use the observation in reply to the constant questions: 'Why did you leave Europe?' and 'Why did you become a monk?' The latter question is a specifically orthodox Indian one; it means literally: 'Why did you choose houselessness?' To become a monk is to choose houselessness. My Guru, who gave me my name—Agehananda, which means houseless joy—knew how important the act of going away was in my specific situation. In the last resort it is a very different matter for a Viennese to become a houseless monk than it is, say, for the son of a Brahmin from Tanjore or Banaras—or even the son of an Indian king. 'Different' has many degrees—my step was very different.

I don't really know whether this book will succeed in giving an answer to the question. I could try, of course, to give the answer in the form of a dissertation, but I don't want to; I feel that to do so would profane the experience itself. I am very fond of theses and dissertations but not about my private experiences. No doubt a psychologist could light on various answers. He could say that the beautiful, recalcitrant, red-haired Gretl, who had been the patient's first love, ultimately turned him down, and that the effect on this hyper-sensitive and somewhat manic person was the cause of it all. To some extent that could even be true, but it would not be the whole truth. For example, there were also the rather unedifying family experiences; then the indoctrination first by the Catholic catechists and afterwards by the Nazis. That is all too true, but still not the full explanation. You could go on like that for a long time, and draw up an impressive list of individual reasons, but not even their sum would provide the full explanation. There are, of course, rational grounds, and many of them; and I put them forward and defend them in academic discussion, but they are not the only factors—they are not even the most important factors—just as the academic side of a thing is never the most important.

My belief was strongest when I left Europe, and its intensity remained more or less stable for a couple of years. Belief—in my own language now means simply: to see one's own cause as the only worthwhile one. But where the Mediterranean religions—Judaism, Christianity and Islam—are concerned, belief, although not contrary to my definition, is a narrower thing. All three of them make the claim to universality which I reject; all three declare that their particular way is the only one. At the time I thought that I had got beyond belief. For me belief is something negative, something which must be rejected because it leads to dogmatic evangelism. It is only comparatively recently that I have realized that, at that time I, too, 'believed'; because I postulated that everyone who had approximately my background, my education and my level of culture, and approximately my background experience, must necessarily go the way that I was going. That, of course, was nonsense; but—much worse—it was belief. And I fear that Kant's categorical imperative is similarly dominated by belief, since his own definition betrays a universality-claim. To-day I realize that the path I took was ethically neutral—it was neither good nor bad, because choice of this nature is aesthetic and not ethical. If I had realized this at the time I should probably have been ashamed of myself; as it is today I approve of it.

In my youthful disputes with the intellectual and spiritual representatives of the post-war Western world I didn't do too badly, because unconsciously I more or less shared their view that conviction is a virtue; that one is entitled to claim truth for what one thinks about nature, the world, the soul and God merely because one is convinced that what one believes is correct. But, in fact, that is a germinally anti-humanist, bigoted, fanatical attitude. With mild men it is mild enough; with hard men it is unbending; and with fanatics it is disastrous. It is the conviction which inspired Francis of Assisi, Calvin, Giordano Bruno and Torquemada. Conviction is no proof of anything; it is merely an indication of the emotional intensity of the person who feels convinced. It is not even an indication of the possible truth of what is believed. Conviction is therefore an appropriate field of investigation for, in the first place, psychiatrists, and then for literary critics, and finally perhaps for lawyers. But as far as the truth about the world we live in is concerned it is im-pertinent in the literal sense of the word, and grossly misleading.

Does this mean that conviction, or belief—I regard the two words as practically synonymous—is valueless? And should one therefore have no convictions? Not at all. If we are to attach any value to an attitude which cannot be judged by the criterion of success or verifiability, then belief, or conviction, has its justification. But at the same time we must remember always that 'value' in the ethical or aesthetic sense does not mean truth or validity. Whoever holds beliefs, i.e. has convictions, has something valuable, but on that account it is not necessarily truth that he has. Truth must be obtained by other means: by investigation, by discursive thought, by comparison, by an exchange of ideas, by strict and uncompromising tests with objective criteria—by logical, experimental or documentary proof.

When I made that oath in the Indian Club to fight for India's freedom, and when I subsequently took up arms in that cause, running personal risks and suffering personal tribulations, I thought that the conviction, or belief, which lay at the basis of my aims, actions and sufferings was an aspect of 'truth', just as I regarded the content of certain mystical experiences as an aspect of a special and higher 'truth'. At the same time I thought that they were truths, or aspects of truth, which had the same validity as those more banal truths which we apprehend discursively. I have since—much later—recognized this as folly. The question which now arises is: had I recognized this complete independence of truth from belief and conviction at an earlier stage—say, before I decided to take my chance as an Indian political prisoner—would I have chosen another and different path? Hardly. Belief or conviction, action and risk, are valuable and worthwhile even though they do not imply truth. They have nothing in common with each other because they are on different logical planes, and they can therefore not be logically brought together in one sentence or one system—just as you must not confuse the seemingly identical words 'in' in such sentences as 'She went off in a huff and in a taxi'. Truth has value, and belief, or conviction, has value, but they are quite different kinds of value; and the fact that we are all inclined to see essence and identity when merely the same word has been used is due to the influence of that venerated father of philosophical confusion Aristotle—and still more to the fossilized and uncritical homage subsequent generations have paid to his work, coupled with the confusion of thought which lies in supposing that important little words such as 'in', 'with' and 'is' always mean the same. Truth 'is' valuable. And conviction, or belief, 'is' valuable—but 'is' doesn't mean the same thing in each case; nor does 'value'. It is high time that we emancipated ourselves from the arbitrariness of language.

In my own case I can say: it is good in the sense of value—for me, for my self-realization, and as an example for others similarly constituted—that I turned my attention to more remote, heretical and unprecedented matters; that as an outsider I joined in the struggle for Indian freedom; that I became a Hindu, and ultimately a Hindu monk; that I quite deliberately became an apostate from the teachings and the traditions in which I was born; and that according to this teaching, and to the many, many letters I have received from worried Christians in all parts of the world, I must now look forward to eternal damnation in Hell fire. Yes, all that is good, and it was right for me to choose it. But—truth has nothing to do with it, nothing whatever. Indian and Asian ideas have no more truth in them than occidental ideas. In fact, occidental tradition has produced better logicians and better scientists, since truth is, as already indicated, something banal; that is to say, something which is analytical in Kant's sense, or verifiable in the sense of modern logical empiricism.

If, on the other hand, every exalted feeling, every mystical revelation, every religious doctrine—whether 5,000, 2,500, 2,000 or only ten years old—every poetic outpouring is 'truth', then we shall have to find some other word to describe objective, logical banal facts. Otherwise 'truth' is liable to become—as it unfortunately very often does—a vague, fortuitous and trivial word like 'philosophy', as, for example, in the expression 'philosophical faculty', which allows a man to become a 'Doctor of Philosophy' for his prowess in mathematics, biology, agriculture, music, angling and landscape gardening—and in some future United States, perhaps for baseball. In some way the meaning of important words—and 'truth' is an important word—must be limited, as otherwise they will mean everything, and consequently, nothing.

My actions and my intentions were not 'truth'. Nationalism is not 'truth'; that is to say, its theses are not truths in the sense that the perceptions of mathematics or logic, or of historical data are truths. And this applies both to consciously dutiful patriotism and to brutal chauvinism; neither is 'true'. It is true, of course, that they exist; but such a statement is neither nationalistic nor patriotic, but a mere historical or psychological fact. I was under no sort of compulsion to join the Indian Legion. I volunteered because I believed at the time, as I believe now, that India ought to be free. That is the truth, and at that time the word had a charismatic effect on me. To-day it no longer has that effect, and I'm no worse off in consequence. India is free. That has been true since August 1947, but this truth is historic and banal, and not charismatic—or, at least, it isn't if we do our best not to allow it to be.

As I have said, what I did I would probably do again despite what I know now—if it were necessary, and if the possibility of doing it were still given. But I would not do it now because of its supposed truth, as I did then, but because it would still exalt me, because it might enrich me again; in short, because I am—at least, I hope I am—an epicurean; an epicurean in the spirit of Epicurus, and not in the spirit of philistine misinterpretations. Epicurus said: 'We act as we do not because it is pleasing to the gods, or to the State or to the Areopagus; and also not because it is customary and traditional, or because it is the thing our forbears expect of us; but purely because it is delightful so to act.' I approve this at the risk of being thought a hedonist; though, incidentally, I would sooner be a hedonist than intellectually confused.

And all this applies, *mutatis mutandis*, to my weightier decisions. Although today I know things I did not know then, and did not want to know—for example, that India is no nearer to truth than any other highly-cultured part of the world—I should choose the same thing again because it satisfies me completely, and whether its doctrines have more 'truth' than the Christian teachings, or the Western humanistic teachings, doesn't interest me in the least. The truth would no longer play any role in such a decision—in any case, the multiplicity of possibilities involved is so great that it is impossible to grasp them all—and what counts is simply and solely what suits me in the long run; which doesn't usually mean what gives me the greatest pleasure. If I were merely out for pleasure then I should spend much more time listening to Bach and Mozart—and probably a good deal with beautiful women. No, what suits me means what allows me to give the most of which I am capable. India may have as many, or as few, truths as the Occident; Hinduism or Buddhism may have a sounder theology and a more attractive mythology than Christianity; Christianity may have a more expedient moral code and more constructive social teachings than Hinduism. But these things just do not matter to me; all that matters to me is that I am more at ease in the sphere of Indian mythology, Indian theology and Indian ritualism. Even if I regarded Western philosophy as sounder than Indian, it would still remain true that my path lies in India and not in the West, because a man can live fully only where he shares both ritual and mythology; and not where men think as he thinks. You can think what you want to think anywhere you like. I can live in the Himalayas or on the banks of the Ganges. I can think anywhere, there or in the West, since thought is free, and will remain so—unless Big Brother comes along with his injections in 1984. I can think analytically and critically in India whilst living as an Indian. Thoughts and theoretical systems do not determine a way of life: that is done by ritual and culture.

Quite often I am asked whether I am an Indian or a European; whether I am a Hindu or an occidental humanist. Unfortunately the answer is not that simple. There was a time when I should have been insulted at the suggestion that I might perhaps after all, be a European—not because of any psychotic or artificial resentment, but just because I was dead keen on being an Indian. But for some time now I have found it embarrassing when well-meaning people attempt to laud me by calling me an Indian. I do not want to be both, or, indeed, either. It might be said that this is a brand of humanistic-cosmopolitan outlook. But unfortunately that is not altogether true either; because as a humanist you cannot be a monk and live like an anchorite. A monk desires to be emancipated as an individual from all spiritual bonds, no matter of what nature. The Buddhist Bodhisattva wishes, it is true, to save the whole world, but first of all a man must save himself, because only then can he show others the way to salvation—that is an undoubted because perfectly clear preliminary condition. The humanist is interested only in the human being, or, rather, in the finest achievements and possibilities of the human individual. The monk may be interested in that too—I am, for example—but it is not enough, and in any case my main interest does not lie in such matters, but in ritual, in meditation, and a postulated emancipation from all bonds, including those of humanism.

The divinity in its thousand radiant forms as taught in India, and in Asia under Indian influence, as both manly strength and female beauty, as philosophically neutral, as an abstraction, as non-existent—this divinity is my ultimate interest. But not in the sense that I believe that it exists, in the way that I am quite certain of the reality of the moon or of the human digestive system; because, in fact, I do not know whether it exists or not, even though I may have experienced something which I will call divinity. My individual experience proves nothing; mystical experience does not confer the status of objective existence on what has been experienced. I, myself, postulate this divinity, or Godhead, and it interests me beyond all humanism or aestheticism. And if Kant were alive to ask me whether this is a moral postulate like his moral law, I should say no. If this postulate is to be qualified (and I hesitate to do so) then I would sooner call it an aesthetic postulate—even though theologians keep telling me that aesthetics is far inferior to religion.

It does not in the least follow that I therefore believe in the objective existence of this Godhead or divinity; in fact this existence is totally unimportant. As everything must be attained in person, and as the concept of mercy does not appeal to me, and repels me, just as does the ethically harmful concept of vicarious atonement; in short, as the Godhead does not intervene except when it is identified with some part of the conscious or unconscious, it is a matter of indifference whether It exists or not. Its existence or non-existence makes not the slightest difference to my meditation or my ritual.

The same applies to more concrete ideas and actions. There is no such thing as Mother India; no ancestral or hero-spirits; there is also no nation and no people apart from the very few individuals we can meet in a land in a lifetime. Nevertheless, we can choose a ritual as though there were a Mother India, or as if there were a nation—Vaihinger would certainly have agreed with me. To take up arms, or to refuse to do so as damaging to the nation, or to the Motherland, all this is ritual informed by a postulate; and 'Mother India', the 'Nation', 'Our Ancestors', and so on, are all aesthetic postulates. In the West you wear evening shoes at a party; in Japan you take them off. In the one case as in the other it is ritual. If the country whose passport you carry goes to war you have to be a soldier, and if you happen to be a pacifist and you refuse to be a soldier then you take risks a soldier is not called upon to take. In the one case as in the other it is ritual; in the last resort each decision is an aesthetic choice. Let no one object at this point that they are moral choices; I could quote too many diametrically opposed behaviour patterns in the same situations, all of which could be morally justified. It reminds me of the young man who went to Sartre for advice; he wanted to know whether he should stay with his sick old mother (as the Bible teaches) or whether (as the Bible also teaches) he should go off to serve his people—which meant in his case joining the Resistance. The choice that this young man then made was an aesthetic one. Actually he had already made his decision before he went to Sartre; otherwise he would not have gone to a notorious anti-Nazi, but to some collaborating padre.

Thus I became a Legionary because I chose a certain ritual—except that then I believed that 'freedom', 'heroism', 'Mother India' and so on, were real things; whereas now I know that they are names. All those who have been brought up to mistake names for things—and that means all of us, because we were all taught that the 'People', the 'Motherland' (or 'Fatherland' as the case may be), 'Freedom' were real things, like gold, or Gandhi, only much greater; and we were also taught about a loving Father in Heaven; and as though they were things—things in the most general sense, as anything which can be said to *exist*. All of us who were brought up in this old and dangerous confusion find matters very difficult when we begin to abandon it, since only clear thinking can help us, and a recognition that much about which we thought as real things, and which gave us courage and confidence, was only names all the time. That is a bitter awakening, a deflation worse than any other we can experience.

There is, decidedly, no People, no Nation, no Motherland, all that really exists is 'people'. It is a collective name for a set of indescribable, fully satisfying experiences which resolves *all* problems. As the Upanishad puts it:

> 'The knots of the heart are untwined;
> All doubts have disappeared;
> Mortal man becomes immortal;
> Since he has seen the Highest.'

There is, of course, a practical intellectual difference between the name 'God' and the names 'Nation', 'People' and 'Motherland'. Apart from the name 'God' and the experience of God, there may actually be a God. Unfortunately, however, you can never know it, or deny it. In the other instances there is nothing whatever to which they could possibly refer beyond the names. But one thing with regard to the former must definitely be stressed; namely that the God who may actually exist apart from the experience of 'God' is completely meaningless, completely unimportant, and just as closed and unapproachable to us as Kant's thing in itself. Perhaps, in fact, God is that 'thing in itself' of which the punctilious Königsberger wrote.

CHAPTER III

HIMALAYAN ACOLYTE

'Die Meisterregeln lernt beizeiten'
(Hans Sachs in the *Meistersinger*)

On January 30th 1949, the first anniversary of the assassination of the Mahatma, the S.S. *Taurinia* put into Bombay. The voyage had taken just a month. You would find it difficult to travel as slowly now, even if you wanted to.

The great moment arrived. I set foot for the first time on Indian soil—slipped and measured my length; my first prostration *in situ*. My first Indian host was a rich and elegant Mohamedan, and the invitation had been extended weeks before. The first evening in his house was like any similar evening in a cultivated household in Vienna. There was nothing new at all, except that I had a chance to display my sparkling Urdu. Oh, yes!—just one thing was very different, for me. I ate meat, a thing I had not done in Europe for many years, except once by accident. It was in the Tirol, and it depressed me for days. Here, on the sacred soil of India, it didn't seem to matter, and I experienced no subsequent pricks of conscience at all.

The following morning I strolled almost as though in a dream along Peddar Road. From there I took a bus into the centre of the town, where I bought myself a khaki suit and a Gandhi cap; after this I ambled along Hornby Road, Colaba and the neighbouring streets. I felt at ease and at home, though not in Eliot's sense. I felt relaxed and at peace with the world, and that for me is the test of being at home, in the simple way that a child feels at home. During the eight years I spent in Southern Asia I may sometimes have felt out of sorts, upset, annoyed, but I never felt tense, and my nerves were never jangled—not in the way that happens to me as soon as I am on occidental soil. There need not necessarily be any profound or mystical reason for this; I first thought that the specific physical environment, warmth, tropical vegetation, and dark-coloured people who share my own symbolism, together with spiced food, produced a certain relaxation in me. Later on, however, once more in temperate zones, I observed myself with sufficient attention in a Chinese or Japanese restaurant in San Francisco, or at a Sikh party in British Columbia, and felt the same feeling of relaxation and levity.

What exercised me most of all during my first strolls on Indian soil was the reaction of the people around me. Would the Indians to whom I spoke regard me as an Indian? At first there was surprise, followed usually by a friendly glance, and then by the question—not always spoken—where do you come from, huge, fair-skinned monk? And then, of course, the Indian languages I speak are spoken without an accent, in a way very few non-Indians can ever have spoken them before. This is not immodesty; it is a fact which has been confirmed even by Indians who were not particularly well-disposed towards me. On one occasion in a government office in New Delhi I overhead a remark I was not supposed to hear: 'He talks exactly like one of us, and that's why he's so dangerous.'

However, it must not be supposed that—as can be seen from this particular incident—this was always an advantage. Ninety per cent of the Indians I talked to were friendly and pleasantly surprised. But the other ten per cent were there, too; particularly in the industrial towns, in which communist and other extraneous ideas are spreading rapidly. In such places I would be treated to unfriendly and sarcastic remarks, not from religious Hindus, of course, or even from religious Mohamedans, but from working men and students. They were inclined to regard me as some sort of a spy or charlatan, some sort of missionary on behalf of a hostile confessional or political power—and the fact that I wore the ochre robe and spoke their language as well as they did only increased their suspicion. This was particularly true at the Universities, which are breeding grounds for imported ideas. And quite apart from such artificial resentments, the urban poor are naturally suspicious, as any class would be which had lived, as they have, for generation after generation without hope. But you see only about half the population on the streets of an Indian town—the men. Today it is the same as it was in more restricted times: nine out of ten people on the streets are men. The queues for the cinema are enormous; they often wind round and round the building like a snake, and they are composed entirely of men. Women never queue up for anything. And it's all the same whether the cinema is showing a sentimentalized Hindi film or *Guys and Dolls*. The queue starts forming perhaps three or four hours before the performance is timed to begin. I often wondered when—and if—the men in the queues ever did any work. The fact is that this mass cinema siege had become a factor intensifying Indian urban impoverishment. The men spend too much money in this way, and in consequence have less than ever to take home to their families. You can get into the cheapest seats for a few pence, which sounds very little; but isn't all that cheap for people whose weekly earnings are less than a pound!

Once or twice I took my place in those queues. Provided I did not open my mouth I was immediately treated with the greatest respect, even reverence, and invited to jump the queue and go straight up to the box-office and buy my ticket. This consideration, be it said, was not due to any respect for my religious habit, but entirely to the colour of my skin. There is xenophobia in India, but there is also an obsequious respect for the lighter colour of a man's epidermis. On three occasions I queued up for the cinema and each time exactly the same thing happened: at first obsequious respect; and then, as soon as I began to talk, an immediate change of tune. I was one of them at once, to be jostled even out of my rightful place if possible. If I had spoken broken Hindi with an English accent, the reaction would have been very different. And when once I shouted at them in unmistakable English the effect was electrical.

You might, of course say—and English-educated Hindus would say—that a monk shouldn't go to a cinema. But there is no basis for this beyond prejudice, particularly when a sacred subject is treated on the screen; and perhaps a quarter of the films shown in India have a mythological background. Incidentally, the Indian film industry is second or third only to the U.S. in the number of films produced per year. India produces films in thirteen languages, but chiefly in Hindi, and, *nolens volens*, the film has become an All-India teacher of the national language. Films are often based on the Mahabhārata and Rāmāyaṇa epics, and on the god and hero legends of the Purāṇas. The beautiful princesses, goddesses and snake-women wear close-fitting saris intended to leave no doubt as to their physical assets, and they sing and dance and flirt, and there is a good deal of lustful ogling—but no kissing. The censor would cut that out at once, though he doesn't cut it out of American films, perhaps because there would be little film left if he did. In any case, Americans can be as immoral as they like, but Indian films must respect India's pure and virtuous past. Personally, I find the beautiful goddesses poured snugly into their saris more aphrodisiacal in their effect than the big-breasted popsies of Hollywood, but that, of course, is a question of taste.

After three days in Bombay I went by local train to Khar, a small and beautiful little residential town on the coast perhaps 40 miles away and quite near Santa Cruz, Bombay's airfield, where big air liners from all parts of the world land daily. In Khar I went to the *āsram* of the Ramakrishna Order, and there I experienced my first monastic retreat—three memorable days. And yet for me there was nothing particularly new or strange about it, because I was already well versed in the jargon; and whoever has completely mastered the jargon of a social group, or of any kind of hierarchy, is accepted at once. Westerners are so often startled and puzzled at the idea that anyone could wish to spend the rest of his life as a member of an Indian ascetic Order primarily because they just cannot imagine how one can come into real communication with such an exotic environment. But it's really far simpler than they imagine. First of all, you must have mastered the language—really mastered it—because you cannot establish real communication with an Indian monk by means of English, no matter how well he may speak and understand it. But even the language, although necessary, including the complete idiomatic use of the written and spoken word, is not everything. You must also be completely at home with what I have called 'the jargon'.

Every society, whether it has grown up naturally or been deliberately organized, has its own particular jargon. And if anyone wishes to identify himself with that particular society he must fully master its jargon. But once he has done so, then in my experience 80 per cent of the preliminary difficulties have been overcome. But to master the jargon does not mean merely to know and be able to use it, but to love and enjoy it, just as a real musician loves and enjoys the music he plays—if it's good. This qualification is important for the comparison, because the jargon must strike those for whom it is intended as completely authentic. At the most they must merely wonder how the user obtained such a mastery. Now my fellow monks did just that, but only for the first few minutes of our acquaintance, and sometimes not even that, because they often assumed that I had been born with the same cultural background as themselves, and in that case they were never given any reason to suppose otherwise. But even if there was that preliminary astonishment, I was quickly one of them, because I spoke and loved their jargon, and was prouder of it than of those scholastic attainments in which I was, and am, their superior.

Monastic jargon in India consists of a certain somewhat archaic Sanskritized way of speaking, delivered in a certain rhythm and with a peculiar intonation, and with a very clearly defined content. There are, for example, many things which are never referred to, and if you should refer to them, then by that very fact you would stamp yourself as an outsider. Do not run away with the idea that this jargon is used only for religious-philosophical monastic discourse, and that profane conversation is not conducted in it! You could quite easily draw up a vocabulary and phrase book of monastic jargon; not according to the ordinary rules, but by collating the subjects dealt with. For example, politics *are* discussed in this jargon, but never critically; sides *have* to be taken. Technical achievements are also discussed, but in two definite ways: either adversely, because they lead to materialism; or approvingly, when they can be traced back to Indian mythological sources—at least in talk. In this way the atom bomb is a favourite subject of discussion amongst Indian monks in their jargon, because they can trace it back to related phenomena in the epics of Mahabhārata and Rāmāyaṇa; for example, the weapons of Varuṇa, Brahmā, etc. Thus the first thing is to learn what subjects may not be referred to; and then, what subjects may be, but always in the accepted phraseology. And finally, you must learn what things may be said outright and without beating about the bush. This is very easy—because there is so little that may.

I am well aware that what I have just said may startle European readers, and even offend some of them, but at least my explanation accords well with my intention in writing this book in the first place: to state facts, even when they are soberly uninspiring. Very many Occidentals firmly believe, and desire to believe, that everything connected with the East is mysterious, magical and mystical. It is an article of faith with them, and to shake it is to arouse their indignation and resentment. But one of the most important tasks of the field worker out to establish true communication between the West and the East is to explode this deplorable attitude of mind wherever he meets it. And this must be the rule for the Orientalist, the philosopher and the priest, who consciously attach themselves to the traditions of the East, but who nevertheless retain their critical faculty where both East and West are concerned. The people who are really to be regarded with suspicion are those who praise the West at the expense of the East—and vice-versa. Let the Believer dance and sing and shout hosannah; but otherwise let him keep his mouth shut except in the presence of those who feel the same way as he does and share his beliefs. An exception may naturally be made in the case of those rare believers who are disciplined enough to control their emotional beliefs when they set out to teach, and are therefore able to teach objectively. When a believer does his best to teach objectively, then his very effort entitles him to teach, even if his beliefs do colour his teachings. But then he should always make it quite clear to his pupils: this is what I believe, but it is not necessarily so; and this is objectively so, but I do not necessarily believe it.

The Ramakrishna Mission is a modern Hindu Order, consisting of fully ordained monks and novices. It has 138 centres, 86 of them in India; about a score in other Asiatic countries and in Africa. There is a centre in Paris, and another in London. There were at one time two in London, but the Swami in charge of one of them suddenly discovered to his satisfaction that Vedānta was the same as Communism, and Communism was Vedānta; the order did not see the point. In the United States there are about a dozen centres.

Towards the end of the last century there lived a young ascetic Brahmin, the son of a poor village priest in Bengal. He himself became a priest in a new temple erected not far from Calcutta. Today you can reach it in half an hour by bus. Its name is Dakshineshvar, or 'Lord of the South'. The Lord of the South is Śiva, of course, and he is installed with his consort Kālī, the *magna mater*, the dark Goddess of the All, who is venerated by all Bengalis. An incarnation of Viṣṇu is also venerated in the same temple. In almost all Indian temples there are, apart from the particular Godhead to which the temple is primarily dedicated, various shrines to the honour of other aspects of the Godhead. They are not other gods (though guides and missionaries still persist in saying that they are) because there is only one God—if any—in India, though that God presents himself in a great variety of varying aspects and forms. Now this young Brahmin priest was known to everyone as Ramakrishna, although his original name was Gadādhar Chattopādhyay. He was a strange and unusual priest, unlike his fellows: more devout though less civilized, and perhaps even a little off his head. It is in any case not easy to draw the line between mania and trained mysticism. In fact if there had always been trained psychiatrists we should probably have far fewer mystics and holy men in our various calendars than we have now.

This young Ramakrishna was a devotee of the goddess Kali. There is nothing extraordinary about that; other Bengalis also venerate her formally and ritually, singing hymns and saying prayers in her honour. But with Ramakrishna it was rather different: he not only saw her but he talked to her, danced with her, and even squabbled with her. The image which his superiors had appointed him to venerate in the usual ritualistic fashion was to him a living person. But he was not one-sided in his devotions, and he practised all the religious exercises known to him. He meditated on Sītā, and she appeared to him under the Pañcavaṭi tree and entered into his body. He also saw and united himself with Śiva. He saw Kṛṣṇa and Rādhā, and he became one with them, one as the wine becomes one with the drinker. For a while he became a Moslem Dervish, because the Prophet appeared and spoke to him, and he then recognized Allah as the God of gods. He meditated on Christ, and Christ appeared to him, and showed him the Christian truth. And finally he was initiated into the profoundest mysteries of the pure spirit. A sannyāsī monk, the naked Totapuri, initiated him into the doctrine of the Absolute, the impersonal aloneness of the Brahma, into the monistic Advaita doctrine, and in the total oneness-way which Śamkarācārya had taught as the *summum bonum* 1,200 years ago. And finally a Brahmin ascetic female appeared to him and she initiated him into that dangerous knowledge in which the Godhead is apperceived in the union of man and woman to the accompaniment of complex rites and ceremonies known only to the initiates and a few, a very few scholars—the Tantric initiation.

The reputation of this young priest spread to a worldly, educated, bored and hypertrophically aesthetic Calcutta. Some smiled, some mocked, some went to see him—and went away shaking their heads. Some stayed. But many of those who came and went took away the feeling that they had seen and talked with an interesting maniac. Amongst the visitors to Ramakrishna were three of the outstanding representatives of Indian metropolitan culture at the time; Calcutta was then the capital of India, and it was only later that the British authorities moved away from Calcutta to the more central and temperate town of Delhi, which had itself once been the capital of the great Mogul Empire. One of these three visitors was Debendranath Tagore, known to his contemporaries as 'the Great Seer'. He was a scholar, a poet and a reformer—and the father of Rabindranath Tagore, the great modern Indian poet who was awarded a Knighthood and the Nobel Prize for Literature. For a time Debendranath Tagore was fascinated by this strange new holy man, but then he dropped him—allegedly because Ramakrishna refused to dress himself properly when he came as a guest to Tagore's house. The second of the important visitors was the famous Sanskrit scholar Pandit Ishvar Chandra Vidyasagar, 'Ocean of Knowledge', the leading Sanskrit savant and scholastic of his day, and the founder of many educational establishments which are still amongst the best in India. The third of the trio was the Bangali dramatist Girish Chandra Ghose, famous in his day, and a great drinker and fornicator before the Lord. But the holy man made Ghose no reproaches on that score, though otherwise he was implacably strict in matters of behaviour and would sharply rebuke a man even for smiling at a woman.

One day a very young student visited the Master. His name was Naren and he came from a good but impoverished middle-class family. He was a sceptic—at least he thought he was—and he came with the intention of amusing himself at the Holy Man's expense. A whole group of students from Calcutta had decided on the outing as a sort of jape. But he repeated his visit, and when one day Naren came into the presence of the Master the latter put his feet on his chest and Naren fell into a deep trance. When he came to, Naren abandoned his studies, left his family and stayed with Ramakrishna as his first disciple, devoting himself tirelessly to the Master and his teachings. This Naren subsequently became the great Swami Vivekananda, who travelled through Europe and the United States as the first missionary of Hinduism and Indian religious teachings.

In recent years a good deal has been written in most Indian languages and in the leading languages of Europe about this mission, which met with both triumphs and set-backs, and I do not feel that I need deal with it here. Suffice it to say that an important reason why many people in the West feel themselves drawn to India and her teachings to-day is to be sought in the work of Swami Vivekananda, in his books, all of which have been published and translated into many languages, and in his indirect influence.

It was the Ramakrishna Order with which I first corresponded from Europe. I hoped that I would find what I sought in the Order. In fact it took me two years to discover that this was not to be so, that Ramakrishna was not my saint, nor Vivekananda my teacher. This may be the first occasion on which the Ramakrishna Order is criticized from inside knowledge in an occidental style. Let me say at once that there is nothing to be said against this famous Order in any banal moral or moralizing fashion. It is, incidentally, the only Order amongst the Indian monastic institutions which enjoys the full confidence of the Indian Government, primarily on account of its samaritan mission, in which the Ramakrishna Order stands alone. It has founded schools, colleges and other educational institutions; it runs excellent hospitals, maternity homes and crêches, and in times of trouble, such as floods and famine, it is always on the spot to succour the victims. All those things, which a modern Welfare State provides for its citizens, are provided most admirably by the Ramakrishna Order. It is the institutional embodiment of active and responsible citizenship. Its leaders are monks with a good English education. Its monasteries are clean and well-run, and its discipline is exemplary. All these things are beyond dispute; its members are never accused directly or indirectly, of misusing the ochre robe as a cloak for gluttony or sensuality; which, be it noted, is more than can be said in modern India about monks in general.

Generally speaking the parable of the Good Samaritan plays no very great role in Hinduism, and in this respect the Ramakrishna Mission has certainly introduced a new factor into Indian religious life, perhaps under Western influence in general and Christian influence in particular. But it was Swami Vivekananda and not Ramakrishna himself who set this new ideal before the Order. Vivekananda was a very active man; the kind of man who cannot sit still for long. All forms of quietism were foreign to his character, though quietism is much more typical of orthodox Indian monachism than social and charitable service. Vivekananda and his followers justify their attitude from the Bhagavadgītā, in which Kṛṣṇa calls on Arjuna to be active. Others have appealed in the same way to this sacred book—those who fought and worked for Indian independence for example, and Tilak and Gandhi in particular. Gandhi was obviously influenced by Vivekananda's writings, though he did not mention it specifically.

However, despite this activist conviction of Vivekananda and his followers, and despite modern Indian nationalism, it remains true that the spirit of native religious observance in India is primarily contemplative and quietist, whatever one's views about the value of this attitude. When Swami Vivekananda founded an activist Order and preached an ideal of service he was setting himself up in crass contradiction to his Master Ramakrishna, though the Swami and his followers are not prepared to admit that. His present-day devotees, both monks and laymen, claim that Vivekananda's Western influenced activism actually goes back to secret instructions imparted by Ramakrishna to the young Naren, but there is not the slightest documentary evidence to support this contention. On the contrary, there is one authenticated episode which suggests the opposite. On one occasion Vivekananda confessed to Ramakrishna that he would like to found hospitals, schools and rest homes for the sick, poor and aged of India, whereupon the Master replied: 'If God appeared to you, would you ask him for hospitals, schools and orphanages? I don't think so. Instead you would beseech Him for wisdom, the love of God and Salvation'.

A lay follower of Ramakrishna, who is referred to as 'Master Mahāśay', and in the English translation of the original Bengali by the cryptic letter 'M' (his name was Mahendranath Gupta), made it his business to note down the words that fell from the lips of the Master. Now this Gupta, though an honest and a saintly character, was apparently not too richly endowed with intelligence. In consequence, he failed to understand a good deal of what the Master said; and, in addition, when the Master said anything which did not appeal to him he did not record it at all. Ramakrishna himself was not a scholar, though it is probably wrong to assume that he was totally illiterate. However, he did have the traditional peasant mistrust of all erudition, which, he taught, was an obstacle to holiness. In so doing he was introducing nothing new to Hindu tradition, because from the fourteenth century on there have been a great many men of peasant origin who have been wary of the pandit and the scholar. There are, by the way, plenty of parallels for this sort of thing in Christian tradition. The holy man who has nothing but his holiness is inclined to suffer from a feeling of inferiority where erudition is concerned, and to compensate for it by anti-intellectual sermons. For reasons which are not far to seek, such an attitude naturally appeals to the masses.

This has not been without its influence on the Ramakrishna Mission. The monks and its lay followers are not, generally speaking, great scholars, but they are very much better educated than the average Hindu. In addition they are all staunch nationalists, and they believe with Vivekananda that, whilst the West can teach the world scientific technique, only India can teach it ethics. They also believe that all religions ultimately teach the same, and that a man can find spiritual salvation in serving his people. In fact this outlook is very typical of modern India, but although it is attractive, it still does not satisfy everyone. It did not satisfy me for long. The fact is that Ramakrishna—certainly quite unconsciously—and Vivekananda after him, not too consciously either, have sown seed which have produced much good fruit and a big crop of weeds as well. Modern India is suffering from it to-day, though it will not admit it, indignantly denying the charge through the mouths of its foremost representatives. The rejection of that humanistically-directed, theoretical, speculative knowledge for its own sake, to which India has always given the highest place in the human hierarchy from the earliest Vedic times down to the beginning of our own century, has become the official attitude of India in our day, canonized by Gandhi's teachings and trumpeted to all the four corners of the earth by Gandhi's world-improving political and ideological followers.

And the germ of it all is to be found in Ramakrishna's words: *śuddha pāṇḍityate kī ha'be*—what is the use of mere erudition? Since the days of Ramakrishna this has come to mean: knowledge for its own sake, not coupled with piety and pious meditation. This attitude has swept through India like a prairie fire—not, of course, through learned India, but through the half-educated India, which speaks English and hunts for good sinecures in the Government Service; the world of petty-bourgeois lawyers, teachers and civil servants which is so pervasive in India; the world of people who are unwilling to learn Sanskrit because it is too difficult and not practical; a world which is naturally unable to assimilate the humanist tradition of the West either, because that is just as difficult and just as 'unpractical', and has the added disadvantage of being more remote.

My own answer to Ramakrishna's *magnum dictim*—'what is the use of mere erudition?—is a counter-question: what is the use of nothing at all? For pious meditation is attained by very few people, and in Ramakrishna's sense by hardly anyone. The Paramahaṃsa was uniquely suited for it, but it is perhaps just as well that only a few are built that way. The modern Hindus are people who lap up Ramakrishna's axiom eagerly, millions of them; and they certainly have no talent for intensive, protracted meditation. Fortunately they know this and admit it usually. However, their attitude involves a disastrous conclusion: namely, that if one hasn't, or hasn't yet, pious intuition, then erudition isn't necessary either. And, further, one needn't even strive for it, because 'erudition is an obstacle to holiness'. My answer to that is that one cannot draw a conclusion from something which does not exist. Europe has been well aware of that since the days of Aristotle, and probably even earlier. And India knows it too, from the days of the logician Gautama, and probably even longer. Holy men like Kabir in the middle ages, and Ramakrishna in our own day, who taught that erudition is an obstacle to holiness did so from emotion and not from knowledge. After all, since they had not erudition how could they possibly know whether it was an obstacle to holiness or not? On the other hand, there is clear proof that erudition is not necessarily an obstacle to holiness; namely, the existence of that other category of holy men in India—those holy men who were also scholars. The same thing is true of the West of course: on the one hand you have Francis of Assisi and John Chrysostom; and on the other Thomas Aquinas and the Spanish Theresa. Who would dare to decide which category is the holier?

My answer, which I began to formulate very soon after my entry into the Ramakrishna Order, was the beginning of my abandonment of Ramakrishna and Vivekananda. While I was yet in Europe I had chosen them for my Gurus, but when I got to India I was in due course compelled to abandon them.

In Khar I was received at the door of the Mission House by a portly Bengali. I was, of course, expected. He showed me in and told me I should have to wait for the Abbot. We then sat down together on the floor and he began to talk to me cheerfully about this and that. He asked me nothing about myself and treated me as though I had always been there, with the result that I felt more at home than I had done for a long time. At last the Abbot was ready to see me. He was a short, fat and rather ordinary-looking man, also a Bengali, and perhaps fifty-five years old. He looked at me rather sternly and then demanded somewhat reproachfully how it was that I had not arrived three days earlier as arranged. My spirits immediately sank, but I explained to him that the ship on which I had travelled had taken longer for the voyage than it should have done. He shook his head as though this were a wretched excuse and not the sort of thing he was prepared to accept.

At first he spoke English, but then he used slow and badly intoned Hindi, setting out my duties. As I was to stay only three days with him and then go on to the big monastery near Calcutta I should consider myself an onlooker as far as discipline here was concerned, and for the rest I should follow my own devices—except that I must be present at the *āratī* evening service. It was possible, he indicated, that whilst I was here he would call on me to take dictation. I could use a typewriter presumably? After about half an hour of this he dismissed me more amiably. Two novices then showed me the cell in which I was to have my quarters, after which they brought me the garb of the novice, the *brahmacārī*: a white *dhotī*; that is to say a piece of cloth about two and a half yards long by a yard and a half wide which is wrapped round the waist and when in position should reach down to the ankles. My first *dhotī* didn't, because in India there aren't many monks my size, and they had nothing to fit me. Then comes a white shirtlike garment, a sort of cotta, and finally a *cādar*, which is also white, and which is worn over the left shoulder and under the right arm. Everything the novice wears is white; the ochre robe is the sign of the fully-ordained monk. The novice wears his hair in a *śikhā*, a sort of tuft about the size of half a crown at the base. All the rest of the hair is shaven off. The shaving is done twice a month, preferably in the days of the new and the full moon, although this is not strictly adhered to.

I put on these garments, and there I stood, a *brahmacārī*, or novice, and felt free and comfortable. The light cotton garments are clean and agreeable to wear; there is nothing to restrict the movement and nothing to make you uncomfortable. At first it feels rather like a nightgown and when you leave your cell in the morning your first impression is that you are striding through the waking world in your nocturnal attire. However, after a day or so you get so used to it that it is a toilsome change to get back again into the heavier, tailored, stiff European clothing.

Nowadays *brahmacārī* is quite properly translated 'novice', 'neophyte', but etymologically its origin is much more interesting, and certainly much more important to India religious culture. Semantically it has nothing to do with being a tyro. There are, for example, eighty-year old *brahmacārīs* before whom men entitled to wear the ochre habit bow in deep respect. Literally *brahmacārī* means 'moving in Brahman', i.e. spiritually confirmed in the Absolute. The simplest, most valid and at the same time the oldest Vedic definition of the word is solely: 'Who constantly fixes his mind on the *Brahman;* he is a *brahmacārī*'. It does not apply merely to a man who lives literally without a house and without indulging in sexual intercourse, but implies directing his mind towards *Brahman*. The god Kṛṣṇa had sixteen thousand wives, all of whom he enjoyed simultaneously, believe it or not, yet he was a brahmacārī. However, before long the meaning of the term changed and it came to refer, as it does to-day, merely to sexual continence, primitive celibacy. For my own part I have always held to the original meaning of the term, in which mere sexual continence is the least important characteristic. In fact in many esoteric disciplines which are taught to lead to spiritual emancipation, it is probably a hindrance—not from the psychological angle of threatening complexes and disorders (I couldn't care less about them), but on the path of deepest intuition. Thanks to the perseverance of Hindu philistine medievalism, to Christianity, to Gandhism, and to the puritanism of an inceptive industrial India, the infinitely delicate and profound balance between celibacy and erotocentric ritualism has been lost in a welter of narrow-minded, collectivizing religious observances which are Hindu only in name, and the one particular meaning of *brahmacārī* as primitive celibacy has taken root.

When I was finally alone in my cell I squatted down on my bed, drew my mosquito net around me and meditated quietly.

I was still uninitiated in this complex art; but already I completely identified myself with the core of Indian monasticism—the meditational attitude and practice. Towards evening, a warm, tropical January evening, the conch horns sounded. I was expecting to hear them but I had never heard them before. I pulled my unusual garments more tightly around me and made my way towards the beautiful little temple of the Mission. There were about thirty people present for the evening devotion, including, of course, all the monks and novices of the local Mission. There was also a small portable harmonium, a pseudo-European and pseudo-Indian instrument which, unfortunately, Indian music can no longer discard. On it was the inscription 'Made in Dresden'. A monk performed on it whilst a novice beat out the rhythm on a small bipartite finger-drum known as a *tablā*. In addition, there were cymbals and *kartāla*, or wooden castenets. The laymen present were well-to-do Hindus from Khar, followers of Ramakrishna's teachings, or just plain pious people. Apart from this they were men with both feet planted firmly in the everyday world: Gujaratis, usually quite wealthy men.

A senior swami conducted the formal ceremony, performing the censing, the offering of food, the prayers, and the appropriate finger movements (*mudrās*); and finally came the *ārati*, the concluding hymn in which the whole congregation joins, whilst the master of ceremonies revolves a five-fold oil lamp clockwise round the idol, which in this case, as in all the temples of the Order, was an effigy of Ramakrishna Paramahaṃsa himself. By the side of his picture, a large photograph, were smaller pictures of the Śāradā, the 'Holy Mother' as she is called in the Order, namely the wife of the Paramahaṃsa, and one of Swami Vivekananda. The *ārati* which was composed by Vivekananda in completely sanskritized Bengali is very impressive and beautiful. The smell of incense and sandalwood became stronger, whilst the striking of gongs and the ringing of bells made a not particularly harmonious but nevertheless musical sound which rose in a crescendo and ended in a final crashing accord. Whenever the *ārati* is performed it produces an almost narcotic effect, bordering on the magical; an effect probably due to the combination of very intense visual, accoustic and olfactory stimuli.

It all made me completely happy, and this deep feeling of satisfaction lasted almost twenty-four hours. And then unexpectedly came a disturbing experience. It was not an important episode in itself, but chronologically speaking it was probably the beginning of my sempiternal criticism of the Indian monastic life of our times. The following afternoon a beautiful lady of modern outlook invited me and two other *brahmacārīs* to tea. She was the wife of a rich Jaina merchant. Together with Hinduism and Buddhism, Jainaism is one of the three great religions of India. Its historical founder, Mahāvīra, was an older contemporary of Buddha, having been born about eighty years before the Gautama. He was active in the same part of India, and it is not impossible that the two great Masters actually met. The Jainas are strict atheists; that is to say, they deny the existence of any kind of absolute divine being or entity whatever. Only the *tīrthaṅkara-s*, those who by appropriate meditation have become perfected hierophants are called *Bhagavān* or 'Lord'. The Jainas are the most radical upholders of complete physical non-violence, and as they may endanger no living thing they may not be peasants or cattle breeders, and they have no option but to live from trade. In consequence they have become one of the richest communities in India. They are also—as a matter of course—vegetarians.

This elegant Jaina lady, whose name was Sushila, or 'the well bred', a name which she bore worthily, gave us wonderfully aromatic tea, *pakaurās* (a spiced Indian pastry), *jilebīs* and other Indian sweetmeats. After the good but rather monotonous food of the Ashrama it all tasted very good indeed. Sushila was keenly interested in the work of the Mission, although the teachings of Ramakrishna have little in common with Jainaism and did not appeal to her personally. Whilst we were sitting there chatting amiably and having our tea, two beautiful girls stepped into the room. One of them was almost a child still, but the other was about eighteen and fully mature. They behaved modestly and stood there with folded hands, but they were not shy; they smiled freely and laughed out loud at a remark of mine which was not particularly diverting. Sushila now told us that Malini, the elder of the two, would soon marry a worthy young Jaina, who had just returned from Cambridge University and was about to take up a good position in one of the Ministries in Delhi. In his case the great ambition of all modern young Indians—to obtain a well-paid government post—was being achieved very promptly. In the middle of this agreeable conversation, one of the other two novices, Brahmacārī Bomkesh—that was how his Sanskrit name Vyomakeśa, or 'Heavenly Mane', was pronounced in Bengali—turned ash-grey, threw his hands up over his freshly shaven head and rushed from the house out into the afternoon sun and back to the Mission House.

Sushila looked upset at this extraordinary behaviour and asked me anxiously if I had any idea what had caused the sudden departure of the worthy Brahmacārī. I was as puzzled as she was, and I was unable to venture an explanation. Shortly after that I took my leave and went back to the Mission House and straight to the cell of Brother Heavenly Mane to find out the cause of his sudden flight. I found him sitting on the floor weeping, his abandoned rosary laid out beside him on the mat like a question mark. I spoke to him in a friendly and soothing fashion, and finally he looked up at me with swollen eyes and half-sobbed: 'I have given up all that. I want to hear no more of the dirty world and its love and marriage broking; and then she speaks of marriage and the base enjoyments of the senses—ah, how disgusting all that is to me.'

His words would probably have impressed a Hindu-born novice as an adequate expression of the renunciation of earthly things, but I had not been born and brought up in the home of Sigmund Freud for nothing, and the pathological reality behind the appearance was immediately clear to me. I made no such comment to Brother Heavenly Mane, but inwardly I discounted him as a serious candidate for the monastic life. In fact, less than two years later he abandoned the Order and married a Bengali nurse. Other monks and novices of the Heavenly Mane type are frequently less fortunate, and quite a few would end up in a psychiatric ward if there were a sufficient number of them in India. But most of them retain the cloth, because that's the simplest thing to do once they have taken it; particularly as they fear the opprobrium attaching to the spoiled monk more than the constant gnawing inner frustration.

The monasteries of India are full of ill-concealed frustrations; and in such primitive and psychologically simple matters Freud was certainly right. A man can be happy in a monastery only if he respects the senses and does not gnash his teeth against them, even risking that they get the upper hand once in a while. The legends of India are full of holy men, like Viśvamitra, who became fully holy only after his 'fall'. Seen from the heights of mystical experience such a fall is no real fall but a boon. The temptress responsible for the fall is always a manifestation of that goddess whom the monk venerates as the form of the universal divine principle, the *Brahman*. She is *Śakti*, the only force, the force which not only makes the world go round but through which it rises through renunciation to spiritual life. She is the All-Goddess to whom the ascetic sings daily hymns, to whom he devotes his meditation. At the same time she has for the contemplating mind all the characteristics of a beautiful woman. Her rounded breasts protrude firmly, and they are so close together that not even a lotus stalk would find room between them; her large eyes are flushed with the desire for love; her waist is slim; and her hips are curved. She is the Indian ideal of female beauty—which is very different from that of the Greeks.

Before the end of the week the portly little Abbot sent me off with his blessing to the big Mission House of the Order in Calcutta. I took the train in Bombay, travelling third class. To enjoy such journeys, which often last from twenty-four to forty-eight hours, you must be either an Indian born or a keen ethnologist. The Mahatma himself always travelled third class, though in his case it was in a third-class compartment which had been reserved for him and his following. That was a sort of ritual, though I am not suggesting that the frightful crush in the ordinary third-class carriage on the Indian railways would have disturbed him. As far as I am concerned, and although I love ritual, that one experience was enough for me. After that, whenever possible, I travelled first or second class.

The sun was going down behind the River Hooghly when the train steamed slowly into the great hall of Howrah Station, which is the main station for Calcutta, and lies on the far side of the bridge over the Ganges. The two sons of Sarat Chandra Bose, the elder brother of Netāji Subhas, were there to meet me. I stayed as a guest in their beautiful house in Woodburn Park in Calcutta. There was something symbolic about it for me because it was the last house in which Ramachandra, alias Leopold Fischer, was to stay; from there he went out into homelessness. The following morning, after having been treated most hospitably, I went off to the monastery in which I was to be received into the Order. It is called the Advaita Ashrama, and it lies in the centre of the city. It is also the editorial and publishing centre of the Order. There were perhaps half-a-dozen monks there who all spoke good English and were expert in everything relating to printing and publishing. The Abbot was Swami Yogeshwarananda, a senior monk from Southern India, and an M.A. of Madras University, highly skilled in

Sanskrit, English and theology. For the next two years he was to be my immediate superior.

The first thing he asked me was how long I should need to wind up all my worldly affairs before entering the Order. He did not mean this in any metaphorical way, but was simply offering me a few days to look at the life of a layman for the last time from the standpoint of the almost-novice. I therefore took another week, and went back in the car with the two Bose boys to Woodburn Park. During that last week in the world I experienced, really for the first time, that feeling of merely looking on, which makes the life of the monk possible in the darkest hours of the soul. Unless he masters this art he will inevitably turn a misanthrope, at best a pious misanthrope, like most monks both in the West and in the East, or at the worst a Torquemada.

This mere looking-on is not meditation, and I must make a clear distinction between the two. Meditation here is what is called in Indian terminology *dhyāna* or *yoga*—a guided, deliberate, acquired immersion in the metaphysical object in an intuitive and not a discursive fashion. 'Mere contemplation' is also guided, but it is not intuitive; it is discursive and intellectual, and therefore I fear that a stupid monk will be incapable of it. Stupid monks—and there are many of them—are dull and gloomy monks, and woe betide the novice or young monk who is unfortunate to have one of them for his superior or teacher. Nothing is more depressing in monastic life than symbiosis with this type of monk, particularly if he happens to be a superior and may therefore not be put in his place.

Goethe was probably thinking of something of the sort when he declared that the looker-on was always right and the man of action always wrong. Transferred into the monastic context I should feel inclined to say that the looker-on is always right, and the depressed and melancholic monk always wrong. Depression and melancholy are the two most frequent and most dangerous cankers of monastic life.

The wife of Sarat Chandra Bose had invited a number of guests to take part in my last secular meal. They were all older men and orthodox Hindus, and no member of the family took part, since that would have been against the feelings of the younger generation—and also of the father. However, it is regarded as particularly meritorious to speed the parting monk with a meal; and what was set before us was an example—the first for me—of the almost superhuman art of a pious cook under a pious mistress. There were three kinds of rice, four kinds of fish, many spiced sauces and vegetables, three kinds of *dāl*, and many sweet dishes. I sat in the middle with the guests around me, and I ate a very great deal. But when I finally—or as I thought, finally—came to a halt, the hostess urged me to eat still more, which, with some difficulty I did. That night I slept heavily and far on into the morning—that is to say, far on into the morning by Indian standards, I woke up at eight, whereas in India even the layman rises between five and seven.

In the afternoon everyone took leave of me, the men shook hands whilst the women touched my feet, which is the traditional mark of respect for an ascetic—and I was about to become one. I had learnt this gesture on my first day in the monastery in Bengal, and I had used it to the senior monks, but now that it was used towards me for the first time I found it a little embarrassing and felt a great impulse to withdraw my feet; but that would have meant refusing the requested blessing, so I remained still and suffered it—but with a lump in my throat, for I suddenly realized how far I had left Europe behind me.

I entered the monastery from Wellington Lane, a very dirty lane leading from Wellington Park, where all those political parties whose representatives do not happen to be in power hold their protest meetings. All the great leaders of the Indian national movement have spoken there at some time or other, including Gandhi himself and Nehru. The Abbot now presented me to all the brothers; two of them were young, intelligent Bengali novices, and three were fully-ordained monks. All of them made a good impression on me. We ate an excellent evening meal, and then the Abbot told me to be present at the evening reading, for which the monks assembled in the balcony room. There were readings from the conversations of Ramakrishna; first of all in Bengali, which I understood at that time mainly through my knowledge of Sanskrit and Hindi. The Abbot then handed me an English translation and asked me to read it aloud. This I did with delight, and although I was still wearing European clothes I took a full part in the proceedings. The next morning I was to be shorn and to receive at last the garb of the novice.

I slept in a room with two other novices, on the stone floor, which was covered with coconut matting. As a matter of fact, in India and in all tropical countries this is quite the best way of sleeping, and it has nothing to do with the practice of asceticism. It is so fitting that if by some chance you subsequently have to sleep in a soft European bed you no longer find it comfortable. You sink into it; there is not sufficient resistance; you sweat and you suffer discomfort.

It did not take me long to realize that I was now in a very active and highly efficient house, with regular hours for editorial work, the sale of books, and so on. Every monk had his own particular tasks to perform. The work was the same as it might have been elsewhere in a more secular publishing house, but, as the older monks taught me, the spirit behind it was different. Secular publishers, editors and booksellers work to achieve a certain object, but here the monks worked for the sake of Thākur and without relation to the fruits of their labour. After a year or two here a monk would be transferred to quite different work elsewhere, perhaps nursing the sick, helping at refugee camps, or succouring the victims of flood and famine. This regular change in the kind of work performed was intended to prevent a monk from becoming inwardly settled and rooted. The classic *sannyāsī*, the orthodox sadhu outside the modern Ramakrishna-Vivekananda Mission, obtains the same result by being on the move constantly; and the rules of his Order forbid him to stay in once place too long. The length of time he may stay varies from Order to Order, and also according to the maturity of the monk or novice; it varies between three days and six months.

Vivekananda introduced one ingenious innovation into the practice of the Ramakrishna Order. Previously (and it is still so in the more orthodox Orders) the neophyte was subjected to a particularly strict regime. He received little food, he had to wear an old habit, and he was given the most uncomfortable place to sleep in. Only gradually, as it became clear that he really had a vocation, was his life made easier. Vivekananda decided that exactly the opposite procedure was better: in the first period of his life with the Ramakrishna Order the novice is particularly well treated, and if he happens to come from a poor family then at first he lives better and more comfortably than he has been accustomed to at home. He has good, clean clothing; he is fed well with good and very tasty food; and he sleeps no more uncomfortably than anyone else. Then gradually these special privileges are withdrawn, but so gradually that he hardly notices it. In fact, what usually happens is that the monks themselves voluntarily abandon first this and then that privilege of the novitiate; they no longer desire this relatively high standard of comfort. Thus in the Ramakrishna Order the situation is paradoxical for the more orthodox: the young acolytes live, for monastic ideas, almost in luxury, whilst the older and senior monks practice the privations which are usually reserved for the younger men. In the more orthodox Orders the novices live meagrely, the senior monks well, and the abbots sometimes almost luxuriously. In the Ramakrishna Order the situation is reversed. Each method has its advantages and disadvantages. Although Vivekananda's innovation is psychologically sounder and pedagogically more effective, it certainly has one disadvantage: the older monks, having lived ascetically and frugally for so long are often dried-up and disagreeable old sticks who can, and sometimes do, make life difficult for the younger men—not necessarily directly, but perhaps in a subtle monastic way which is not easy for a novice to understand, but tends to produce permanent guilt complexes.

Within three days I had settled down into the routine and discipline of the publishing centre of the Ramakrishna Order. As the monastery was centrally situated, we constantly had visitors from other Missions in Calcutta. The Ramakrishna Order has over a dozen houses in Calcutta, and the headquarters of the Order, which is in Belur, is only about ten miles away. Every evening I went out for a two-hour walk, and during these walks I quartered the whole town, interesting myself for the moment in its topographical features; the opportunity for sociological investigations was to come only in later years.

At first I was always accompanied by Brahmacārī Sudhir, or 'Very Wise One'. No doubt he had been instructed to go with me for fear that I might lose myself in the confusion of streets, and the still greater confusion of sins, which Calcutta affords. In one respect in particular we were unsuited to each other. He was short and wiry and had hardly a third of my weight, and even if he had not known his way about as well as he did, he would have walked much more quickly than I was accustomed to. In short, he was too quick for me and I was too slow for him. After a few days, to my relief, he came with me no longer, went off on his own, or just stayed behind. He had probably convinced the worthy Abbot that I was really in no danger of getting lost in either sense. However, in the 'Very Wise One' I met, for the first time, a modern educated young monk who was at the same time devoted to the old traditions with a good deal of feeling and a certain dogmatic toughness. There are not very many of his kind in India, and whether their numbers will increase in the future is problematical, for the general trend in India to-day is towards secularization; and the wearing of the ochre robe is coming to be regarded as a cloak for laziness, which indeed it very often is, though certainly not amongst the members of the Ramakrishna Order.

Now Novice Sudhir had fallen into one serious error, which he shared with all the other monks and lay followers of his Order: he was perfectly certain that all the problems of space and time had now been finally solved in the teachings of Ramakrishna and Vivekananda, and that all anyone had to do was to follow them conscientiously. Such an attitude is typical of all converts in all countries and at all times. The early Buddhists, the early Christians, the National Socialists, the Communists—they all have the same confident and comforting feeling of personal salvation and inner security: they have found the answer to all problems. 'Inner certainty' is, of course, a very edifying possession but it has nothing whatever to do with fact. All religions and all ideologies suffer from the same prejudice. Whoever believes, judges before he knows. This uncritical, naive certainty first set my nerves on edge, then it embarrassed me, and finally it drove me out of the Order of Ramakrishna and Vivekananda into an older, unreformed and not progressive, but intellectually far less prejudiced monastic tradition.

Swami Vandanananda, who was at that time in charge of the Book and Publication Department of the Order, and who is now assistant to the famous Swami Prabhavananda in the Ramakrishna Vedanta Centre in Hollywood, performed the main physical initiatory act: the shaving of the head. All the hair is shaved off except the *śikhā*, a cranial tuft. It is thus a sort of inverted tonsure. The *śikhā* has always been the outward sign of Brahmin orthodoxy. It varies from one part of the country to the other: sometimes it is larger, sometimes smaller; sometimes farther forward on the head, sometimes farther back. Afterwards I took a bath, and then I was given two new lengths of cotton and a tailor came specially to measure me for my *kūrtā*, a kind of long-sleeved shirt. This *kūrtā* is a quite unorthodox garment, and the older and less modern Orders look askance at it. Ancient Indian clothing has nothing sewn, and the shirt and trousers are of Persian-Mogul origin, i.e. a foreign innovation. The orthodox Indian rejects them as impure, uncongenial and untraditional. To-day, however, only very orthodox Brahmins, monks and novices—in short, all those who identify themselves actively with religious traditions—wear the unsewn drape. And, of course, the women; for the sari is nothing but a long length of silk, brocade, or other material, though what the urban Hindu lady wears underneath is becoming more and more Western.

The Ramakrishna monks are the only Hindu monks to wear a shirt. It has long arms and hangs down over the *dhotī*. The *kūrtā* of the novice is white, that of the ordained monk ochre. But the habit proper, in so far as it is orthodox, consists of the aforesaid two equal lengths of cotton. The third orthodox item of monastic clothing is the *kaupīna*, which is a cross between a loincloth and a chastity belt. In some Orders this is the only item of clothing, and there was a time when it was so for all Indian monks.

The same evening I went for a walk on the Chowringhee in my new clothes, and the reaction of the people around me changed at once. The effect of my appearance produced on Hindus throughout the years would provide a basis for an interesting psychological or sociological study. For the Hindu the garb of the monk is the undisputed symbol of the teacher—the highest form of human being; even the divine human being, the God-Man. According to tradition the celibate monk stands above the wedded gods in the cosmic hierarchy. When he enters a temple he blesses the images—he blesses them because celibacy stands higher than matrimony, celestial though it be.

My stay in the Advaita Monastery in Calcutta lasted just four months. Every evening I strolled across the Dharamtalla, the busiest street in the centre of the town, the elegant Chowringhee, then through Park Street along one of the streets running parallel to the Chowringhee, and back to Wellington Place and the monastery. This itinerary formed a square with sides about half a mile in length each. It was already very warm, and by the beginning of March the sweat was bursting out on my forehead at every step. Although by this time I was used to wearing my new garments, I still was not very good at fastening the *dhoti* round my considerable middle. There is no kind of belt to assist the process, and the *dhotī* has to be so folded and tucked in that it holds up on its own. The same is true, of course, of the women's saris, and to adjust them properly is an art. On one occasion when the Abbot was looking me up and down he pronounced the words 'And the drape will fall from the middle'. I took his words metaphorically, but I would have done better to have taken them in practical earnest and pay more attention to the careful adjustment of my *dhotī*. Usually he spoke in an elevated fashion, invariably with some reference to the Absolute. Most other forms of conversation were a waste of time in his opinion. I therefore interpreted his words in some such sense; e.g. that after long meditation the drape, i.e. the veil of untruth, would fall from the middle, i.e. from our phenomenal existence, in order to reveal the truth. And with that elevated interpretation I went on my unsuspecting way. But that evening, in the middle of the Chowringhee, the drape did fall from the middle. My *dhotī* came loose and dropped around my ankles, and there I stood in my shirt. As it happened too, I had omitted to put on my *kaupīna*, on that old-established and usually expedient Viennese principle 'No one sees it anyhow'. Of course I made a swift dive for my disarrayed *dhotī* and managed to get it round me again somehow; but not before curious eyes had witnessed the embarrassing scene. They remained fastened upon me to see what I would do next, and there was even a certain amount of giggling. I hurried to the nearest open shop, where a small tailor sat behind a pile of cloth. He was too small to have noticed anything beneath the level of his bales.

'What can I do for you, Great King?' he inquired politely for 'Mahārāj' is the only possible way to address a monk in India. Feeling like anything but a Great King I asked him hurriedly if there were any place where I might be out of sight for a moment or two. He had no idea what it was all about and he bowed low and answered: 'The Great King may withdraw into whatever place he desires, seeing that the whole world belongs to him.' This was all very well, but it didn't help me much at the moment. However, I managed to hide myself behind his bales and there I wound my *dhotī* around me with all the attention it deserves. After that there were two things to which I paid special attention: First of all I always tried, in the words of my superior, to separate the practical from the metaphorical, which wasn't easy; and secondly, I always folded and tucked in my *dhotī* with the greatest possible care.

As soon as I arrived in Calcutta I had been told that I should stay there only for a few months; my training proper was to take place in a monastery in the Himalayas, and Swami Yogeshwarananda himself was to accompany me into the mountains. The Abbot of Advaita monastery always spends six months in Calcutta, in the cool of the year, and six months in the Himalayas, in the hot period. I therefore made systematic use of the time I still had to spend in Calcutta, since once I started my training in the Himalayas it was unlikely that I would see the plains again for quite a long time, and certainly not Calcutta. Till my departure, there was plenty of opportunity to study the urban life of the monks. Almost every week there was a *bhaṇḍāra* in one of the many houses of the Ramakrishna Order in or near Calcutta. A *bhaṇḍāra* is the favourite change from the everyday jogtrot for all Hindu monks. Literally translated it means a 'clearing out of the pantry', and that is sufficient to indicate its character. Some rich Hindu of the neighbourhood decides to celebrate some special occasion, such as the marriage of a son or daughter; or to give thanks for some blessing; or perhaps just to give particular expression to his own piety. So he gets into touch with the nearest monastery and announces that he is prepared to have so many monks as his guests at a *bhaṇḍāra*. When the date is fixed the women of his household start the preparations well in advance; there are sometimes as many as a thousand monks at such a *bhaṇḍāra*, though such mass affairs are growing rare nowadays.

When they arrive for the party the monks sit on the floor on rush mats in accordance with the monastery hierarchy, forming a *paṅgat*. *Thālī-s* are then placed before them. These are shallow dishes, of silver or some other metal; and then the feast begins. The rich man's servants, and sometimes his wife and daughters, and himself too, bring in great dishes of food—never less than ten courses, and naturally all vegetarian: vegetables fried in butter, various kinds of rice, *chapattis* (Indian unleavened pancakes, very much like Mexican *tortillas* in appearance), baked pulse pancakes, many sweet dishes and mounds of fruits. And when the meal is over the host produces a sack and distributes money amongst his guests, or perhaps, and certainly in a more orthodox fashion, ochre *dhotīs* and *cādars* or woollen blankets.

Indian monks usually have good appetites, and when they get the chance they eat heartily. But the amount a monk can get through in his prime is astonishing. His food is, of course, always orthodox: no meat, no fish, no eggs, no onions, and many other prohibitions. The objection to such dishes is not so much that life must be taken in order to prepare them, because the Hindu sophist will say, quite correctly, that there is life in a grain of corn, but because the forbidden items are believed to have an aphrodisiac effect. However, there is still a very great deal of good and tasty food that a monk may eat: many kinds of vegetables prepared in many different ways with many varieties of spices, while onions are replaced in the cooking by asafoetida. Then there are the sweet dishes, and they seem to belong to the gastronomic essence of the monk's economy. The Vedāntic literature even allows itself a joke or two about the sweet tooth of Brahmins and ascetics. There are hundreds of sweet dishes in India, and certain areas are famous for their goodness and variety, especially Bengal. The ingredients are chiefly milk, curds and whey, cream, flour, *ghee* (butter fat) and large quantities of sugar or *guṛ* (molasses). These dishes are not baked, but cooked for a long time on a very low fire, or steamed. With few exceptions I have never been able to take kindly to these sweet dishes, and for this reason pious eyebrows have often been raised in disapproval: a real monk ought to like sweet things and be able to consume them in large quantities. The more you eat means the more virtue to the credit of your host, so he does not like to see you not doing full justice to what he sets before you. In one form or other that logic is not confined to India.

A lot of nonsense has been written both in India and elsewhere about food customs and food prohibitions in India. The fact that perhaps 70 per cent of all Indians are vegetarians has little to do with their religions and traditional ideas. The real reason is more a matter of economics. Meat is just too expensive for the average villager or factory worker, so he has to live on rice and *dāl*, and perhaps yoghurt. And even where Indians are vegetarians as a matter of orthodoxy it is impossible to point clearly to the reason for the tabu in the same way, for example, as you can point to the doctrinal prohibition of pork for the Moslem. In the Vedic days when the canonical writings of the Brahmins was being codified, meat was eaten, and not just meat, but beef; in fact it was the main food. Rāma and Sītā, the heroic pair of the great epic, and the heroes of the Mahābhārata, had no objection to eating meat or to drinking alcoholic potions. It was only gradually that the eating of meat went out of fashion; probably, as I have suggested, for economic reasons. The Indo-Aryans, who were beginning to settle down needed the products of the cow more than they needed its meat and abstinence from meat-eating gradually began to be coloured by religious considerations; and then came Jainism and Buddhism to reinforce the abstinence. However, the Buddhist monks in almost all countries eat meat—beef, pork and chicken—and whatever the pious layman in Ceylon, Burma or Siam cares to put into their begging bowls.

If you ask the orthodox Hindu why he does not eat meat he will tell you it is the law for Hindus—but only if he supposes that you know nothing about Hindu law. If this is not the case then he will give a series of reasons, none of which is particularly convincing—at least, they do not strike me as convincing. Manu the law-giver does not forbid the eating of meat, though he does say that it is a virtuous thing to abstain from it. Similarly, however, he says a lot of other things which arouse misgiving; for example, concerning the status of women, who do not come off very well at his hands. And as for the objection that meat has an aphrodisiacal effect, I wonder what good food has not. The only way to be free of all lusts of the flesh is to eat nothing at all. The best explanation of the vexed question is also the most reasonable: in certain families and castes it has been the custom from time immemorial not to eat meat, and they maintain the old tradition. It is a fact that a Hindu who has never tasted meat is often revolted by the sight and smell of meat dishes. Indian students from orthodox families who come to England and the United States to study often find it very difficult to accustom themselves to eating meat, though it is true that once they do most of them grow to like it. But some of them cannot or do not want to get used to it. *Chacun à son goût*. Further, it is not at all certain that because a particular Hindu does not eat meat he therefore believes in the teachings of Hinduism. The truth is that abstinence from meat is a social matter in India and not a religious one.

You can get by bus from Howrah Bridge to the headquarters of the Ramakrishna Order in Belurmath in just under half-an-hour. It is the centre of a community of monks which unites the traditional and the modern India in a way never done before, and there is an impressive relationship between the community and the outside and importunate world. People simply swarm out from Calcutta to honour the pupils of the Holy Master, and often to ask them for advice. Well-situated citizens, a bank official, or a doctor, or a lawyer, will turn up at the monastery, with wife and seven children. He parks his good English car in the spacious Math grounds and they all get out. It doesn't matter whether it's a Morris Minor, which is now being made under license in India as the 'Hindusthan', or a big American Studebaker; the whole family has to get in it somehow. Very likely the man's father took him out to Belurmath when he was a little boy, and he is keeping up the tradition. The father will have visited Swami Brahmananda, who was one of the most beloved of all the pupils of the Paramahaṃsa. A layman can have a Guru, and he picks himself out one from amongst the many monks and holy men available, choosing one who suits his own character, which he now hopes to perfect with the aid of his Guru. The Guru gives him a secret *mantra*, a formula which the pupil will repeat a million times in the course of the years, and at the same time he will meditate on the Godhead in the form evoked by his *mantra*, which is the key to that aspect of the Godhead which is chosen; the aim being to win emancipation from the chains of life and rebirth.

According to the rules of the Ramakrishna Order only the President, i.e. the Abbot General, of the Order may perform this *mantra* initiation, technically known as *dīksā*. The reigning Abbot-General will now initiate the man as his father was initiated. There is no compulsion, and no indoctrination from father to son: The spirit of the thing is passed on, and the son voluntarily seeks the initiation. People who receive the *dīkṣā* from the same Guru are then '*Gurubhāī-s*', or '*Gurubhagini-s*' for life; that is to say Guru-brothers or Guru-sisters, and a close bond exists between them, whether they know each other personally or not.

The family—as do all the hundreds of thousands of others who come out every year to Belurmath—now greet the swamis by touching their feet, and an amiable and pious conversation begins. But although pious, the conversation is not entirely devoted to pious things, for the swamis are shrewd, worldly-wise and practical as well as being holy men. The family then makes a tour of the temple, always keeping the shrine on its right. This procedure, *parikrama*, the clockwise circumambulation is a symbol of devotion not only in India but throughout the whole of Buddhist Asia. When the circle is completed they enter the temple and pay their respects to the particular Godhead enthroned there; in this case it is Ramakrishna Paràmahaṃsa, who represents an incarnation of the Godhead to all true believers, something which is canonically very easy to substantiate in a case like his. There is hardly a holy man in India who is not regarded by some religious group or other as an avatāra, an incarnation. The obeisance is not performed by full length prostration on the ground, as is the case in Southern India, but by kneeling down on both knees and touching the temple floor with the forehead in front of the cult object, whatever it may be. It may be a swami, a holy man or an image. With the Sikhs it is the Holy Book, the *Guru Granth Sāhib*. There is a short form of greeting which consists of touching the feet with one's right hand and then touching one's forehead.

Apart from the monastic community, two worlds converge in this Ramakrishna temple at Belurmath, but almost without mutual contact. These are the worlds of the poor Hindu, the worker or peasant; and the world of the Calcutta middle class. Peasants and working people visit Belur in the same way as they visit any other holy place, out of untutored piety handed down by their parents—and perhaps mingled with curiosity. For the poor Hindu the temple has been a kind of museum from time immemorial, the only museum he knows. The members of the Calcutta middle class visit Belur because Ramakrishna and Vivekananda, and particularly the latter, signify a sort of middle-class apotheosis. The holy men here belong to the parents generation; they come from the middle or lower-middle class themselves, and they have awakened a tremendous renaissance of religious culture in India. All the direct pupils of the Master, the immediate colleagues of Vivekananda—with one exception only—belonged to the middle class, went to middle-class schools and learned a certain amount of middle-class English; and in consequence the better situated citizen of Calcutta projects his own traditional and spiritual idea of freedom on to the monks, who have all grown up in his own environment, but who have succeeded in emancipating themselves from worldly chains and obligations and in winning through to freedom.

The great celebration in Belur is the anniversary of the birth of Ramakrishna, and it is kept up with tremendous enthusiasm. Thousands of poor people are fed, and hundreds of thousands of visitors come to the temple. Loudspeakers set up in the grounds broadcast pious exhortations for 24 hours, including sermons by swamis themselves, and by specially chosen laymen: *bhajans*, litanies are chanted, and there is sacred music. The birthday of Ramakrishna is solemnly celebrated wherever there is a Ramakrishna Mission. As Ramakrishna and Vivekananda were both eclectics, and because the hallmark of the Hindu renaissance is a belief in the essential oneness of all religions, speakers from all the available religious communities in India are included in the programme of the celebrations. In Indian Mission centres you find Mohamedan Mullahs, Hindu monks and Brahmins, Jaina scholars, and even Christians together on the same platform. In the United States a Rabbi and one or two Christian pastors are always invited to take part but, of course, only those who themselves believe in the oneness and equality of all religions—or those who at least do not positively deny it.

I, for example, am not qualified to stand on such a joint platform because I am not an eclectic and because I am firmly convinced, and, I hope, in a position to support scholastically, that the great religious groupings of mankind are fundamentally different. Whether the scene is a Mission House of the Ramakrishna Order in Calcutta, Madras or San Francisco, the argument is always the same: Moses, Buddha, Christ and Kṛṣṇa all meant the same in their teachings—and that applies in particular to Ramakrishna. They expressed it differently, that is all. The Ramakrishna monks are particularly fond of quoting the facile axiom of the Upanishad: 'There is only one truth, but Wise Men call it by many names.' Unfortunately, however, this axiom was uttered at a time when only one truth was taught, that of a single, absolute essence. Buddha, who rejected the idea of any such absolute essence, had not yet come upon the scene; and the radical atheistic Jainas had as yet little influence. It is also interesting to note that although all Ramakrishna Mission Centres proclaim that even Buddhism teaches essentially the same, one, uniform teaching, no Buddhist monk or Buddhist lay scholar is ever invited to take part in the celebrations of Ramakrishna's birthday, because Buddhism never teaches what Moses, Kṛṣṇa and Christ did teach in common in their various ways, namely a Being or essence in all eternity.

I was much more taken by the *Durgāpūjā* which I experienced in the Belur temple at a much later date. Durgā is the female divine mother principle; mythologically she is the consort of Śiva, and the most sophisticated aspect of the Brahmin universal conception. Kali, the goddess whose name is much better known in the West, hungry as it is for mythical sensationalism, is identical with Durgā, and represents a not-quite Brahmanical modification of Durgā. Kālī may be ritually venerated by priests of a lower caste, but only Brahmins may ritually worship Durgā. The 'honouring of Durgā', known as *Durgāpūjā,* takes place in October. This is a specifically Bengali celebration, and for ten days the whole of Bengal looks unhinged. The municipal services cease to operate, the Universities close down, and tremendous crowds of people dressed in their best surge through the streets gaily taking part in the celebrations and paying honour to the many decorated effigies of Durgā which are set up everywhere. These effigies which are life-size, and sometimes even larger, have been made for many generations by artists who specialize in clay modelling. There is the goddess Durgā herself and her divine companions, and also the bull-demon Mahiṣāsura, who is killed by Durgā: he symbolizes the evil powers of violence and male aggressiveness. The effigies of the divine ladies usually have real human hair.

Every year Durgā is supposed to leave her consort for ten days to return to her parents, and all married Hindu women follow her example, and their return is a joyful event for the whole family. These returning wives are then the younger sisters of Durgā. They wear their most beautiful saris and they decorate the picture of Durgā, daubing her forehead with cinnabar, which brings good fortune. Throughout the ten days of the celebration priests recite litanies in praise of Durgā; he-goats, and sometimes male water-buffaloes, are sacrificed to her in the forecourts, since in her own home in Bengal Durgā is no vegetarian. On the 'Tenth Day of Victory', *Vijaya Daśamī,* her image is carried in solemn procession through the streets to the nearest river or pond where it is cast into the water. Water, the still, endless element, is Śiva. And so Durgā unites with her eternal consort until she returns again the following year.

For the Belur temple a large and very beautiful effigy of Durgā and her divine companions is made annually by the best artists. The ordained monks themselves take no part in the *Durgāpūjā* and during it they sit to one side, because a *sannyāsī* is dead to worldly life; therefore the ceremony is left to the *brahmacārī-s,* who perform the ritual, sing hymns in Durgā's praise, sit around the holy fire and pour *ghee*, i.e. melted butter, into the flames with the proper incantations.

In April Calcutta is so hot as to be almost unbearable even for the native Bengali. The electric ceiling ventilators work day and night—in the houses of those who have them—but they bring little relief. It was at this time that we began to prepare for our journey to the Himalayas. The Secretary-General of the Ramakrishna Order, Swami Madhavananda, and the Abbot of the Advaita Ashrama, Swami Yogeshwarananda, and I were to go together. A score or so of Ramakrishna monks were assembled at the Howrah Station to see us off, and in particular to say farewell to the Secretary-General of the Order, because after many years service in the highest administrative post of the Order, Swami Madhavananda now proposed to retire to the mountain monastery to spend the rest of his life in meditation. Many garlands of flowers were hung around the necks of all of us, and the general atmosphere was lively and gay. When high members of the Order go away this is always taken as a cause for rejoicing in the centres of the Order, even if they are popular and well liked. I have never been able to discover why this is so.

Our bus reached Champawat only three hours behind schedule, and we continued on foot. The climb was steep and unpleasant, and I got very annoyed with it after an hour, for I detest climbing of any sort. Another reason for my dismay was the conversation of the Brahmacārī and the Bhaṇḍārī-Swami behind me. Not the content, but the linguistic pattern: they spoke their own vernacular Kannada, but their vocabulary was largely English, interspersed with Bengali expletives. It took me a long time to learn that the cultured Hindu's small talk is this sort of blend, as soon as he has had even the smallest amount of English education, which is virtually inevitable in the classes from which the Ramakrishna Order monks are recruited—the lower-salaried government servants, small town lawyers, teachers and *babus* in general. The orthodox monks and priests who are brought up in a totally uncritical, intensely purist atmosphere of traditional rote learning speak a chaste vernacular—their terminology in common parlance derives from Sanskrit just as does their learned, scholastic discourse. The professor of philosophy or literature teaching at a British university and his Indian student, now an I.C.S. officer, speak chaste English with Latinized terminology, the exact occidental counterpart of the Indian tradition availing itself of Sanskrit roots; and whatever lies between them uses the sort of mixed patois which now irritated me beyond description.

The orthodox orders seem also to disapprove of the Ramakrishna Mission's worldly activities, its charitable undertakings. No orthodox Hindu order indulges in large scale organized charity. The Ramakrishna Mission, unconsciously following the model of the Christian monastic denominations, runs hospitals, maternity wards, schools and colleges. The orthodox objection is not born of jealousy, but follows the argument: food is given by the king, worldly knowledge by the scholar, the intuitive realization of oneness with the Supreme can be given only by the monks. Why do the Ramakrishna monks stoop to a lower level of giving? The notion that we attain self-realization through service to humanity is a Christianized notion propounded by Swami Vivekananda, who had had the Puritan protestant education of the British-inspired Calcutta college, and I believe that this made him give a start to the teachings of Ramakrishna Paramahaṃsa, the preceptor of the movement.

It was late when we reached Lohaghat, the only market place near the monastery, and the last halt on the way. We lodged at the house of Mr Mohanlal Shah, referred to as 'Shahji' as a term of endearment by all the Ramakrishnites. He had seen and served Swami Vivekananda, the founder-builder of our monastery, and he had been visiting it every fortnight for forty years. Shahji had remained a bachelor. He never gave any explicit reason (which Hindu society expects to be given, for nobody just happens to be a bachelor, unless he is a monk, or very sick, or afflicted by some other serious trouble), but it was commonly agreed that he felt inspired by the monastic ideal, without quite making it though I always felt certain Shahji would have made a good monk. His elder brother was very different: a married man with the usual number of children, dead and alive, a very pious man in the un-reformed sense. For in spite of the proximity of the Ramakrishna Mission, he lived the life of an ancient Hindu, the renaissance had not touched him, because he had no need for it. His lips were constantly moving in *japam*, he was humble, friendly and totally taciturn. He had an uncanny way of making servants and villagers do what he thought necessary, without saying a word; he just looked at them and twisted his facial muscles for what seemed to be the bare fraction of a second, and his lips never ceased mumbling the *mantra* as he issued these silent orders. None of the other monks ever noticed this strange phenomenon, because persons *per se* are somehow not interesting to the hagiocentric monk. They are mentioned or discussed and attended to only if they act mischievously or if they do something charitable beyond their expected duty; they are noticed only if they divert the monks from their routine, one way or another. The same applies to servants and cooks: they are pure functions, and they become persons only when they are caught doing something impermissible or disturbing. They are treated well as patients, and are given the same medical care, no doubt, as the Sub-Divisional Officer if the latter happens to be in need of medical attention; for serving the sick adds to spiritual freedom, it is a *sādhanā*-like meditation according to the monastic schools of the Hindu renaissance—the Ramakrishnites foremost amongst them. And this lets the cat out of the bag. The servant, the poor man, the S.D.O., they are all instruments for the practice of *sādhanā;* as human beings they hardly figure. The Bhagavadgītā—that first and oldest text of the Hindu renaissance—puts it quite clearly: see the Lord in all beings, treat all beings as the Lord. Which implies something most depressing to the critical humanist: human beings are interesting and to be served only *sub specie divinitatis*, not as autonomous individuals in their own right—for the status of the individual qua individual is *māyā*, a sort of illusion and something to be transcended. It is the individual qua individual one has to get rid of, so that God can shine forth.

My cell was tolerably wide, very neat, with a large *takhtā* and the unexpected comfort of a woollen mattress on top of it, a writing-table, a stool, and a little shelf for the basic literature a monk must have with him: the Rules of the Order, which is just a small booklet, the Words of Ramakrishna and Vivekananda and of some other great monks of the Order, and of course the Upaniṣads and the Bhagavadgītā, plus any canonical text of which the individual monk or novice happens to be particularly fond.

The next morning had the ring of regularity: the inmates assembled for their morning tea in the central hall, and then my rotund Brahmacārī beckoned me to follow him. He showed me the monastery in daytime. Along the walls there were bookshelves filled with numerous books of widely disparate merit. The library of the Advaita Ashrama, a congeries of donations and exchange tokens, contained some excellent material, a lot of mediocre stuff, and some real trash—pious trash, that is, and more nauseating to me than outright pornography. The unique mixture of sentimental, cultural chauvinism, the idea that what is old in religion is better, that everything Indian is the oldest and therefore best, that all religions mean essentially the same namely 'be good' and 'trust God', that the East is utterly spiritual, the West utterly materialistic, and that naïve yet most depressing attitude of the propounders and protagonists of the Hindu Renaissance which seeks out and lovingly lingers on similarities between various cults, religions, and philosophies (and in this monastery, the additional sectarian slant projected in the jejune yet brazen idea that Ramakrishna and Vivekananda had summed up Indian culture in its quintessence)—this mixture of well-meant confusions readily makes for a collection such as this cloister library.

Apart from the books, there is the tea table, a typewriter on a little table, and an old, old H.M.V. gramophone. A dry-battery radio was a recent acquisition, and it ushered in many heated political discussions, commentaries based on the news broadcasts of All India Radio from Delhi or Lucknow, the closest station, or from Tashkent, farther away, but much more powerful.

The dining-hall is under the same roof, and it contains the orthodox *paṅgat*, a long, low table, with wooden boards as seats along the wall; the kitchen is outside this main complex, yet in the same building, as are also the two bath-cells.

The smaller building opposite the main one is the Editor's Office. The Advaita Ashrama is the publication centre of the Ramakrishna Mission, and the pious periodical *Prabuddha Bhārata* (*Awakened India*) is edited and published from here, the Editor-Swami's office and cell being located in the smaller building, which also contains the post-office, a little room where the peon from Lohaghat leaves and fetches the mail. Although there is no direct rule against having private correspondence, there is some degree of reserve against it. The post office serves the editorial office—all but the Editor-Swami frown, or ought to frown, when they get mail from below the mountains.

From the garden square between the two buildings, the bridle path to Lohaghat branches off to the third building of the Ashrama, the Hospital and Dispensary, and to the Guest House. The hospital is well run, and of course purely charitable. Medical and pharmaceutical firms in Calcutta and elsewhere donate drugs and instruments every year.

The last station on my tour of introduction was the cowpen, where quite a few milch-cows were kept tidily by Ram Singh, an incredibly dirty Kṣattriya (there are only Brahmins and Kṣattriyas in the indigenous Hindu population of this region) who had been in the Army, and who could swear with a fairly rich vocabulary in Punjabi. But he loved the animals, and that is why the Ashram kept him in spite of many minor frictions. His love of animals was rather self-defeating from the Ashram's viewpoint, for he pinched the cows' udders when milking them, lest they should give too much for the monks and keep too little for the calves. Hence a *brahmacārī* or a monk was delegated at milking time to watch the good man with a lantern, lest the milk should be less than the daily requirement due either to Ram Singh's theriophile udder-pinching or the addition of water, which flows plentifully near the Ashram.

On the crest above the monastery complex, there is a well attended orchard and vegetable garden, with a little hut in it. Usually, one Swami feels like retreating to this lonely, lovely spot for a few months to perform solitary meditation and to tend the garden. For some reason which did not become clear to me, it was also considered the healthiest spot in the monastery, for monks who had been in poor health for a while were put up there. Last but not least, there is the lavatory—a euphemistic term, be it said. It never offers any problem to the born Indian, but to me it loomed formidably wherever I went in Asia. My bones are heavy Central European bones, and I cannot squat in the manner required for the Indian sanitary equipment, which is always on a level with the ground or at least not meant for the occidental approach. Here in the Ashram there was a little hut alongside the main buildings, some planks and about half a dozen holes in the planks, until about a year after I had joined, when, owing to the munificence of a devotee, septic tanks were installed.

From the library to the lavatory I had thus completed my first monastic circumambulation. The rotund Brahmacārī told me my secular commitments: I would have to do some cleaning in the main building, a chore done by rote by the *brahmacārī-s;* I would have to rearrange the library and catalogue all its books, because that had not been done so far; I would have to help the Editor and the Publisher in their Office work, proof reading and so on, and I would have to do all these things in a spirit of dedication, for although they look worldly, the spirit of dedication renders them spiritual, on a par with meditation, and with the study of the scriptures. So long as I stayed at the Advaita Ashrama, the Abbot was wholly in charge of my studies and of my spiritual progress—yet this did not mean I could not also study subjects I felt personally interested in: the library was at the disposal of every inmate, and I could read and think at all hours when there were no other duties, holy or otherwise. I felt happy. The atmosphere was congenial. I was a regular novice now. I would stay at this Ashram for about four years, studying and meditating; then, I would be sent down to Calcutta and Belurmath to get my first ordination as a consecrated *brahmacārī;* then I would come back for another four or five years, whereafter I would obtain my final anointment as a *sannyāsī* in the Holy Order, again at Belurmath. This was the first and so far the last instance in my life when I kept believing for over a month at a stretch that my course was settled for the next eight years.

That evening, Swami Yogeshvarananda took me aside again and made me sit facing him in his room. 'It is understood', he said, 'that you meditate regularly twice a day. It is understood that you study. It is understood that you do whatever work is given to you in the name of Ṭhākur, and that you do it for Him. For the daily office work, menial work in the Ashram and in the garden, we all are witnesses, and you will be rebuked if you do not perform them properly. But meditation and study are up to you—if you do them, you will advance toward the goal, which is total freedom, perfection. If you don't, you will not advance; but there is no control over these inner activities. No one will tell you to meditate if you don't, even if one of us should observe that you are not meditating; no one will tell you to study the scriptures if you don't, but not studying them will tell on you—for this life in the spirit requires fortification by reason. Not in all our Hindu traditions, but in the *sannyāsī* tradition study is incumbent on the monk. True, *mokṣa* and the life of contemplation have nothing to do with learning. The sage may be illiterate. Ramakrishna was almost illiterate, other great souls were completely illiterate. But if learning is added to sagehood, then it is like some beautiful flowers kept in a beautiful, elaborately fashioned vase: the flowers are perfect without a vase, but the vase adds to their beauty nevertheless. Learning is not essential to achieve salvation, freedom from birth and from death, oneness with the Brahman; but it adds something to the seeker of freedom, nevertheless.'

I remembered this instruction of my urbanized Abbot in the Himalayas, when a more powerful teacher, a woman-saint, taught me the same with a different simile a few years later: 'Learning does not add greater freedom to *mokṣa*, for *mokṣa* is complete freedom. But it adds grandeur to the seeker. It is like a beautiful woman—she is most perfect when she is nude, but when she drapes herself in charming raiments and puts hibiscus flowers into her hair, something seems to be added to her perfection. Knowledge, learning are like the raiments, logical speech is like the red hibiscus.'

I had not had my *dīkṣā* yet—I was to be summoned to the General Abbot later in the year, but within the first three days Swami Yogeshvarananda gave me sufficient instruction to begin my meditation provisionally. This is the customary procedure in almost all Hindu monasteries, not only in the Ramakrishna Order: the authority to give *dīkṣā* vests in the very senior monastic personalities, and as seniority is frequently tantamount with fame, and as fame decreases accessibility the individual novice must often wait for quite a while until he gets his *dīkṣā*. In the Daśanāmī Order some have to remain without it for twelve years, some just never get it. It is impossible to say how far this is intention and how far accident. Monastic lore tends to ascribe a lot more intuitive pedagogy to such delay than would seem warranted to me. Things simply are not so well organized as in the monastic orders of the Roman Catholic Church; this lack of organization has proved to be of immense spiritual advantage, which compensates, to my feeling, for the fact that it is slipshod. This charge, however, does not affect the Ramakrisha Mission, for this is the one monastic organization in India which would hold its own with the Society of Jesus in matters of efficiency. The Abbot General was very old and not too well—this was the reason for the delay.

Hence, the meditation I learnt previous to my *dīkṣā* had the outer form of initiated meditation, but it was short of the main instrument, the *mantra*. This can be imparted only by the Guru and he in the case of this Order, was the President or Abbot General. What is meditation in its technical, anchorite sense? It is an entirely mental process—nothing in it is related to what occidental faddism conceives as 'yoga'; the only physical requirement is a correct *āsana*, which has to be learned within the first two or three months by simple experiment, by trial and error. Then, the aspirant has to learn to eschew objective and discursive thought by a gradual process. He advances from rational thought to supra-rational thought, or, if this term is unpleasant to the analytical ear, to intuitive, non-discursive thought. He has to learn to grasp the object of meditation, not through an act of inward description or objectification, but through a mental act as direct as perception. Hence the mystics speak of 'seeing God', 'talking to God'—the fact that sensuous terms are used to describe successful meditation points to the directness of the process; yet, it is an entirely non-sensuous 'perception' that is achieved. Impossible to make this clear to anyone who has not experienced it—or even to anyone, who does not care to experience it—or, in other words, who is not attracted by the flavour of ineffability which permeates all mystical literature. Mystical language is that in which consummated meditation is discussed; mystical literature describes this consummation and to some extent, the steps that lead to it. The claim to pronounce truths about nature or God or man apart from experiences in meditation, or by way of discursive generalization about the things experienced in meditation is fanaticism if the teacher generalizes on the basis of his own experience and hoax if he does it on that of anyone else. The difference between a prophet and a mystic is just this: the prophet is a mystic who insists that his meditative experiences correspond to things or facts outside his mind, who thinks they are 'true', like tables, beer and philosophers. The mystic is one who draws no objective conclusions from his experiences, who either keeps them to himself or imparts them merely as an incentive to others to seek the same experiences, very much in the manner a Bartok lover tries to make others love Bartok. The Judaeo-Christian-Muslim tradition is replete with prophets and has a few mystics; the Hindu-Buddhist-Jaina tradition is replete with mystics and has fortunately had no prophets so far. 'Prophet' to my way of thinking at least, is a derogatory term.

Now though meditation is a purely mental process, it aims at eradicating mentation in the end: the mind experiences a complete catharrsis, it gets emptied of all contents. This is totally different from sleep, stupor, drowsiness, imbecility and certain drug-induced states, for there are all sorts of contents in these states, albeit misarranged, or pathologically distorted. Meditation leads to an emptiness of mind which, again, just cannot be described to anyone who has not gone through it; or, at best again, it will strike a note for those who are attracted to the way teachers and saints and mystics have been talking about this 'emptiness' for well over 3,000 years.

The method by which the novices of the Ramakrishna Order learn to meditate is as old as systematic yoga; it was laid down by Patāñjali about 2,000 years ago, and even he was drawing on sources which were ancient by his time. There are certain innovations in the method of meditation taught to the disciples of Ramakrishna, but this is nothing unusual, for every founder of a new school—such as Ramakrishna and Vivekananda—expanded traditional matter by his own insights, adding to an interminable process of eclectic variation. This is extremely important. In fact it is a cue to the understanding of Indian spiritual practice, epitomized in the canonical words *ekaṃ sadviprā bahudhā vadanti*, 'there is one truth, but sages approach it by different methods'. All teachers from the days of the Veda have taken it to heart. Vivekananda once said it would be the ideal thing if every human being had his or her own religion. The methods differ widely indeed; from extreme asceticism to extreme indulgence, there is an almost infinite gamut of intermediary methods toward the supreme realization. The Ramakrishna Order stands somewhat in the middle, but it leans toward asceticism, in the main because its outlook is ascetic and because its denominational background is that of the most austere group of monastic orders, the Daśanāmī Order.

Meditation itself, and the process of learning it, is not by any means painful or even strenuous, though the concurrent disciplines do appear hard to the person who has had a 'soft' background. Yet the daily routine around the meditative kernel is certainly less hard and unpleasant than that of a recruit in the Wehrmacht. And then there is a most amazing thing about it all, one that might make a Christian monastic frown and a psychologist smile: nothing is enforced. There is no check on whether one does one's meditation regularly, or on how long one sits for meditation, and the check on matters of general routine is extremely loose; in the Ramakrishna monasteries it is virtually absent, and it is probably this freedom from any kind of disciplinary pressure that makes the monasteries function with the utmost precision. I have not seen any Ramakrishna Monastery where inmates, either novice or monk, would absent themselves from their chores. I have, however, seen that the intensity of formal meditation—the actual sitting down for the complete process—differs very widely within individual monasteries. Here in the Advaita Ashrama, supposed to be a contemplative cloister par excellence, only three out of ten inmates sat down for meditation with the prescribed regularity, i.e. twice a day. Those who meditate regularly and for a long time at a stretch, are soon known for it and treated with deference. Those who do not do so regularly, or hardly at all, are not blamed for it and their own rationalization is this: we serve by doing the work of Ṭhākur, and this service *is* meditation. They find their scriptural corroboration in the *karma-yoga* concept of the Bhagavadgītā, which concept has had influence on all the leaders of the Indian Renaissance, both secular and religious. This concept militates against the quiescent tradition of the Upaniṣads and effects a broad distinction between contemporary monastic groups. By far the greatest number of them retain the quiescent, contemplative spirit. The modern, 'reformed' organizations serve in the name of *karma-yoga;* the direct Christian model is evident, though denied by these orders. The Ramakrishna Order is the most radically *karma-yoga*-minded of all. This is the reason why of all monastic organizations in India, it receives full support from the Government of India, which resents purely contemplative monasticism; *ārām hairām hai*, 'rest is taboo', is one of Mr. Nehru's famous obiter dicta. He is certainly the least enamoured with the ochre robe, but he exempts the Ramakrishna monks, because their ways fall in line with those of his teacher.

The monastic timetable begins around 5 a.m., when the novices and monks rise, mentally greet the Guru with folded palms, and take their bath. Before that they should move their bowels. The adage among good Hindus is that a man who does this once, early in the morning, is a *yogī;* one who does it twice is a *bhogī*, viz. a worldling, a man going after creature comforts; and one who goes thrice is a *rogī*, i.e. an ill man. Occidental physicians might not fully agree with this diagnosis. The bath in the Advaita Ashrama is a simple affair—the little cubicle is about 6 ft high and 4 ft long and wide; there is a bucket which is filled with water from the well and a little mug with which the water from the bucket is poured over one's head and drips over the whole body. A cauldron with hot water is ready in an adjacent cubicle, and the degree of ablutional austerity is left to the individual—he can use ice-cold water, or mix it with the pleasantly hot water from the cauldron. *Mantras* are murmured during the process, and I found that cold water makes them more intensive and more frequent. The monk then puts on a fresh *dhotī* and a fresh *cādar* as well as a fresh *kaupīna* as underwear. Each monk owns two sets of these three garments, which are his whole wardrobe—a long-sleeved loose shirt is a Ramakrishna-Mission addition, frowned on by all orthodox orders. These two sets are worn and washed every other day, so that what the monk wears to-day is rinsed the next morning (as part of the bathing procedure) and hung up on a line; then the other set is taken from the line where it has been hanging for 24 hours. It is an eminently clean and hygienic way of wearing clothes, and it is by no means a monastic monopoly: almost all highcaste Hindus do their washing and wearing in the same sequence.

Thus, fresh and comfortable, the monk returns to his cell and sits down crosslegged on his *āsana*. His main opus begins. The novices start with a period of less than 10 minutes; about five minutes are added every month, and the span of concentration is lengthened very gradually. By the time a *brahmacārī* obtains his full *sannyāsa*-ordination, he should be able to sit and meditate for three hours at a stretch.

I shall not now dwell on the process of meditation, but shall proceed with the external routine. Around 7 a.m., the inmates assemble around the breakfast-table in the main hall. This is another compromise with the modern world; there are no such tables in more orthodox cloisters and breakfast is taken in the *paṅgat* like any other meal, if indeed there is any breakfast at all. Many orders take only one solid meal a day, and for the Buddhists and Jainas this is an important rule. The Buddhist monk is not supposed to take any solid food after midday. Here, however, culinary regulations are more sophisticated: there is excellent, hot, strong, sweet tea, and there is puffed rice, '*mūlī*', a Bengali breakfast favourite, of which huge quantities can be consumed without any negative effect on the system. The convention is that there should be no talking at breakfast, as it destroys the meditative atmosphere which lingers for a few hours after the morning opus. However, there used to be some harmless small talk and none of the senior monks took it amiss. The newspapers are perused at this hour—they are about five days old, for this is the time it takes the mail to come up from Calcutta. On Sundays (again a calendary compromise with the modern world) breakfast extends pleasantly over an hour, and the old H.M.V. gramophone is wound up to play Bengali *bhajans;* the selection was good in my time, but not very large. I came to know those naively charming compositions very well indeed and I thought I had had my fill of them after a while. Not so: when in America I ordered them one by one, prompted by a strange nostalgia, and I frequently play them on Sunday mornings.

After breakfast the monks and novices get down to their various secular commitments for Ṭhākur—cleaning, washing, supervising the kitchen and the store, tending the gardens and, for the more literate inmates, editorial work, which is, on the lower rungs, almost synonymous with proof-reading. At that time the eighth volume of Swami Vivekananda's complete works was being issued, consisting chiefly of his unpublished letters. It was in course of my sub-editorial work at the Advaita Ashrama that I first realized how much superciliousness and how much inane generalization that great man had propounded, both in his talks and in his wide correspondence, together with genuine wisdom. I felt rather upset about statements like 'the Germans do not drink beer with their food', and rhetorical interjections like 'who says the Aryans came from outside India!' I voiced my apprehensions to the Publisher, but Swami Yogeshvarananda lifted a threatening finger at me: 'Are you cleverer than Swamiji was?' 'No doubt, in such matters as these', I retorted. Such retorts on my side ultimately led to the Order's dissatisfaction with me. I learnt to keep quiet even when I knew that I was objectively right; but I learnt it too late, at a time when I had made many enemies in the monastic and the lay Hindu world.

To the average Hindu, objective statements directly or indirectly comparing the Indian tradition and other traditions are welcome only if they tally with the notions inherent in the Hindu Renaissance—spiritual superiority of Indian culture, ethnical autochthony of the Indian realm, and ethnical oneness of the Indian people. Swami Agamananda, a very learned Ramakrishna monk, abbot of the *āśrama* built at the birthplace of Śaṃkarācārya in Kerala, rebuked me for 'perpetuating the Aryan-Dravidian myth': 'the Aryans and the Dravidians are the same people, they both originated in India, all languages derive only from Sanskrit'. Why? 'Because this talk about different backgrounds has done a lot of mischief, has destroyed unity'. I want my readers to note this proposition as paradigmatical. It is in line with scores of other statements made by pandits and monks all over India against their better scholastic knowledge. That beef was eaten by the Vedic Indians, that heady beverages were drunk by Rāma and Sītā in the 'Rāmāyana,' that there was some sort of polyandry prevalent in certain sections of the Aryan population—all these things are known to most of the learned orthodox among the Hindus, but woe betide the person who mentions them: he leads the pious astray. However, it was probably advantageous that I realized this trait at the very beginning of my Hindu monastic and scholastic career and that I learnt the fact that it had its basis at the very top of the hierarchy, in the brains of the very best of the inceptors of the Renaissance. This realization gave me an important scholastic tool for later days of research: to seek for the roots of religious inbecilities, not in the erratic minds of the later protagonists of a religion, but in the words of its founder. Pious sentiment has ascribed impious interpretations to teachers who misunderstood the founder. I knew in those early neophyte days, as I read and reread the galley proofs of the eighth volume of Vivekananda's works, that I would have no commerce with either deceptive scholasticism or with this particular sort of piety. Facts remain facts and their dignity must not be impugned by any motives, not even spiritual ones.

Around 9.30 in the morning, the Abbot assembled the monks and novices in the main hall and, squatting on the floor, he gave us textual instruction. The Indian monastic tradition, which covers all the three indigenous religions, trains its scholars by a process of joint exegesis and homiletic. Here is the canonical text and commentators have explained, or tried to explain, every word of the text; on their commentaries, subcommentaries were written, either by themselves, or by their disciples, or by later generations of scholars. And this process of constant commentary is kept alive in oral instruction in all seats of Indian thought, monastic and lay alike. Our Abbot read the canonical text—about a verse, at most—then its commentaries and subcommentaries, and then he added his own explanation as a sort of final commentary. There has never been such a thing as independent philosophizing in orthodox India: almost everything can be said, almost every thinkable ideology may be held, but it has to be shown as derivative from the canonical text. Swami Avyaktananda, who ran a Ramakrishna Centre in

London for a while, saw dialectical materialism and, so it seems, Communism in the Vedanta. *Per se*, this would have been well within the Indian exegetical tradition, but other considerations, not pertaining to the tradition, made the Order decide that this particular interpretation was not expedient. Avyaktananda no longer belongs to the Ramakrishna Order.

During the first few months after my entrance, the morning text was from the Bhagavadgītā. I tried to play truant for a while, because I view this particular piece of scripture with much reserve. In the first place, it has been too much popularized, too often translated, and hence too banalized; in line with the Tao-te-ching and many of the worlds 'great holy books', it has become an epitome of profoundly 'different' thought for the escapists in the West who must be tickled by the mysteries of the East. This is no fault of the Bhagavadgītā itself, but my graver misgivings about this poem derive from its inane eclecticism, and from its blatant moral contradictions. It preaches violent Junkerism in one place, and extols complete withdrawal from worldly affairs in another; it propounds a half-hearted absolutism, avoiding offence to the monistic teachers who seem to have dominated the theological academies of its time, and then it disports a naive theological dualism with a strong sectarian flavour as its doctrinal consummation. Śaṃkarācārya had a hard time to explain away the fundamentally dualistic purport of this scripture, and he did not really succeed. Later rationalizations were legion and to-day the apologetic tells us that the recipient of this teaching starts off as a crude mind and is taken into the deepest truth step by step, so that the doctrines in the later sections supersede the earlier ones. This is an argument which I find not only unhelpful, but decidedly nauseous, for if the earlier teachings—especially the ones entailed in such a charming deal as 'if you are killed in action, heaven will be your lot; if you survive, you will rule the world. Hence fight!'—are directed to a crude mind, why should they be quoted as profound wisdom whenever they are expedient?

Finally, the Bhagavadgītā is not a canonical text in the strict sense, but it has become one of the emblems of the Hindu Renaissance, and it is hardly any use resenting its popularity. Politicians and saints, philosophers and secular teachers have been editing it, rendering it into their own idiom, commenting on it, emphasizing the aspects that corroborated or condoned their particular interests. This is the main difficulty: the text lends itself to any ideological slant. The modern politician sees *karma-yoga* in it and minimizes its other teachings; the esotericist expounds its scarce and vague references to yogic techniques, and the devotionalists chant its abundant passages on the supremacy of *bhakti*. Objectively, the last group has certainly the greatest justification, for the Gītā is essentially a text for devotees of a strong, personal god devoid of the naive anthropomorphisms of the Judaeo-Christian tradition. However, I do not see how anyone who has rejected this tradition largely on account of its dualism and personalism can feel attracted to another personalistic teaching. I suspect that to many frustrated ex-Christian seekers of Eastern mystery anything is good if only it has been composed in and around India, regardless of its doctrinal pattern.

However, there is no doubt that the Bhagavadgītā is a masterpiece deserving literary attention: it is written in simple, elegant and beautiful *ślokas* and it is the finest didactic text of the Mahābhārata. It is written with enormous conviction, and I remember from my childhood days, when I first read it in Leopold von Schroeder's good, albeit somewhat bombastic German translation how contagious that conviction was. Yet, power of conviction does not prove a text's value save as an instrument for conversion, and as such the Gītā has been eminently successful. I would say that it had an important part in my own conversion; but I was fifteen then, the right age for religious inspiration. Later on, the mind must learn to be critical and to chasten its enthusiasm. I strongly disagree with the Nazarene's musings on the state of the child as a commendable state, and still more with the gospel of the poor in mind.

I tried to stay away from the Gītā classes in the morning, but there were too many frowns—so I did join after about a fortnight. My reserve about the text remained unaltered. I voiced my doubts; I brought forward all the criticisms which I have listed here, and some others of a more technical sort. This is perfectly acceptable in the monastic tradition—there is no gospel-truth to anything a teacher, however senior, may say to his flock; in fact, argument of this sort has been encouraged from ancient times. But Swami Yogeshvarananda, a veteran teacher of the writ, rebutted all I said; rebutted, mind you—he did not refute my points. It was here that I learnt the stereotyped method of rebuttal common to all teachers of religious doctrine in India: the moment discursive arguments would jeopardize the axiomatic perfection of the text, the critic is given a simple line: 'Your argument may be intellectually valid, but what of it? Only those who have seen the light can see the consistency of the text; only those who have experienced the truth from within can see that intellectual argument is of no avail in the end, etc., etc.' This would hardly be objectionable were the atmosphere among Indian theologians purely non-discursive. But this is not true: they avail themselves of refined scholastic argument all the time, but they jettison all of it the moment their axioms are impugned.

I vividly recall one instance of this exasperating trend: the second canto of the Gītā teaches, 'Do not abandon such actions as are born with you. It is better to perform these actions, even though they be bad, than to perform others' actions', where 'others' actions' mean actions to which you are not entitled by your birth, actions, that is, to which persons of different birth are entitled. This passage, of course, is crass theological casteism; it goes without saying that the representatives of the Hindu Renaissance which rejects innate rights belonging to any particular social group cannot accept it at its face-value. On the other hand, it is such clear and unambiguous Sanskrit that esoteric interpretation would look too artificial even to those who are impressed by metaphorical verbosity. I took objection to this passage, noticing that Swami Yogeshvarananda passed over it rapidly. He finally said, 'Being born and bred in a society which does not understand religious purity and the sanctity of a noble spiritual bequest, you cannot understand that we are born with certain actions which we must do. A soldier, loyal to his country, does not murder even when he kills hundreds.' This argument I had heard elsewhere before, but not decked out with any religio-intuitive apparatus. 'Can it be', I asked the Abbot, 'that when a thought is propounded by a political dictator, it is to be rejected, but when the same thing is taught by a religious leader, it should be accepted?' 'You cannot understand the fine distinction—you lack sufficient inner vision. If you had had such vision, these doubts would not occur to you.'

Lunch was served at twelve, and the monks and novices converged on the *paṅgat*. The same hymn is chanted as grace in all Ramakrishna Monasteries. It is very beautiful, and it is from the Bhagavadgītā: 'Brahman is the dedication, Brahman is the sacrificial food, the oblation which is that Brahman is poured into Brahman by means of Itself—in Brahman are to be resolved all the actions, as from Brahman they proceed'.

Food at the Advaita Ashrama was always delicious, wholesome and nourishing, though light. It was as though a dietician had compounded the menu of purely Indian, orthodox ingredients. Ninety per cent of it was vegetarian, but if a monk did like meat—Bengali monks usually eat fish and eggs, both of which are considered non-vegetarian in orthodox India—they can have it occasionally. After lunch, most of the monks sat for a while in the main hall for what I secretly styled the tooth-picking-break; drowsiness was a permissible weakness at this juncture, and soon the monks and novices withdrew for about half an hour to their cells, lying down to relax. The Indian tradition is wise: you sleep fewer hours at night, and add an hour at midday. Although there is no ordinance of any sort about it, this wonderful after-lunch siesta is almost a rule in all monastic institutions in India. It is a contemplative sort of siesta—the monk does not fade out into a total slumber, but repeats his *mantra* in soporific silence.

Around two, all the inmates of the Ashrama converged on the main hall for the afternoon class, which is a thorough affair lasting two hours or more. This lesson was very much after my own heart. It formed the scholastic opus of the day. The Abbot was a man of fine Sanskrit learning. A South-Indian Brahmin by birth, Swami Yogeshvarananda represented the rare combination of the orthodox Sanskrit tradition of learning both text and commentary by rote, with the occidental approach to the study of a classic through grammatical and syntactical analysis. The texts were the Upaniṣads, with their classical commentaries, although only the works of commentators who wrote in the monistic tradition were adduced, together with the Bhāgavata-Purāṇa, the most thoroughgoing orthodox compendium of mythology. It was here that I attuned my mind to Hindu exegetical sophistication, which utilizes acute intellectual tools, and which suspends these tools the moment axioms are challenged. Now it so happens that axioms are not really challenged by any teacher within the variegated Hindu tradition. The *pūrvapakṣa*, i.e. the assumed opponent and dialectical critic of the propounded thesis, is a sort of Advocatus Diaboli à la Hindu. The *siddhāntin*—the propounder of the argument—refutes his challenges in minute detail. However, an axiomatic outsider would not be answered: be he a Buddhist, a Jaina, a Moslem or Christian, or a humanist, anyone who rejects the Veda as authority and the Brahman as the substratum of the Universe. The Hindu scholastic has no quarrel with any of them, he just refuses to argue with them. He does not claim that they are inferior thinkers, even less that they are following a wrong path; theirs is just a path or an argument which is outside his own ken. He is concerned only with disputes that occur, or might conceivably occur, within the Hindu tradition, which insists on a few axioms: that the Veda is *śruti*, that there is rebirth, and that there is an absolute spirit that is both immanent and transcendent. Each of these dicta can be interpreted in innumerable ways—there has never been such a thing as a standard interpretation, or a compulsory commentary; new interpretations are always welcome, even interpretations so radical that they seem to undermine the very axiom. Only the axioms themselves must not be impugned.

There was a voluntary tea-break around five, and then each monk or novice was left to himself. A brisk walk through the lovely forest was recommended and regarded as a pleasant part of the *sādhanā;* I undertook many long walks in those hours between five and seven, and they are most certainly conducive to contemplation. The soft robe, the staff, the knowledge of the Himalayan presence—all these together create a meditative mood. I would walk about one mile away from the monastery in either direction; I would then settle down and practice something which I had thought I would forget: I sang scales—good old *messa-voce* scales, topping with the high 'c'—I had learned many years ago at Uncle Harry's abode. I am almost sure that this region of the Himalayan foothills has not until then at all frequently witnessed a monk singing *Recondita Armonia* and *E Lucevan le Stelle.*

Around seven, everyone returned to the Ashram where he was supposed to sit on his bed again for an hour's meditation. The 'Moment of Brahman'—daybreak and sunset have been declared as the ideal time for meditation. Supper was eaten around 8.30—and all settled in the *paṅgat* again. There was the same invocation and light, lovely, nourishing food. There was no meat under any circumstance for supper, nor any spicy dishes: fundamentally, meat and spices are thought to be aphrodisiacs, and a monk can ill afford to risk their effects when he retires for the night, *Ne polluemur corpora, ne conspicemur phantasmata*—

The Gregorian nocturnal chant has a universal application for the anchorite profession.

After supper, all settled on the floor in the main hall for the last time. A reader was appointed, who read aloud some text of the Order's own literature: the Gospel of Ramakrishna, the works and speeches of Vivekananda, the instructions of Brahmananda. This reading was usually conducted in English—and the honour of being reader to the evening assembly descended on me for quite a while. As Hindi was just then coming into fashion, I was asked to read from the Hindi translations of the Ramakrishna-Vivekananda literature now and then. None of the inmates of the Ashram knew Hindi too well—during my time with the Ramakrishna Order at least—there was not a single monastic member in the entire Organization who spoke Hindi as his mother tongue. This has been an object of considerable criticism on the part of other monastic orders in India, for though the Ramakrishna Order is no doubt an all-Indian, and in a very real sense a cosmopolitan Order, all its Indian monastic members are either Bengalis or South Indians. There are valid historical reasons for this shortcoming, but a mild type of parochialism is certainly amongst them. Paradoxically, then, I happened to be the only speaker and reader of elegant Hindi in the Ashram.

This reading was usually followed by a free discussion, and it was here that the first serious friction on points of doctrine arose. Swami Madhavananda, who as I said was spending a few months of temporary retirement from his almost inhumanly exacting commitments as the Secretary General of the Ramakrishna Order and Mission, used to listen to those readings. Apart from being the most efficient administrator of the Order, this saintly, aged monk is also a scholar of considerable scholastic merit. He has published quite a lot, and his magnum opus was his English translation of the Bṛhadāranyaka Upaniṣad with the commentary by Śaṃkarācārya. Now this ancient canonical text contains, towards its conclusion, a section of candid erotics: how a woman should be courted, how she should be consummated, how male offspring is to be begotten in her womb, and how she ought to be treated if she refuses the earnest suitor's wooing. Puritanism had not yet clogged the Brahmin mind in the canonical age, and was not to mar its abundant freedom for many centuries to come. However, as everywhere in the world when the philistine takes over from the thinker, puritanism encroached upon the bountiful Indian mind, in due course to envelop it completely, and the Hindu Renaissance is the consummation of Indian puritanism, its great men sharing it with the holy simplicity of enthusiastic reform. Vivekananda, to my mind, was the epitome of puritanism, or if he was not, his successors have made him out to be.

Now the relevant passage in the canonical text is no doubt exceedingly direct. In Swami Madhavananda's Bṛhadāranyaka Upaniṣad the full text is printed in the Sanskrit original, but these passages are simply omitted in his translation. It was to this omission that I took strong exception. For if every word in the *śruti* is truth, then there is no human being who can tamper with the text itself; he may interpret it by all means, and make it speak about the preparation of vegetables, if he can torture the text sufficiently and if sexual matters are an abomination in his ears, but he simply must not omit it without explanation. Swami Yogeshvarananda gave me a sort of *entre nous* apology: Nirmal Maharaj does not attach importance to these passages; they are *kāmaśāstra* and not really relevant to metaphysics. Also, he is an old man, and if anyone takes objection to these omissions, he can make his own complete translation. Needless to say I was not satisfied—in fact, I felt very unhappy about it, for I had been hoping that Hinduism would keep its promise for me, that it would include what Christianity denied, the relation between woman and man as an aspect of the divine, not as a work of the devil. I did find what I had hoped for, but not in the Ramakrishna Mission, for the attitude of this Order in matters of sex matches that of the most literal Presbyterian. Years later, I related this matter to a senior, learned, immensely human Maṇḍaleśvar. He laughed aloud and said: 'If God does not mind creating a human or an animal penis or a human and an animal vagina, and if he does not mind arranging a particular relation between their carriers, why should He hesitate to talk about them? Who are we to tell Him what is decent and what ought to be said, or what ought to be omitted?' These words were late grist to my mill. No doubt, the chief abbot's mind was closer to that of the *śruti*-revealing seers than the reformed minds denigrating natural processes and the aesthetic quest linked with them.

Swami Virajananda, 'Kalikrishna Maharaj', had been the President and Abbot General of the Ramakrishna Mission for many years. He was in indifferent health when I met him—no scholar, but a saintly, kind man, a *bhakta* in the most ideal definition. His frame was small, he had a long beard—rather rare in the Ramakrishna Order. I did not see him on the first day; early next morning I was summoned to his presence, and was formally introduced. He spoke to me in Hindi, for though his English was excellent he obviously wanted to verify the grounds for the linguistic fame that preceded me. There was a tiger-skin in his room, a couch draped with ochre cloth, and pictures of the Holy Mother, Ramakrishna, and Vivekananda. There was the soft smell of sandalwood incense, and the atmosphere was exactly what it should be in the abode of an exalted monk.

The day and the night before *dīkṣā* are usually spent in light prayer and meditation, and no cereals are eaten. On the day of the *dīkṣā* itself, the novice fasts completely until after the initiation, and so does the guru, his health permitting. An hour before the auspicious time for my initiation, the young secretary-Swami of the Shyamlatal Ashram dropped into my cell and said, 'Swamiji will instruct you in Hindi'. I often wondered, in later days, at the significance of this decision; Swami Virajananda spoke Bengali as his native language, and his English was, as I said, excellent. Was it that he welcomed me as the only Hindi speaking person in the flock? Or was it that he felt shy of speaking in English with me? But he had initiated and instructed many people in English before, for South Indian novices have rarely learnt sufficient Bengali by the time they get their *dīkṣā*.

At the appointed hour I was called into the Abbot General's room, and a tray with fruit was placed in my hands: the *dakṣiṇā*, which I should offer to him after the initiation was over.

The moment was the consummation of many years, but I was far less excited and felt less exalted when I entered his room than I had expected and hoped I should be.

This was the gist of the *dīkṣā:* a sacred formula, the *mantra*, is imparted to the disciple by the guru, and its methodical use in the process of meditation is then explained. This is done in camera—it is strictly a one-to-one relationship. Only the imparting of the *mantra* proper, however, is a charismatic act—the rest of the ceremony is perfectly practical though secret instruction: how to harness your mind, how to relax it, how to sit in a proper *āsana*, how to do *prāṇāyāma* efficaciously, how to place the objects of worship and of actual meditation before the mind, and how to exclude other objects from the mind, one by one, what initial and concluding invocations are to be performed, how happiness and well-being must be sent out to the entire universe, how the spiritual lineage beginning from the personal, immediate guru, traced back to the original preceptors and to the tutelary deity itself are to be invoked as witnesses and helpers.

The *mantra* is secret, by definition; for although there are manuals by the dozen which contain all the mystic words and syllables used for initiation and for subsequent practice, these are not *mantras*, and hence not potent, unless they are imparted by the guru to the disciple. Without this process they are either bare scriptural passages or quasi-morphemes; they are like bombs without the fuses, there is the semblance, but there is no effect. The *mantra* loses its force the moment it is divulged to anyone, except through the process of *dīkṣā*, when it has found its fruition in the adept, when the disciple has become fit to be a guru in his turn. Then he must pass it on to a new disciple, or disciples ad infinitum; this is the spiritual lineage of India, and all the three indigenous religions share this functional element in but slightly modified forms.

I prostrated before Swami Virajananda—and now I belonged to the fold: I was part of an in-group, to use a very different terminology.

The march back to Mayavati was exacting, but not unpleasant. I was very happy to have the *mantra*. On my climb—let us remember that Mayavati lies considerably above Shyamalatal—I reflected on the implications of the last day: it was Mahālaya, an auspicious day in the Hindu calendar. The guru's task is to decide which mantra he will give to the disciple—will it be the *mantra* of a personal aspect of the deity, will it be that of Ramakrishna, that of the Goddess, or the most austere, the *mantra* of the impersonal, monistic absolute? For this decision moulds the disciple's life more than any other single decision ever could; 'what a man thinks, that he becomes', the text says. Would I become what I was to think of forthwith? Would I intuit the significance of the *mantra*? I realized that this was the most important question so far; everything else, up to this point, had been either facetious or trivial; and the few moments of transporting exultation found on rare occasions in perfect sexual love and in the sudden rupture of individuality through the intrusion of beauty, had been few and far between. Above all, they were unplanned, they could not be summoned at will. The *mantra*, when it succeeds, yields all that—it allows the successful adept to switch on that bliss at will, and to build it up: for there are degrees of bliss, well delineated in the relevant scholia—and the infrequent moments of human bliss which make life seem worthwhile, seem to be on the very lowest rung of the ladder. I could not formulate the situation as it applied to myself. Bliss as I knew it had two chiffres: that of woman and that of music. Not, of course, just woman or just music, but some few experiences of heightened perception through their medium—not just, to choose the somewhat less delicate paradigm, a particular phrase of a particular composition by Bach or Vivaldi, but one apperceived at a particular performance under very specific conditions, most of them subjective. From these experiences I could now infer, or at least postulate, the possibility of learnt, or skilled bliss—that which the texts and the teachers promise. Perhaps their promise would not fulfil what I aspired: that was a calculated risk.

Following my return to the monastery, I was zealous in my observances, regular in my meditation and, from an initial period of half an hour a day, I learnt to meditate three hours at a stretch. The regular pensum was two hours and a half in the morning, and one and a half hours at night. I studied a lot: not only the scholastic texts of our tradition, but also western philosophy, to which I now returned with a new outlook. I went through the available histories: Erdmann, Überweg, Windelband, Russell; I read the first and the second Kantian Critiques from cover to cover for the first time—for in earlier days I kept postponing this task. I had brought the Reklam Editions with me from Vienna, and there were two ticket stubs between the first pages: Staatsoper Wien, they read, and: *Die Walküre.*

Two years passed almost unnoticably. Nothing outside his own mind really seems to matter to the monk: political strife, wars, all of it appears removed and the relation to the extramural world is somewhat like that of the cinema-goer to the events on the screen. The novice's *sādhanā* is absorbing: it leaves scant room for things and thoughts which do not directly pertain to it. The only difference between individual monks practising *sādhanā* in the monastic residence seems to lie in the degree to which each of them regards extrinsic things and thoughts as pertinent to his *sādhanā*—and there are of course considerable differences. I have been regarding the study of discursive philosophy, of logic and contemporary analytical thought, as pertinent to my *sādhanā* on a par with the study of scripture, though not as directly pertinent to it as meditation. I have the backing of the Scripture itself, for all discursive effort is *sādhanā*, and the study of the Veda, the Upaniṣads, and the entire body of doctrine, together with the performance of ritual—all belong to the discursive sphere—meditation alone, and its subsequent experiences are non-discursive. This being so, it is really irrelevant what disciplines the individual monk includes in his studies. Indian monastic history has abundant proof of it: there were fabulously learned monks, and there were illiterate monks; there were teachers who regarded learning as important to *sādhanā*, as a controlling instrument and there were teachers who denigrated learning.

There is a Bengali custom to write letters or notes, short or long, to friends and relatives during Durgā Pūjā. I had written a number of *Vijaya*-letters in the two preceding years, and this time I wrote a long one to our Abbot, Swami Yogeshvarananda, who had gone to Calcutta for the cooler part of the year as is the custom with the Abbot of the Advaita Ashrama. On the day when he left, he blessed us all jointly and singly, and he said to me: 'Well, Ramachandra, pray to Ṭhākur, take the name of Ṭhākur, think of Ṭhākur, that is the best and the only thing you can do.' These words of farewell had lingered in my mind, as I felt there might have been a slight sting in them. I had been voicing my feelings about the founder of the Order, and I had made it clear that I could only regard him as a teacher of spiritual practice, albeit one of the greatest that had lived in our time. For this, I thought I had Swami Vivekananda's sanction, for in a little booklet which is distributed among the novices and which serves as a kind of private manual—it had been compiled by Vivekananda when the Order was new—he had expressly stated that each monk and novice of the Order would be free to regard Ramakrishna in whatever light he deemed fit: as an *avatāra*, as a great teacher, or an ordinary, saintly person. I chose the last of the three and made no secret of it. I was given an indirect hint once by a young Swami in Mayavati: 'though we are free to hold our individual views about Ṭhākur, it is nevertheless understood that we, as his spiritual children, see him in a very special light.' I came to feel, in due course, that the attitude toward Ramakrishna did matter a great deal, though this was not said, and that monks and novices who refused to regard him 'in a very special light' did not last in the Order. I resented this very much, for it amounted to the assumption of a virtual sectarianism. If I join an organization which offers me a wide choice, say of factors *a*, *b*, *c*, *d*, and if the founders of the organization declare that factor *a* is important to them, but not incumbent on all who would join it, I may well join it for its factors *b*, *c*, *d*, and factor *a* may leave me cold. I felt that the Order was falling short of its promise in this very point: if offered monastic training in the rich, ancient tradition of Hindu monasticism, and this offer had been inspired by one who stood deeply rooted in that tradition. As it is, the Order has fallen victim, so I feel, to the great temptation which hovers around every religious movement inspired by personal charisma: the temptation to apotheosize the founder. I also fear that Ramakrishna himself gave some encouragement to his subsequent apotheosis. He is reported to have said: 'He who was Rama and he who was Krishna, is now Ramakrishna—and not in the Vedantic sense.' The last clause implied that he did not want this statement to be understood as a metaphysical proposition corroborating the fundamental doctrine of Brahmanical monism, according to which, of course, all individuals coalesce in an intuited substratum—but that he did mean it in a personalistic sense which would condone sectarianism.

I wrote in my letter to Swami Yogeshvarananda, my Abbot: 'When you left Mayavati, Maharaj, you blessed me, telling me to pray to Ṭhākur, to take the name of Ṭhākur, and to think of Ṭhākur, etc'. Maharaj, if by *Ṭhākur* you meant a paraphrase of the impersonal, allpervading, ineffable Absolute, the Brahman that is everything, then I take your blessing as a reminder of my own worship; but if by 'Ṭhākur' you mean the little village-priest, the great Paramahaṃsa whose disciple Vivekananda founded this Order, then I am afraid I cannot fall in with you. And, Maharaj, I thought you knew this—I do not regard the Paramahaṃsa as an *avatāra*, because the notion of *avatāra* does not mean much to me, just as the word 'father' had meant nothing to me when I decided to abandon Christianity; in fact I detested that word—likes and dislikes just cannot be imposed on a thinking mind'. I added the reference to the little pamphlet of Vivekananda, stressing that I did not see why my attitude should be objectionable, or not in accordance with Swamiji's behest.

Two weeks later, the peon brought a letter from the Abbot. The envelope was addressed to 'Mr Ramchandra Leopold Fisher', and I knew immediately that this meant dismissal, for otherwise it would simply have said 'Brahmachari Ramchandra'. Yogeshvarananda's letter was not very long. It said 'I have long noticed that you are not keeping up with our discipline. You have outgrown this Order; perhaps you will find greater freedom outside its fold. Make your own arrangements from now on—there is no need for hurry'.

I packed my bundle about two weeks after Swami Yogeshvarananda's letter had come, and set out for Lohaghat early on a cold December morning. One of the Ashram lads carried my bundle. I took leave of the monks, touching their feet in the traditional token of respect to the senior. I touched everyone's feet, for everyone was senior. But I did not manage to touch the rotund Brahmachari's feet; I liked him, but he was so round and his voice was so high, that I felt I would burst into laughter if I tried to touch his feet. A very irrational sentiment, but then I had followed irrational sentiments in weightier decisions. It is not reason that makes one decide personally important issues—not the most important ones.

The bus from Tanakpur drove right up to Lohaghat at this time of the year, so I had to walk only a few lovely miles to the village. The sky was perfectly clear, the birds were dipped in all colours, and the snow-range was close.

A good-bye to the Himalayas, for the time being. My novitiate was approaching its end. I bought some *gerrua*-clay in Lohaghat, for I would need it soon.

As the mountain-bus descended, I thought of many things: was I different now from what I had been two years ago? Certainly. I felt I had lost one of the five great obstacles: anger. But I might be wrong. I should have to be tested. As to the other four: lust, infatuation, avarice, and egotism? They never exist in a vacuum. I should have to subject myself to tests. Could I have obtained my present poise, my present blissful equanimity outside the monastery, away from the Himalayas? Possibly. But it might have been of a different order. There is something unique in this residence—monk or layman, those who learn meditation in the Himalayas are different.

CHAPTER IV

PILGRIMAGE

'yadahareva virajet, tadahareva pravrajet'
(On the day on which he renounces,
on that very day let him sally forth)

THE Panjab Mail is one of the three fastest trains in India. It took me to Banaras Cantt. in seven hours. I was now entirely on my own—for I did not know anyone here, except the monks of the Ramakrishna Monastery, and I would hardly seek their company. A monk is supposed to be on his own, and I felt strong and free. I thought of Ramakrishna's advice: find a place to stay, in a new city, then put your bundle there and with that burden off your mind, go sightseeing. His counsel had been meant metaphorically: first place your mind in the divine resting-place, then only go and enjoy whatever this world has to offer. But the amazing thing about the Indian teachers' advice is that it usually works both ways—and I took it literally. I deposited my bundle at a Dharamshala near Assi Ghat and went to the Ghat of the Ten Horse Sacrifices for my bath. I hesitated for a moment, pondering if I should buy some sort of container for the Water, to offer it to Lord Viśvanāth. A tallish man of about 50 approached me, and said: 'Here is your *kamaṇḍalu*, Maharaj'. I took it and was fascinated by its exquisite shape. When I looked up enquiringly and to thank him, he had turned and was walking away.

I had *darśan* of Lord Viśvanāth, and then I walked back to the Ghat. I knew what I was looking for: a sannyāsī to give me *sannyāsa*—it was as simple as this. There were some sadhus sitting near the Chausatthi Temple wearing the robes of Daśanāmī monks. I approached them, saluted and they beckoned me to sit down. I told them my story. They were silent when I had finished. Then the oldest among them, a stern-looking man in his late fifties, said in an unexpectedly gentle tone: 'Your effort is laudable, brother. I have not seen anything similar in all my life—you could probably earn 500 rupees or more and have a nice family in Germany and drive in a car. And yet you want to be a *sadhu*. But you cannot have *sannyāsa;* I believe you know that only the twice-born can enter this state?' I told Swami Sumedhānanda—that was his name—that I was well aware of the stricture, yet Vivekananda had been a *śūdra*. 'That is true, brother', Sumedhānanda continued, 'but you see, it is easier with a person who has had some sort of *saṁskāras;* and where will one draw a limit? But you are from across the ocean. I don't think any *daśanāmī* would give you *sannyāsa*. And if he did, most of us would not regard you as a sannyāsī.' That was it. I bowed and walked away.

The next two days were days of acute suspense and dismay. I must have contacted over a hundred monks and abbots in three dozen monastic establishments. I got three types of answer: the first, given by most of the orthodox Brahmanical orders, was that I was not entitled to *sannyāsa* because of my wrong birth. There could be no question of acceptance into their order. The second answer was the sectarian one: 'We will gladly accept you as our own, wherever you may come from, but you must realize—and promise you will try to realize—that Viṣṇu is the only Lord of the Universe; that Guru Kabir taught the quintessence of the Veda and that it is upon him that you will look forthwith as your own guru; that onion and garlic are the main culprits obstructing the path to perfection'. Of this type, I had had a thorough experience in the two Mayavati years just concluded. The third type of answer was procrastination: 'Live with us for a while, see how we think and meditate and serve, and if we find that you fit into our way of life, and if you feel you can endure it, we shall make you one of ours in due course.'

I would not have any of it, I would not be a lay hanger-on: I must be in it and of it. One way was open, and I was about to decide to take it. At Hardvar and Hrishikesh formal *sannyāsa* is easy to have; one can have it for a very modest sacrificial fee, or for rendering services to the monk who initiates you. Many of the hundreds of thousands of folks wearing the ochre robe in India took their *sannyāsa* this way, I presume, if they took it at all. For there is the possibility to be what is called a '*svatantrasādhū:* one dons the ochre robe, takes a monastic name and sets out as a monk, or settles somewhere. Nobody asks a monk what he was before he became a monk—except perhaps city-folks and college-students. I could be a *svatantra* monk, and might even be the better for it, with no affiliations of any sort, and no need to vindicate my thoughts and actions to any formal superior. Among the *svatantra* monks, there are hundreds of excellent, learned people. There are also thousands of rogues, but then there are also thousands of rogues among ordained and established monks. There is no uniform control in the Hindu monastic realm; this may change—there is the talk of some sort of identification paper for a person donning the robe—but so far nothing of the kind has gained ground and the orthodox orders vehemently oppose any such movement as infringing upon their basic freedom.

As I went to retire to my rest house late at night, I saw a small crowd of devotees sitting on the steps of the Harischandra Ghat listening to a man with a pleasant, high, and even voice. He spoke in chaste Hindi, and the people around him were listening in rapt attention. I drew closer and saw a feeble, friendly old man in the ochre of the *Daśanāmīs*. He was discussing *Māyā*. It is *Māyā* that cannot be described; the Supreme is defined and described—it is being, consciousness and bliss. We should rest on what we know, and not on what we do not know. He chanted some passages in support; his voice was thin but not shaky; and there was a lilt in it, as there was a very slight smile on his face. It was a moonlit night, and I could see his face quite well. When the men around him dispersed after the discourse, I remained where I was. He had noticed me earlier and now he said: 'So you have come to join the fold.' He did not mean this in any esoteric sense; nor was it a statement of clairvoyance. He saw me in the novice's clothes; he saw I was not from Banaras, and he saw me listening to his discourse. He was old and experienced, and he must have seen many who wanted to 'join the fold'. I told him my problems, and recounted in detail my experiences of the last two days, for he seemed to be interested. At the end of my narrative, I added, 'Of course I know by now that you will not make me a *sannyāsī;* that is why I am off to Hardvar to take it from any monk who will offer it to me, regardless of his own standing and his knowledge.'

The old monk held up his hand, gesturing me to silence. I fell quiet immediately, for I saw he was thinking hard. This was a strange experience and a novel one to me—novel as a Hindu monk's reaction to a problem. There was nothing sanctimonious in his face, nothing of the 'I know of course' mien so common on the faces of the *sannyāsīs* who are asked a question. This was the face of a scholar pondering a difficult problem, or of a defence counsel in court. He was fingering his rosary; I do not know how long we sat in silence. After a long time, he said: 'I shall give you a trial, *Brahmacārī*. If it proves a failure, it is still a worthwhile risk. There is a passage in the scriptures which can be so interpreted as to entitle a man like you to *sannyāsa*. "Whenever he renounces, he should set out." This injunction does not necessarily refer to a Brahmin. I shall initiate you on the basis of this passage.'

I was struck with awe and supreme delight. Monks at Mayavati had quoted the same passage—it is from a somewhat apocryphal Upaniṣad—but in a totally different context. They regarded it as a weapon against the challenge frequently put forward by the more orthodox; that one has to go through all the three *āśramas* before one can enter *sannyāsa*, the fourth stage.

I felt very humble and grateful. I did not ask any questions and sat with folded hands; there was nobody around now except a few boatmen at some distance, smoking their *bīḍīs*. 'I shall give you *sannyāsa* on the day of the new moon, so you will have to wait for a week. Meet me tomorrow for *bhikṣā* and bring some *dakṣiṇā*. My name is Viśvānanda Bhāratī—you have only to ask for the Swamiji from Madras at the Hanuman Ghat.'

I obtained half a dozen fresh plantains, a coconut, and some oranges. I performed my meditation, attended the formal worship at the Viśvanāth Temple and kept a full fast the next morning. As I crossed into the Ghat, a young, sturdy looking man approached me—was I coming to see the Sādhū from Madras? Indeed I was. The man was the son of the Swami's host, an old Banarsi family, originally from western India but settled for over 300 years in the Holy City. Swami Viśvānanda hailed from South India. In each generation of his family there had been a monk and Viśvānanda himself took orders as a boy of 18, a week before he was to have married. He studied at one of the head monasteries of the Daśanāmī Order and meditated at Gangotri in the Himalayas for 7 years. He had taken his bath at four *pūrṇakumbhas*, and had travelled the length and breadth of India several times. He was equally conversant with Sanskrit, Hindi, Canarese, and his own mother-tongue Tamil, in which language, as well as in Sanskrit, he had composed some exquisite religious treatises and hymns. Moreover, he could read English, though he would not speak it. But when I entered his room on Hanuman Ghat and prostrated myself before him, he put aside a copy of the English *Amrita Bazar Patrika*, Allahabad Edition, and took off his rimless spectacles. He beckoned me to sit before him, offered me betel, which I thought rather strange on that occasion, and said, 'Don't you think Bengal will go communist in the elections?' I said I did not think so and, on his request, with some hesitation, I told him why I thought it improbable. He nodded, then he asked abruptly: 'Have you brought your *dakṣiṇā*?' I pointed to a piece of cloth in which I had the fruit. 'I shall instruct you now until the sun sets; then you can lie down here and rest for a few hours; at midnight I shall take you to the Maṇikarṇikā, and will make you a sannyāsī there.'

It was about 1 p.m. when he began, and it was 7.30 when he finished talking to me. He spoke about *sannyāsa*—but in a rather different manner from what I had expected. For he did not say what a sannyāsī should or should not do, nor what he or other sannyāsīs are doing, but what *I* could and should do. That was very different, in many ways, from the cut-and-dried notions Hindus entertain about *sannyāsīs*. I hardly remember any specific thing he said; but in the years to come, whenever I heard something I thought important, or whenever I felt that I was striking at a new idea, it occurred to me that it had somehow been contained in my teacher's instructions before he gave me *sannyāsa*. He told me that sex was the one great obsession of the monk's mind—in various shapes and under the pressure of control; internal control on account of his vows, external control on account of society. Now I had been worried by sexual thoughts during my Mayavati days, yet I had not really suffered. And as though the Swami had anticipated my thoughts, he said: 'It is not now, when you are a young and active monk, Brahmacārī Ramachandra, that your mind will be much troubled by sex. The real trouble begins well after 45—between then and 60 you will have a hard time. For then your body revolts, your mind panics—they want to enter into their rights ere the gates close. Chastity will come relatively easily to you for the next 10 years, with no more than a little care. At your age, it is hard no doubt, and it is a very great sacrifice; but it is not at all impossible. And if you do fall, occasionally—let that not worry your mind either. Perform your prescribed penance and start all over again; that is the only way. I have not seen a monk who did not fall. In fact he must fall to rise. Only the ignorant draw a dividing line between rise and fall. And the lawyers. But we are sādhūs, not lawyers.'

What did he advise me to do after the ceremony? 'That's up to you,' he said. 'You may stay and have your *bhikṣā* here in Banaras for a while, Viśvanāth's temple is always accessible. Or you may make a pilgrimage, as our generation of sādhūs used to do.' I told him that I would rather like to wander and live on alms as the sādhūs had done from time immemorial, but was it right for me to live on alms and feed on the poor, when I was not needy or indigent? Was it in accordance with the times, and with the things this newly independent country needed, that men who could actively contribute should go a-begging? 'This is all nonsense,' he said with an almost contemptuous gesture. 'As you wander through the villages, you don't just stand there and eat. You sit under a tree or at the temple and teach. For that you get some rice or *roṭī* and *dāl*. You could teach in a college, but your teaching in the villages gives the people there a chance to learn what they would not otherwise hear for a long time yet. And if some sadhu teaches the children the three R's and the adults how to make their lives a little happier and wider, is that not worth some food? Would a schoolteacher, who knows so much less and has so much less inspiration, and hardly any enthusiasm, teach in village after village for no more than some rice and *dāl*? No, Brahmacārī Ramachandra, don't be perturbed by secularism; our work is more secular than that of paid teachers. Even if it were not, even if we did just sit and meditate, we should do no wrong—and if people don't feed us, well, we shall not survive as an order, nor perhaps as individuals. A day may well come when there will be no ochre robes in this land. There are many great people in this country who would welcome such a day. But what does that bother us? Each one must go his way. You cannot prescribe interests, and you cannot forbid interests. If you do, you are a tyrant.'

The Swami taught me the etiquette of the mendicant: the poise he must develop in his dealings with other monks and with the laity; the kind of virtues he must build up to make a success of renunciation—patience, forbearance, and a sense of humour in the face of physical hardship. The instructions were numerous. At one point I felt I should take a few notes, but Viśvānanda waved the idea away: 'Don't write these things down, that wouldn't help you. They will come back to your mind as you need them. You don't need all these instructions at once—you need them for particular situations. Why, at times you will have to put up a show of anger, though calmness is a permanent discipline for the monk. There are no hard and fast rules that apply to all situations, and there are none for critical hours: then your own wisdom must decide.'

It must have been around six in the evening and Swami Viśvānanda was about to dismiss me, but as I got ready to retire, he said in a somewhat casual tone: 'There is one thing which you will do well to remember. I shall take you as a full sannyāsī after midnight tonight; others, similarly inclined, will too. But there will be very many who will not take your *sannyāsa* seriously. There will be the orthodox whom your learning and your renunciation will not impress in the least. You are not entitled to *sannyāsa;* you are no Brahmin by birth. You have known this story for some time and you have spent the last two days experiencing it on your own body. Maybe you will grow in spiritual stature to such an extent that some who will not accept you now will accept you later. But very many will never accept you, even if you were the Ādiguru incarnate. Do not mind this too much, even when it hurts. Set up a criterion for yourself: the minimum criterion of the Scripture. What is the minimum criterion? "Having renounced the desire for wealth, for sons, the fear of social opprobrium and the love of social approval, they sally forth, begging their food". This is the minimum criterion. So long as you feel you satisfy this criterion, you are a *sannyāsī*. If you do not, you are not a *sannyāsī* even if you are born of a Nambuthiri father and a Nambuthiri mother. Now go and lie down, and be ready before midnight. Try to sleep—for the Brahmacārī will die tonight—it is your last sleep . . . as a Brahmacārī,' he added with a smile.

I woke up at a quarter before midnight. I took a quick bath downstairs and put on a clean *laṅgoṭhī*—the last white *laṅgoṭhī* I should wear. I had already dyed a set of robes with the *gerrua* colour which I had bought weeks earlier at the bazaar in Lohaghat. I hesitated to take the dyed cloth along and called a servant, asking him to find out from the Swamiji whether he wanted me to take the dyed cloth with me to the ghat. But the Swami had already left an hour earlier. I told the servant to take the cloth and to follow me at a distance.

It was fifteen minutes fast walk to the Maṇikarṇikā Ghat, through the meandering alleys of Banaras. I hastened my steps. The air was bright and incense laden—people looked at me more than usual, as though they sensed that I was on an important errand. There, the four dark silhouettes of the temples near the ghat. I stopped for a moment at the Maṇikuṇḍa, the deep well—allegedly unconnected with the Ganges from which it is separated by no more than 15 yards—into which Śiva's ear-ring fell when he was carrying the dead Sati on his shoulders. From time immemorial, this has been the most important cremation ground in India. Pious Hindus consider it great spiritual merit to die near this ghat and to have their bodies cremated there. Day and night, the pyres burn—one can see them from a great distance, even from the train coming in over the bridge, from Moghul Serai, when one travels at night. Corpses seem to burn brighter on this ghat. I never saw funeral pyres from so great a distance as I did here for the bridge is at least two miles east of the ghat.

I did not quite know where to find the *ācārya;* there were several monks about and several *brahmacārīs*. I found out that about half a dozen novices were to take *sannyāsa* here tonight. Swami Jagadīsvarānanda, a famous monk from Hardvar, was to confer *sannyāsa* on four young men, a monk told me. 'Do you know if Viśvanandaji will give *sannyāsa* to anyone?' I questioned him. 'The Madrasi Sādhū? Yes, I heard he is giving *sannyāsa* to a *mlechcha*! What do you think of that?' 'It is quite impossible?' It was too dark for him to see my colour. 'How do I know.' the monk answered with a shrug. 'It is certainly not customary. But the Madrasi Sādhū is a learned man. He must know what he is doing.'

A tall swami, obviously a Northerner from his looks and his intonation, approached me saying: 'Hurry, Brahmacārī Ramachandra, the *ācārya* is waiting for you.' But when I came within sight of Swami Viśvānanda, he was reclining in a niche in the Durga Temple, and said calmly: 'Oh you have come fast. There is still half an hour. Go and worship the Devī. You have been wanting to, this is the time.' Until that moment I had not known that I wanted to worship Her. I went to her shrine on top of the Maṇikarṇikā, and I worshipped Her. As I rose to leave,

Viśvānanda was standing at the temple entrance. 'Follow me now,' he said. He walked swiftly towards the cremation ground and I followed him. The pyres are about 5 yards from the road that winds its way through the ghat—the stakes are set on a platform that cannot be seen from the road, though it is visible from the river. We ascended the platform. There were three burning pyres: one of them almost extinct, two burning violently with a bright flame and vehement crackling sounds—this is the stage at which even the *dāhasarīs* can no longer distinguish whether they are produced by the firewood or the bones of the corpse. Two dead bodies were being made ready for the cremation, one that of a young woman with her stillborn child tied to her under the same red cloth, the other that of a middle-aged man. The heat was intense, but I was only mentally aware of it—it did not seem to cause perspiration. The stench was powerful, but somehow my mind grouped it with the other external paraphernalia of the consecration.

The moment Swami Viśvānanda appeared the *dāhasarīs* bowed low with folded palms and withdrew from the platform. It appeared as though they had been told there was going to be a *sannyāsa* ceremony that night. There must be many throughout the year, although the time-honoured custom of bestowing *sannyāsa* on an actual cremation ground is fast falling into disuse, as is the taking of *sannyāsa* in general. I had asked the swami earlier whether the injunctions of the relevant texts were incumbent on every candidate. 'They are and they are not,' he had said 'Some take them literally, some interpret them. Some give *sannyāsa* to *brahmacārīs* on real cremation grounds. I always do, especially when we are so fortunate as to have the Maṇikarṇikā at our doorstep. Some wander through the whole land begging their food, practising the text "they set out, begging their food" literally; others declare a well-built house, a fine mansion, or a temple to be the cremation ground, and beg their food in town for the rest of their lives—no one blames them. Why should they not?' Then, after a while, he had added 'You will have to make the choice yourself, Brahmacārī Ramachandra. If you want me to give you *sannyāsa* in this house, I shall, because I have decided that you should have it. And if thereafter you want to take your *bhikṣā* here at Viśvanāth's Darbar, then that will be your great pilgrimage. It is for you to decide.'

I made my decision then and there. I would have *sannyāsa*

on the cremation ground proper, and I would beg my food on the roads, as had the mendicants of yore.

A *maṇḍala* had been drawn near the centre of the platform in red and white and of the prescribed form. I sat down and now I noticed that I was sitting in the geometrical centre of an almost equilateral triangle formed by three pyres. Swami Viśvānanda sat in front of me and did *ācamana* with his left hand: the left hand rules over rituals connected with *sannyāsa*, whereas the right hand functions on all other occasions. He lit another fire from sandalwood, placing it between himself and the *maṇḍala* wherein I was sitting. He handed me two handfuls of sesamum seed and kept about the same amount. The chant began: *tilāñjuhomi sarasāṃ sapiṣṭān gandhāra mama citte ramantu svāhā* . . . (I offer this oblation of sesamum, with its juice, with its ground particles, the well-scented ones, may they delight my mind, svāhā. The bulls, wealth, gold, food and drink, to the Goddess of Wealth may they go. May these sesamum seeds, the black ones and the white ones, liberate me from all the blemishes, may I be free from the debts to the gods, manes, parents, the world . . . the five winds in me may be purified, so I be the light, free from blemish, having renounced. . . . I am now beyond life and death, hunger and grief, satisfaction and dissatisfaction.) With twenty-three *svāhās*, the sesamum and the rest of the oblational ingredients are thrown into the *virajā-homa*, the fire of final renunciation. Lastly the *ācārya* cut off the *śikhā* from my head, the well-trained, well-oiled, stately *śikhā*, and threw it into the fire as the last gift.

The swami asked me to stand up. I followed him to another, much smaller platform which I had not seen before. Here was a small pyre of wood, not yet alight. I was asked to lie on it. The swami approached with a firebrand and some live charcoal. He touched my body in seven places. Symbolically, the pyre was set on fire. Symbolically, I was now being cremated. As I stood up, I made my own obsequial rite, with the *mantras* which are chanted by the living for the dead. I was now dead, though the body lived. It signifies: when the sannyāsī says 'I', he does not mean his body, not his senses, not his mind, not his intellect. 'I' means the cosmic spirit, the Brahman, and it is with This that he henceforth identifies himself. This is the only important difference between the monk and the layman. The layman too is Brahman, and so is all that lives. The monk is Brahman too, but the monk is aware of it, the sannyāsī is aware of nothing else. Or at least, he should be aware of nothing else. I now threw off my white novice's robe, and all the other items of the neophyte wardrobe—they are not many—and walked down the few steps into the Ganges, with the four directions as my garments.

The municipality of Banaras is a puritan municipality, like all the municipalities in India. Even corpses would not be tolerated in the nude. However, it appears that for *sannyāsa* consecrations some special arrangement is made lest offence be given to the occasional late bathers and to municipal orders: people are just asked to move away whenever novices step into their last bath.

As I emerged from Gaṅgā's womb, Swami Viśvānanda, who had followed me, gave me the ochre robe, which I donned immediately. 'Victory to you, HOMELESS BLISS, Victory, Master Agehānanda Bhāratī, be thou a light to the three worlds'—he spoke loudly and distinctly. This then, was the name he had chosen for me—and he must have known why. Bliss through homelessness, bliss that is homelessness, bliss when there is no home—the Sanskrit compound of the privative prefix a+ *geha*+ *ānanda* covers all of these meanings.

He then gave me the *daṇḍa;* I bowed to it, and flung it far into the River, saying 'Keep this *daṇḍa*, Mother Gaṅgā, for I have no more leisure for rules. The Supreme Swans are not bound by any rules, the *paramahaṃsas* do not carry the rod of rules and rites. They are free.'

'Come with me, Swami Agehānanda,' said Swami Viśvānanda softly. 'Choose whom you will honour by taking your first *bhikṣā*.' Then I remembered that I had promised his host that I would take my first food from him. But when we left the ghat, there was a crowd of more than a dozen people, both men and women, with lovely food in plantain-leaves. They thronged around me, touched my feet begging me to take their food, or at least a morsel of it. 'It is thought to be supremely meritorious to give a sannyāsī his first food,' said Viśvānanda. 'Have you already promised anyone that you would honour him or her?' He asked this in slow, but good English—I had not known before that he could speak English at all. I told him, in English, that I had promised his host. 'Then you have to accept his offering. That settles it.'

The swami's host had a large tray of dainties ready for me and placed it at my feet. I sat down and ate. For this corpse was hungry—and very, very thirsty.

I withdrew for the few hours left of this night, and slept as befits the dead. The sun was high when I woke. Viśvānanda was sitting beside me and was chewing betel. He smiled when I greeted him. 'Take your bath first, Agehānanda Maharaj, then we shall talk.'

There was tea and there were *laḍḍūs* and *jilebis* when I came back from my bath. 'What will you do now, Agehānanda?' he asked. 'What ought I to do, Maharaj?' 'It is for you to decide. For as I said, it is your own choice whether you take the traditional directives literally or not. You may set out on a pilgrimage to the seven holy places, or you may walk through Bharat, or you may stay here. I would only suggest that you spend another week here, meditating. Would you avoid the cremation ground for a while?' There was not really any challenge in these words, but there was a mild implication. I said: 'My mind is made up, Maharaj. I wanted to leave this morning, to walk through Bharat. But now as you ask me to, I shall stay on for a week and meditate.' 'It is very good,' he nodded. 'You will be a literal sannyāsī,' he added with a faint smile.

I meditated on the roof of the Annapūrṇā Temple during the next seven days, and on the cremation grounds on the Maṇikarṇikā Ghat during the six nights in between—sitting about 30 yards from the spot where I had died. There is the outward cremation ground; it has to be transferred into one's mind—the sannyāsī's mind is the hypostasized cremation ground. The physical crematorium is but a symbol for the inner one. Without the inner, the physical cremation is of no avail—without the inner cremation, it is like a horror-play on the stage. As a material location, the cremation ground is a farce like all places of burial, but informed by transference into an object of meditation on the inane universal evanescence as well as into a simile for the mind wherein the desires have been burnt up, it is a thing of hallowed beauty and great purity.

After a week, I went to take leave of Swami Viśvānanda Bhāratī. I told him I was going on the great pilgrimage through India. I said I wanted to be as 'literal' as he suggested and I asked him if he would suggest an approximate route. He shrugged his shoulders with what seemed to me a mild annoyance, and then said: 'I have told you already that all this is up to you. What do I care? You are a sannyāsī like myself. You are on your cwn. What difference does it make where you go?' But then he added as an aside: 'When I became a sannyāsī, I was at Hardvar; then I walked all the way down to the Śāradāpīṭha in Mysore. I paid my respects to Narasiṃha Bhāratī. He did not even ask where I had come from. He showed no sign of interest when I hinted at the fact that I had walked 1,500 miles to have his *darśan*—his face showed no more acknowledgement than if I had told him I had just walked over from Shimoga. I do not care where you go.'

I did not say another word nor did I ask for further advice. I decided that I would also walk to Śringerī, just as Viśvānanda had done. At that moment, it seemed to me as though I had heard or read in some monastic manual that it is meet for the new sannyāsī to visit his Order's head cloister. I also hoped that the present Patriarch would bless me with his *darśan*. Viśvānanda seemed to know intuitively what I was thinking, for he said, 'Do not expect too much recognition, Agehānanda. You know the difficulty—this big white body of yours may be fine for almost any other purpose, but it is an obstacle in your recognition, though I do not care, and there are many others like me. Nor should you. But don't be hurt if many do care, whom you would wish to recognize you.'

I prostrated once more at his feet and took leave. 'Godspeed to you, Ageha Bharati, *OṂ NAMO NĀRĀYAṆĀYA*. "*Oṃ namo Nārāyaṇāya*",' I replied, and walked away, leaving my sandals outside the swami's door. I would walk without sandals. Most monks do. It takes about three weeks for the soles of the feet to grow a hard hornlike surface, and walking barefoot becomes fun after some initial toil. It was more hardship to get used to shoes again when I had to.

I took a last bath at the Ghat of Ten Horse Sacrifices, offered *tarpanam* to Mother Gaṅgā, worshipped Lord Viśvānāth at his Golden temple, partook of the *prasād* which the priest gave to me with his left hand: for this is the way food oblations are given to the sannyāsī, in the same manner as to the manes. For ritualistic purposes the sannyāsī is dead and his participation in any ritual can be only that of a witness or else in the same hierarchy as the dead to whose memory certain rituals are directed. When a sannyāsī enters a temple, he blesses the idol, because as one who has shed desires and rebirth and who no longer participates in matters of phenomenal existence, he is above the god of the temple, whose interest in worldly affairs entitles him to dwell in a temple. A *pāṇḍa* at Banaras told me: 'Outside the temple the Lord may be formless, but in here he has form.' Form is lower than formlessness. The sannyāsī epitomizes formlessness; his body is a phantom when viewed from the plateau of intuitive consummation, of the realization of oneness.

I circumambulated Banaras and took a road branching off to the South. I did not know the route, nor I did not have to. It is easy to walk southward or in any particular direction in a country whose topography is founded on shrines and places of pilgrimage. The sādhū is advised to visit the shrines and to avoid big cities unless there are important shrines in them. I did avoid large cities, though I could not avoid wandering past the fringes of Nagpur in the heart of India. When only about one fourth of my itinerary was left, I noticed one morning that I was about to enter Hyderabad, a lovely great city, but I turned away and made a long detour through the villages of that region, and headed for Tirupati, the greatest shrine of Viṣṇu.

There is an almost monotonous routine for the monk on his long wanderings, so much so that the constant sensation of the novel is lost to him: the new sights, the new people, the varying dialects and languages, the different food—all the experiences which would provide many a topic for anthropological dissertations.

This is the routine of the itinerant monk. He rises well before sunrise from his resting place which may be either a temple plinth, a *dharamśālā*, a Brahmin's house, or even the foot of a tree—the latter being the ideal site supported by a dictum ascribed to Śaṃkarācārya, often quoted by monks who follow the ideal and by reluctant householders in their discourse with monks who hint their preference of less austere beds. *Karatale bhikṣā taratale vāsa, bhaja Govindaṃ mūḍhamate*—'With alms food that would just fill the hollow palms, with the tree-root as your resting place, chant the name of the Lord with an ecstatic mind!' Let me add that during my wanderings I availed myself of that arborial hospitality only four times: once to try it out, and the other three times due to the reluctance of all the eligible hosts in some villages far and wide apart.

The mendicant then takes his bath in the tank or the river or whatever watery place there be near his night's rest. He then sits down near the water or at the temple, or even on his last night's bed for a somewhat abridged version of his meditative observances. Then, well before the hour when the village folks leave their own dwellings, he collects his things and starts his day's march, which, from my own experience and that of other itinerant sadhus whom I encountered en route, hardly exceeds a comfortable average of 10 miles a day. The reasons for his early start are two. First, the morning hours are relatively cool, and it is pleasant and inspiring to walk alone with nature, in mystical communication with the flowers and the creatures around one's path. Secondly, a very important consideration underlies the monks' early marches: he has to reach his day's destination at an hour when the men get their morning meal and when food is hot and ready and that is around eight a.m. in most Indian villages. The men are at work in the fields or in their shops around that time, if not earlier. The itinerant monk is not supposed to receive uncooked food—this he gets only when he stays at a place for some time. There are two methods of obtaining *bhikṣā* for the day. One may select a hut at random the less orthodox and, to my taste, the less appropriate way. The other method has the approval of orthodox monastic convention, and it is to take from each donor just about one morsel of rice, or just one *roṭī*, according to whether the region's staple diet is rice or wheat. Here again, the prescribed way seems to me the most elegant one, and I insist that such judgements on the border between ethics and aesthetics apply to many monastic actions. As the monk enters the village boundary he stands still and calls out loudly, but without shouting: OṂ NAMO NĀRĀYAṆĀYA. The villagers hear him, and then usually half a dozen village women, or some men peep out and ask him if he would have some food.

This is the one great complaint of modern India, made even by the pious protagonists of the Hindu Renaissance against the wearer of the ochre robe. He comes to eat, and people give to him without probing his depth, just out of reverence or fear of the robe. The suggestion is that the villagers fear the curse of an unfed monk. It is true that the legendary scriptures are replete with tales of the wild curses of holy men who had not been treated hospitably. But my own experience has not borne out the modern critics suggestion: if people give, it is, with possible rare exceptions, not out of fear. Fear plays only a small role in the complex emotions of the Hindu villager, as he offers food to the monk regardless of whether there is enough in his house to feed his large family. Is it not insolence and parasitism on our part if we claim and accept their alms, knowing their poverty? I do not think so. Education has not yet come to the villages; it will be another few decades before it does. Humanistic and spiritual education, however, will not even then enter the villages—for what a secular ministry of education calls 'moral' or 'religious' values are precisely the values of mediocrity and conformism which the sannyāsī may dismiss. The values of humanistic individualism can be taught in Indian villages, if at all, only by the monk who does not conform to the rules of convention, that is of mediocrity. He may also no doubt teach secular matters, for even of them he usually has infinitely more experience than the poorly paid village teacher with little enthusiasm and little knowledge. I do not imply that the villagers in India show any unusual interest in humanistic individualism, yet values can be inculcated which would merit that description—and in India, from olden days, it is the sādhū and the sādhū alone who has the detached ardour necessary for this job, for he is not bound by society; he acts and thinks freely. In Hindu India, the monk is free to think and to teach as he pleases; the layman is bound by social taboos at every step. Compared to the latter's strictures, the monastic discipline of the Order appears trifling. Monks are not really required to conform to any social norm—hundreds of hymns and panegyrics on the monastic life revel in the description of the monk's unbounded freedom. Maybe it is this which makes the executives of modern secular India so suspicious of the ochre robe: under the uniform garb, there is hidden a congeries of unpredictable non-conformities.

The food is exactly what the villagers eat, because the monk gets part of whatever has been cooked for the day. Its quality depends on the region and the season and the year: from Uttar Pradesh to Mysore there is a wide culinary gamut, and it requires either a very pious or else a very cosmopolitan stomach to thrive on it. On good days and in wealthier areas, the monk will find in his bowl such dainties as vegetable curry, *dāl*, and perhaps even some sweets; but usually it is just *roṭī* and *dāl* in the North, and rice and *dāl* or its equivalent in the South. Monks are not offered meat, fish, eggs, or anything that passes as non-vegetarian diet, even where the villagers eat such things. In the orthodox South, onions are considered either non-vegetarian or an aphrodisiac: the main reason why monks are not supposed to eat high protein diet is the fear for their implicit vow of non-violence. Instead of onions, the orthodox use asafoetida, a most fearful stuff, with an evil odour and as much an aphrodisiac as onions.

All the food has to be accommodated in the monk's bowl, which, together with the water vessel are the only two contraptions he carries on his way. The bowl may be of the shape of a vessel or of a large drinking glass and is made of brass with the less orthodox and of coconut shell or another hard plant shell for the more orthodox monks. It holds everything that is liquid, and the rice as well where rice is given. In the North, and in all wheat eating regions, the *roṭīs* are taken separately and wrapped into a corner of the robe, so as to keep them warm until eaten; the rest—*dāl* that is, or *dāl* and vegetables goes into the bowl. The monk does not utter thanks; that would be very bad style indeed. On the other hand, it is customary that the donors thank the monk for having given them the opportunity to acquire merit. Although there is no such rule, the monk will usually tell the people that he will talk to them, instruct them, and spend the day and the night at the temple, or under a particular tree, or near the river or the well—or he may even ask the villagers' to suggest where he might spend the day. This serves to broadcast his arrival to the village, for it takes less than half an hour for the whole village to know that a *sādhū* has come to be in their midst for a day or two.

As soon as the monk has received his food, he retires to the village temple or to whatever other place he has chosen for his day's sojourn. He must eat alone, and no one goes near during his meal. He then rinses his mouth and sits down for about one hour's reading and chanting of the scriptures. Although he should be alone during this observance, it is usually at this point that the first villagers will approach, prostrate themselves before him and sit down at some distance—having his *darśan*, without of course interrupting his chant. Then usually he will himself begin a conversation, or he will just tell the assembled that they may put their questions.

From this moment the day is no longer his, with the exception of about an hour's rest: he will just tell the people that he would like to lie down for an hour, and that they should continue their questions after his rest. He will lie down on the spot; there can hardly be any question of privacy. It is impossible to ask the villagers to go home, for this would be rude and would deprive them of their chance of *darśan*—for *darśan* continues even when the sādhū is asleep. Sleeping or waking, he is an object of worship. I have sometimes watched dozens of people just sitting as I dozed, some with folded palms, some in a meditative posture; some would come and go even before I had awakened. There is absolutely no parallel to the conception of *darśan* in any religious act in the West; the charisma that attaches to the ochre robe is unequalled outside Hindu and Buddhist Asia. All this will change very soon: there is a lot of sneering in the villages even now. There may be no charisma and no *darśan* after another generation. Secularization in India has begun from two sides—from those who are the political and administrative leaders of the country, including the educationists, and from the people who have taken to reading secular matter and listening to secular radio broadcasts. I have had quite a bit of heckling under the village trees and on the temple plinths. There is always that young or not so young man who disputes the monk's right to exist as a monk—as a parasite who does nothing for the village, nothing for people. And there is the occasional village Brahmin who impugns the *sādhū's* position for orthodox reasons: renouncing family ties, escaping social responsibility is not in accordance with the *śāstras*. The latter is heard in silence by the devoted villagers, and there is respectful nodding without much heeding—the former is usually silenced through the indignation of the majority of the audience.

I would put it statistically, on the basis of my own experience that of the villagers of India, in this decade, 90 per cent are in favour of the *sādhūs* and the perpetuation of their traditional pursuits in the village; 5 per cent are against him for traditional reasons, as devout Hindus considering sādhūism a distortion of the real tradition; and the rest are against him for what I would call secular reasons, which include political, economic, and contemporary considerations, of which the Hindu Renaissance is one, for it does not want the ochre robe as an institution. This would be an all-India average, for attitudes differ widely in the various parts of India. In Kerala and Andhra in the South, and in the Punjab in the North, there is much more antagonism than, say, in Bihar or in Rajasthan—in the regions which are styled 'backward'. Kerala and Andhra are among the best educated areas, and criticism of the sādhū is almost directly proportionate to the degree of secular education. Let me stress, however, that this holds for villages only—the situation is getting to be quite different in the cities, where the civilized *sādhū* is becoming the pivot of a specific cultural reflection.

It is now about 2 o'clock in the afternoon, and the villagers know that they will be treated to whatever edification they desire. Men get home from the fields at different times in the afternoon, but quite a number get home quite early, around 3 or 4, particularly the older ones. Yet, it is the women who come first to the place where the sādhū faces the crowd. Invariably, they bring their children with them, including the ones they carry on their hips. The early afternoon hours are virtually the only opportunity for the women to air their problems, for once the menfolk get close the women fall silent or return to their houses. They never sit together. The men sit on one side of the monk, the women on the other—only the children run to and fro between the two groups, partly because no one stops them, partly as surreptitious little messengers carrying domestic news from one group to the other, for there can be no direct communication between the men and the women once they are sitting in a sanctuary, still less when they are before a monk, eager to have his teaching and his counsel.

The monk never starts a sermon. He has to be asked a question. This sounds more democratic than the religious harangue in other parts of the world. It is, however, a formality introducing a sermon rather than a discourse, because the questions put to the monk are pretty stereotyped and it is usually a village elder, or a Brahmin, or any of the more loquacious of the male population who starts them. The questions asked at first can safely be divided into three patterns: how are we to live in this world and yet perform our religious duties? What is the best way to worship God, for the householder bound to worldly duty? What is the way of escape from the fetters of pain, misery, birth and rebirth?

These patterns are hardly ever transcended at the outset. Neither are the answers new; live in the world and fix your mind on the deity, just as Saint X or Hero Y or King Z did his duty while meditating on his chosen Deity. The second pattern is answered by reference to the ubiquitous notion of *adhikārabheda:* each of you must worship God in the manner for which he is fitted and that manner you must find out yourself, by seeking your guru or by worshipping God with a sincere heart. The last pattern has a rather more scholastic answer, which, for the benefit of the villagers has to be put into simple phraseology: the bondage of human life can be transcended either by the grace of the guru, or by following a path of yoga in accordance with the guru's behest, all the while doing one's duty, and all the while ready to renounce the world when the great call comes, the call to renounce worldly duties for the spiritual life.

Though the questions are identical from one end of the subcontinent to the other, and although the answers are identical, too, in their content, there is considerable scope for the individual monks' narrative genius. In the first place, his skill in adducing the right stories to illustrate the basic teachings, in giving them an interesting or a humorous twist—for homiletical humour is about the only type of socially respectable humour in Hindu India—gives him fame on his way; the orator's good name is an important asset on the long pilgrimage. Secondly, he can smuggle virtually any idea, any doctrine, any ideology into the assembly of the pious if he allocates it to a scriptural injunction, or to the question pattern in general. Thus, I was fairly successful, after a while of trial and error, in planting my special seed among the eager village audiences: the value of objective thinking as against group and traditional thinking; the ludicrousness of naïve superstition; the importance of learning as a tool to achieve intellectual and moral clarity. I have heard and seen other sādhūs, who emphasized their own views: cultural chauvinism, communism, Hindu fascism, and many more or less harmful things. Everything is permissible if it derives from a canonical text; every Hindu, and *a fortiori*, every Hindu Monk, is his own commentator on the Writ.

Fortunately for the mendicant's diversion, the formal part of the meeting comes to an end sooner or later, or rather, it tails away into less general things, and the personal element creeps in. And this is what makes all the trouble worthwhile: the informal part of the daily word gives unparalleled insight into the thoughts and problems of India's rustic humanity—which is a large proportion of that mute, inscrutable humanity about which worried feature writers speculate. Frequently the question-leader will slip in his own personal problem, and others in the crowd follow suit, until the atmosphere is warm and laden with personal communication and with the unique sympathy that springs from the knowledge of a short, sanctified encounter.

What are the problems presented to the monk when the

religious session is at an end? The transition is very gradual and the tenor of the meeting remains *sub specie religionis* even when the actual questions becomes increasingly mundane: illness of man and beast, litigation, avarice of the neighbour, unruly sons and disobedient daughters, and—in the last few years—world news and views. Is it true that the Germans escaped with a part of the Veda and made their successful weapons out of its recipes? Is it true that the Russians have the flower-chariot which Rama used when he took his spouse back from Laṅkā to India? Such, however, are certainly of lesser interest—and the villagers' concern is one of curiosity rather than of inward participation. It is the very local, very temporal problems that concern them—love and hate, goodness and wickedness (not as principles, but as manifest in the dealings of the people in and around the house, in and around the village), this caste and that caste, this piece of land and that piece of land, my woman being barren, other women being prolific, the constant lure of drink and fornication and the abiding horror of both.

Above all there is litigation, in which almost every male who owns just a little more than nothing seems to be involved. Although the monk is not really supposed to give such advice, nor any advice which is not spiritual, it is understood that he does not refuse it. The villager's argument is this: you are a man of God; these things mean nothing to you, but to us poor, fettered souls they mean too much; you are detached, and yet you are compassionate toward our misery; your spiritual strength and wisdom have long penetrated all the great secrets, hence these things are mere trifles which you recognize the moment you are asked, and to which you can give the correct answer the moment you direct but a fraction of your mind toward them. Therefore we approach you with our trivial problems. This is the argument which the monk has to accept as an unspoken premiss. Some monastic diehards of course refuse to listen to these matters, but my object, throughout my peregrinations, was to know the people and to participate in their ways of thinking and I hardly ever refused to give my advice, which, it goes without saying, was no result of my spiritual insight into the mysteries of the universe, but derived from whatever commonsense I had—and an outsider sees more of a problem than him on whom it presses.

I have a fat diary with entries taken during leisurely hours on the road—I used to sit down halfway between the last day's rest and the present day's target, for the road is really the only place where the itinerant sādhū is alone. There was a time when I thought I would publish that diary, but I have decided against it. Many of the things which I heard were of a very intimate nature, and though there would be no difficulty about keeping the persons anonymous, I somehow feel it contrary to the pledge of silence tacitly given by the monk to those who consult him. The monk comes today and leaves tomorrow; he has no interest in the rural body-politic. This is why those who usually do not speak their innermost thoughts to their kinsfolk nevertheless reveal them to a mendicant. Hindu women, unless they are sophisticated beyond repair, do not confide womanly things to their husbands—this kind of complete communication hardly exists between husband and wife, notwithstanding an average of 5 children per family—nor to their brothers, and least of all to their elders. 'Communication' in Jaspers' or even in a less refined humanistic sense is unknown between Hindu wife and husband, not only because there are few ideal matches, but because the humanist ideal (that of total communication irrespective of conjugal duty) conflicts with the Hindu ideal of the wife's complete submission.

Let me adduce only one example: the romantic occidental view of the Indian male as a great lover is not borne out by the average village woman. The plaintive: 'I have had seven children, I have lain with my husband for ten years, but I have not experienced at any time the bliss of which our poets speak, of which our songs sing, and against which our saints warned. I obey, because it is my duty, but I would rather be spared.' In succinct Freudian terms, 'I am sexually unsatisfied'. This provides grounds for a generalization, only because of its pervasiveness. In but slightly varying forms I have heard and noted this statement, during nine months of itinerancy, from village women in Uttar Pradesh, in Madhya Pradesh, in the Vindhya Regions, in Hyderabad, in Mysore, and even in the rather different area of the lovely Coorg mountains, where there is little of the taboo that clogs the mind of the northern Indian villager. In less archaic terms, I have heard this statement from high caste ladies in Delhi, Calcutta, Patna, and Trivandrum—culturally very disparate regions.

The village males are blissfully unaware of this complaint. There is hardly any way to communicate it to them. Although I did succeed in hinting at possible shortcomings when addressing assemblies of male villagers of the pertinent age-groups, there were blank faces on every side. The idea that a woman could be dissatisfied in spite of frequent contact and frequent offspring is unknown to the villager, nor indeed would it matter if it were known, for puritanism, if mainly theoretical, permeates the village. Conjugal sex is a duty, and if it happens to be pleasant to the male, its status is thereby lowered rather than enhanced.

On the whole, religious attitudes rule the mind of the villager in matters which the ethical humanist would regard as morally unimportant or ethically neutral. Sex, food, and the general activities of the household and the family are largely guided by Hindu codes of conduct. In matters which are more important to philosophical ethics no serious conflict seems to be caused by any religious precept. Litigation, fair and not so fair, or harshness towards those who fall foul of village conventions—these do not seem to bother the rural conscience over much, although the Hindu code has as much to say about these matters as about food and sex. As in all puritan communities, somatic 'morality' is psychologically more powerful than bare morality.

The monk's last important commitment is medical. The mendicant is supposed to diagnose and to treat sundry diseases by virtue of his spiritual achievements. Some monks diagnose and dispense either on their assumption of a spiritually inspired intuitive medical knowledge or because they have accumulated genuine experience in symptomatic treatment, and there are quite a few sādhūs who have a profound knowledge of Ayurveda, the Indian medical system. Strangely enough, there are not many sādhūs, nor many villagers, who would regard this medical administration as spiritual healing of a shamanistic or similar kind. Faith-healing, where it is believed in, is not delegated to the sādhūs, but to the most senior or the most revered family member, or to some villager, male or female, said to be specially gifted with these powers. But of course, the numberless temples and shrines, amulets and charms, *mantras* and hymns of sub-philosophical Hindu India derive very largely from their supposed healing power.

I dispensed quite a lot of medicine in the villages I traversed but the only medicament I had with me was aspirin, which I later exchanged for the less aggressive anacin, finding that many villagers get an upset stomach from aspirin. I had no scruples about these treatments, for I would treat nothing more severe than a simple fever or cold. If I suspected something worse, I ordered the patient's people to get some sort of professional medical attention, in whatever form it was available. There are dispensaries and doctors everywhere, very thinly distributed no doubt, but not entirely beyond reach, if there is a will and an effort—at least on the well-populated route which I followed as I marched from the North to the South of the subcontinent.

Whatever else may be said, there is no gainsaying the fact that the Hindu villager is the kindest and most lovable host in the world, at least to the itinerant monk. I never heard a harsh word when I disagreed with people, which occurred fairly frequently. Sometimes, their humility becomes annoying, but the control they have over their minds, subject presumably to fits of anger or sulking like those of all human beings, is astounding when it comes to their dealing with mendicants. Moreover, the villager would rather starve than not feed a guest; this has often happened and it is not only the tales of Hindu hagiology that report this readiness for sacrifice, *atithi devo bhava*, by one who regards the guest like unto a god. This canonical injunction is taken very seriously; why, the Indian word for 'guest' means 'one who comes without appointment' (*a* + *tithi*).

Yet, despite his absorption in the rustic scene, the village and the other places of sojourn are not really what matters chiefly to the itinerant *sādhū*. In fifteen hundred miles across the continent the village, the shrine and the city and their doings never diverted me from the main purpose of the ambulatory which India has built for the monk through long ages; the country road, the forest, the village boundary, the temples, they are a single unit once the monk has set his mind on the fact that his march is an important spiritual exercise—less in humility than in endurance and in meditation. The rhythm of the walk is communicated to the contemplative mind, and I think that pilgrimage incumbent in one form or another on every sādhū, is really meant to teach him a novel way of meditating, different from the sedentary meditation he has learned during his monastic training. This has never been written in any disciplinary text, but I found my purely contemplative experiences considerably more powerful on my march than they had been in the austere, yet sheltered Himalayan cloister.

About 50 miles south of Nagpur, where I had the first difficulties with language (the language border between Hindi and

Marathi passes through that area), I realized one morning that I had strayed from the route for which I had asked the villagers the night before. When I had walked about 11 miles, I saw an old, dilapidated shrine about 50 yards off the path, in the midst of a copse. The rule is that the wandering monk shall make his obeisance at any sanctuary he encounters on his way, and so I left my path and turned toward the shrine. It was simple, even crude, but certainly quite old; the worn bas-relief was of a style which had been common in the 14th century, or not much later. I decided that it must be a shrine of Viṭṭhal, the tutelary deity of the Mahrattas, an aspect of Viṣṇu, the Preserver. There was a *śālagrāma* at the entrance, and the presiding deities were of the Viṣṇuite lineage. I entered through the gateway which was so low that I had to stoop. But then—to my stunned amazement—a strange, lovely spectacle was displayed to my eyes. This was no Viṣṇu Temple! There, in the middle of the debris, stood the lustrous, resplendent image of the Devī, freshly garlanded with *javā*, her hands holding the sword, the lotus and the other emblems, her face smiling radiantly, her mouth half opened as though she had just stopped speaking and was expecting my reply. Incense had been lit before her and the various ingredients and instruments for her worship had been placed in front of her; the sacred lamp had just burnt down its *ghee*-wicks, from which a fragrant smoke still emerged. I thought the priest should not have left the service at this juncture, for it appeared as though the worship was about to draw to its close as I entered. But there was no priest, nor any other person about, only some birds twittering in the trees and on the old stones. I became nervous and called, but then I was drawn to the lovely image again, prostrated before it and remained in worship for a while. An unused garland hung from one of the old pillars standing in the courtyard—the roof had crumbled and the pillar stood free, bereft of its purpose, but no less lovely in its unplanned solitude. I took the garland and placed it round the Goddess' neck, joining it to the other garlands the priest must have placed on her a little earlier. For a long time I sat in silent happiness, but when I noticed that the sun was high and hot in the sky, I rose and called again, this time very loudly, but there was no answer. I took some saffron from the vessel in front of the image, put it on my forehead, bowed once more and withdrew.

I took a chance and walked southward; it was very hot and the country road seemed to meander more than usually. But after about seven miles I saw a few cottages and in front of them some farmers smoking their *bīḍīs*. They greeted me as I approached, and asked me to rest a while, as I was looking tired, as indeed I was. I gladly accepted a big bowl of delicious buttermilk. I told them that I had strayed off my route, and I enquired casually about the Devī Temple; who was looking after it, performing the worship and so on. The villagers gave me a blank look, remained silent for a while and then the oldest among them—a man of about 50—said: 'Maharaj, there is no Devī Temple within 50 miles of here. We all worship Viṭṭhal; some worship Śiva, but not in the villages around here. There is no temple of the Devī.' I described the location of the temple and told them what I had seen. They looked disturbed. The same man paused again and said: 'There is no such shrine, sir. The only thing around here is an old temple of Mārtand, about six miles north of here, but there has been no worship in it for a long time; my grandfather could not remember when there had been a priest at that shrine. Also, we do not like to go there, for the area is haunted by spirits. The soil is barren, and has been lying fallow as long as any living person can remember.'

I felt a mixture of bewilderment and indignation and decided to walk back to the site. I asked the men if they would come along with me. None of them wanted to, but they said there was a lad in the village who would not object, for he had been to that place quite frequently and had seen nothing to rouse his fears. That boy, however, was feeble-minded and this, the villagers said, accounted for the fact that he did not perceive ghosts and spirits where others felt their presence. The boy was called and he went with me, humming a tune all the time. He could speak, but his voice had a strange rattling quality about it. I let him walk ahead in order to see if he was taking me to the same place, he and his kin might possibly have been referring to a different shrine altogether, and there was a faint chance that I had just discovered a site—the archaeological imp in me was rearing its unmonastic head. I was rested and well refreshed, so the march back, under the additional stimulus of curiosity, took about half the time, and soon I saw the outlines of the temple, and the bare pillar from which I had taken the garland.

We entered through the low gate. There was the plinth, and there were the debris. But there was no Goddess. And there was no image of any sort, nor flowers nor garlands; not even a stray petal on the stone; no sacrificial instruments, and no smell of incense. Only the smell of age and bats, ubiquitous in ancient Indian temples. . . .

I walked on my way, and did not look back, motioning the lad to return to his folk, but I often thought of the incident in later years. There are several explanations for it. The simplest is this: for weeks before, during my wanderings, I had been thinking of the Devī, and had been chanting the *Saundaryalaharī*, certain stanzas of which magnificent poem have a powerful fascination for me. May be my mind built up a certain inflation, fatigue and the constant channelling of the mind into the mendicant's inner disciplines adding to it. Some day it had to express itself one way or the other, and any appropriate surrounding might provide the framework for the mental deflation. This is a psychological explanation. The pious Hindus call it '*darśan*'. I call it *darśan*, too—resulting from the psycho-experimental atmosphere in which the mendicant moves as he marches along.

The monk does not wander during the monsoons. The *cāturmāsya* corresponds to the Christian monk's annual 'retraît'; he can halt at a monastery, or make arrangements with a village to put him up for the period, feeding him in return for his instruction and his *darśan*. I spent my *cāturmāsya* in a rather pleasant little town, Bellary, a culturally and linguistically interesting place in South India, with both Dravidian and Indo-Aryan languages spoken by a mixed population. The forms of worship and the attitude toward the sādhū differ from one group to the other, and though my host was a Smārta Brahmin, devotees from all the language communities came and went, and there was a religious meeting for several hours every evening, sometimes lasting until well past midnight. This was pleasant, and it was my first monastic contact with the Hindu middle-class. The men were usually college-graduates, the ladies were cultured and they joined in the discussion quite actively—a thing unconceivable in the villages.

I cut the *cāturmāsya* short and continued my march after less than three months, as the rains were weak that year. I reached Śriṅgerī in the State of Mysore after less than 9 months walking —which of course did not include the monsoon halt in Bellary. At Śriṅgerī is the head monastery of my Order. I took my bath in the tank near the temple, offered my worship to Śāradā, the tutelary deity of the sanctuary, and went to the monastery to seek an audience with the Jagadguru Śaṃkarācārya Candraśekhara Bhāratī. The swami in charge received me with cool politeness. He permitted me to stay in the guest house and told me to see him again next day, he would find out if there could be an audience with His Holiness. The next day he told me that the Śaṃkarācārya would not see me. I did not ask the reason for the refusal, that would have been a solecism. But one of two things must have accounted for the refusal. The late Jagadguru Candraśekhara Bhāratī suffered from some sort of mental disturbance during his reign. The medically-minded suspected schizophrenia; the pious said his advanced state of *samādhi* accounted for long periods of non-communication with people. The Śaṃkarācārya died a few years later during or after his bath in the Thungabhadra, the sacred river of the area. There is the possibility of a joint cause—the strenuous monastic and meditative life of the Jagadguru might have undermined his health, and it is by no means impossible that very advanced stages of meditative absorption brought about an actual schizophrenia. If His Holiness was in one of his states of inward withdrawal, due to either cause, he could of course not see me. But I think his refusal may have been simply due to what Viśvānanda had virtually predicted at Banaras. His Holiness may have felt that the situation would be embarrassing to himself and to me, for he had been informed about my history, my aspirations and my training, and though he probably thought all these laudable, he could not speak to me as a sannyāsī patriarch to a sannyāsī monk, nor could he speak to me as he would to a Hindu layman, for I was neither.

I left Śriṅgerī with a shrug, though with some grief. Injured vanity, I presume. I mounted a bus—my first vehicle since I I had begun my march; I had concluded my part of the assignment, and did not feel obliged to continue my pilgrimage on foot any longer, at least not for the time being, having reached my self-imposed target on foot. I changed at Shimoga, then again at Hassan, from where I went to see the Hoyshala shrines of Belur and Halebid, the loveliest sculpture medieval Hindu India has produced. It was here that I first saw and revelled in the enjoyment of that rich, warm, exceedingly delightful erotic sculpture which has posed many cultural problems for me ever since, for I became one of the most fervent admirers of that segment of the Hindu tradition which manifests itself in those sculptures of consummate loveliness, but which are now hated and regretted by the majority of those affected by the Hindu Rennaissance.

I now felt it was time to return to Banaras and to report to my teacher. Somehow, money comes to the monk when it is needed, for he is not supposed to carry any money as he walks. Barely two hours after I had left the railway station at Bangalore a hansom cab pulled up by the pavement, and an elegant Tamilian gentleman approached me with folded hands: would I be his guest, and would I bless his house and his family and address the circle of his friends? I certainly would. There was excellent South Indian food, strictly vegetarian, with *rasam* and *pāppaḍam* and rich, creamy coffee. (South Indian coffee is the one beverage which really resembles Viennese coffee with cream.) Then I was seated in the middle of the room on a modern sofa, my host's friends and their wives assembled, greeting me in the orthodox style by prostrating themselves 'with the eight limbs'. Then I spoke for about a half an hour in English, and there was a long, interesting discussion, full of wit and sophistication, but not devoid of respect and of a great love and pride in the Hindu cultural values. This was a meeting of the sort I cherished, and which was not to be too frequent in my pastoral experiences, for the sādhū usually speaks to the utterly pious and utterly naïve, to the rigidly orthodox or to the somewhat colourless, anglicized urban Hindu. It was an impromptu meeting, and this may have added to its charm, for when the arrival of a sādhū is announced beforehand, people tend to come tense with stereotyped questions, expecting stereotyped answers.

It was well past midnight when my host asked whither I was bound from Bangalore. I told him my plans. 'How will you manage the train fare?' 'I don't know yet.' 'Then permit me to obtain the ticket on your behalf, sir.' The host said something in Tamil to his friends, and they nodded eagerly. I was put on the train to Madras the next morning, into a clean First Class Compartment, and the ticket was handed to me.

It is a long journey—11 hours from Bangalore to Madras, 24 hours from Madras to Itarsi, and another 15 hours from there to Banaras. There was a lot to see and a lot to think of. India unfolds her scenic charms before the not-too-rapidly moving traveller in the train, and during roughly 100,000 miles of rail travel in pursuit of my monastic and scholastic tasks, the scene never lost its sweet charm for me. I always intended to read, study and write during the long hours of travel, but I hardly ever did. I just looked and felt warm and loving and loved, by that very personal numinous which is the Indian soil responding to the eyes of her lover. For this soil is the most tangible aspect of the *magna mater;* for me, as a votary of Śakti, she is both mother and the ever-beautiful, divine, beloved princess. The green pastures and the fallow fields, the cattle and the people and the peacocks—they are her garb: this is why, so I think, the weavers and dyers of India so often decorate with flora and fauna the more elaborate sarees which they create in gold and colour.

Here it dawned upon me that my reason for deciding to be a monk may have been unique, for the classical reason lies in the realization of grief and pain, and the intuition of the futility of all our efforts to remedy them. This is the common feature of Hindu-Buddhist and Christian monasticism: the motive is one of superseding something negative in order to reach a state in which there is no negation, for even the Buddhist nirvāṇa is no negation (although occidental scholars proclaim it to be, it is a negation only in the logical sense that no positive attribute applies to it). I think I have set a precedent, for my decision was prompted by the intuition of an immense beauty, the perception of an unique joy permeating the things around me. When in the past I loved, when I listened to music which I cherished, played better than I had ever heard it before, I postulated a yet greater perfection, one which could be found only in what seemed diametrically opposite. I had become a monk, not because the world is full of grief, but because it is full of joy; not because of a surfeit of sensuous enjoyment either—although I suspect this might have been the case with the Buddha and with many of his wealthy followers—but because of a desire for more enjoyment, such as the senses alone cannot offer.

Much later I found scriptural corroboration for this last point. The Taittirīya Upaniṣad shows a hierarchy of pleasures and of bliss; there is one man's bliss if he, in the full possession of his senses, has all that is necessary to supply the senses with what they want; there is a bliss, a hundred times more intensive, for a certain category of gods; finally, the bliss of Brahman is a millionfold greater than human, sensuous bliss—this is not a qualitative difference, but a quantitative one, and quantity does not change into quality except in Dialectical Materialism.

CHAPTER V

PHILOSOPHY AT DELHI

Vivat Academia

I left Banaras on the same day and took the train to the capital. I did not go to any of my lay friends, but went straight to the Birla Temple, that biggest, newest, and most popular shrine built by Jugal Kishore Birla about 30 years ago. The rest house attached to the temple is the most beautiful I have seen. It is almost like a hotel, the only difference being that it does not cost anything. The rule is that one should not stay more than a fortnight, but the temple management very frequently waives the rule and I stayed for over a month.

'Why don't you teach and serve, Swamiji?' This question was put to me by half a dozen people, independently, during my stay at the rest house. I felt like a medical man, just graduated and caught wasting his training. One day I mounted the bus which plies from New Delhi right up to the University of Delhi. It has a lovely campus, near the old Viceregal Lodge in the Civil Lines of Delhi. I walked comfortably across the large campus, enjoying an atmosphere of which I had long been deprived. The Library was poor at that time and I browsed through its catalogues with some dismay. The new Arts Building attracted my attention: a very modern edifice, not unattractive. I stepped in and, following a hunch, went straight to the Dean's Office. Dr Ram Behari, sometime senior wrangler at Cambridge, now Dean, Provost and Head of the Mathematics Department entered the office. It was barely ten minutes later that a deal was struck: I was to live in Gwyer Hall, in the Fellow's Court, and teach whatever I would teach: German language and literature, philosophy, or whatever the students might want to hear. It was a wonderful proposition, for it was completely informal. I was to get free board and lodging, and of course no remuneration: that was clear from the outset, for the *sannyāsī* does not accept any sort of salary.

I did not have many friends in Gwyer Hall but two men came close to me. One was an erudite young pandit, taking his Ph.D. in Sanskrit, very orthodox; he did not even drink tea. The other was a brilliant young economist from South India, who had spent nine years in England and who hardly knew any Indian language well enough to converse in it, not even his native Telugu. This was the pattern in all the years to come: those Indians who befriended me were either totally modern, sophisticated, critical and who could have been charged with having no roots in their native soil save for their respect for Indian culture. For there is hardly any Indian in this decade, however westernized, who would not feel and proclaim this respect, although he may freely and radically criticize almost all of the individual aspects of that culture. The other type of men and women who sought my friendship were the orthodox, learned, totally ethnocentric Hindus, the pandits and their kin. They hardly knew any English, nor were they antagonistic to the West as they saw it; to them *English* simply means 'using the language which is creating scientific advance' and *German* 'using the language in which Sanskrit grammars have been written by scholars whose heart was given to Indian culture'.

I made my enemies among those who stand in between the two extremes: those whose Hinduism is based on early memories of their grandmother's tales and legends, and among those of the brahmins and wandering ascetics who visited their little native town or village, memories reinforced by the eclectic, 'reformed' and anti-scholastic literature of the Hindu Renaissance. These books were written or thought in English—in the English of the Mission Schools of the last century—and rethought with some effort in the vernacular. I mean the Ramakrishna Vivekananda literature, the Dayananda-Arya Samaj literature of the Panjab (which, though originally Hindi, for the founder of the movement did not know English, to my mind contains a good admixture of high-school and Christian-College sentiment), the works of Aurobindo, and the thousands of pamphlets and little books put out by the saints and swamis of the last three decades, all of whom, consciously or less consciously, emulate Swami Vivekananda in style and mood. This literature in the minds of the college-graduated Hindu middle-classes tends to create rigid ideas as to what a *sannyāsī* should be and how he should behave. He may smile with a smile which an outsider might call sanctimonious, but he must not laugh aloud. He must say only what the devotees think he should, and he must never, under any circumstances, praise physical beauty; in fact he must give the impression that he never knew or that he has forgotten what it is. This is why Gandhi fulfilled the model of a *sādhū*, though he was not ordained. I learnt too late that when words like 'beauty', 'love' and 'sweetness' are used by and around a monk, he has to show by his reaction and by his own use of these terms that he knows only their ethereal meanings. A sentence as simple as 'that lady is beautiful' is taboo, unless he can so express it that his audience is immediately aware that this is only his facetious way of saying, 'In that person, who happens to be of the female sex, there is a quality described by that divine epithet which vulgar language uses to describe the merely carnal'.

In April 1951 a great event took place in the capital, the first (and last) 'Universal Monks' Assembly'. By the time the actual meeting started, Delhi and the world were agog. The Qudsia Ghat was crowded, day and night, by the pious throng. Hindus converge to worship where *sādhūs* assemble. It was impossible to walk twenty steps without being stopped by dense crowds who, eager for *darśan*, fought to get a close glimpse of the holy ones and to touch their feet, so that the fluid of merit should be transferred to them. It was very hot by that time and as the monks walked barefoot it was no great pleasure to be fixed to a spot for many minutes, one's soles getting parched in spite of their power to bestow blessings. Foreigners entered the *sādhūs'* tents with the same eagerness as the devout Hindu, and somehow there was a feeling of genuine brotherliness between the Indian mass, as poor and as gentle and as devout and as beautiful as always, in its chaste white and grey, and the well-dressed tourists and students and reporters from all lands. They certainly got a first hand impression of India's active mysticism.

There was Narsingh Baba, the leader of the Nāgas, the naked monks. These have nothing whatever to do with the Naga tribe in Assam. 'Nāga' means simply 'naked', and this is the popular name of a rather wonderful monastic organization, the 'heaven-clad' ones. Their spiritual lineage is identical with ours; that is to say, they are Daśanāmīs. They originated as a sort of semi-military group within the *sannyāsī* fold, to protect the unarmed ochre-robed monks from the attack of other monastic groups of lesser lenience, especially during the periodic assemblies of monastic orders. Ideologically, then, the Nāgas are Advaitins, monists like all Paramahaṃsas; Ramakrishna's own Guru had been a Nāga monk. In their monasteries they wear nothing; when they roam about—nothing or almost nothing, a miniature *kaupīnam*. They rub their bodies with ashes, wear matted hair like Śiva, who, as the tutelary god of all ascetics, is particularly dear to the Nāga monks, whose own outer appearance is that given to the Great God in all the descriptions of Śivite mythology. Their insignia are the trident—an emblem of Śiva—a three-pronged iron staff which can be a formidable weapon.

This was my first contact with the Naga monks and it was as delightful as any intra-monastic encounter can be. They are gay, jovial, uninhibited and their leaders possess considerable scholastic learning. They look wild and uncanny; their bodies are completely inured to extreme heat and extreme cold; they walk through the hottest deserts and they sit in the midst of the Himalayan snows with no modification to their dress.

Narsingh Baba (he has nothing but the name in common with Narsingh Giri, the Abbot of the Qudsia Ghat Daśanāmī-Maṭh), the leader of the Nāga group that had come to join the assembly, and his group consisted of about a dozen naked monks. He is a graduate from some Indian university, and had renounced the world soon after leaving college. When he was introduced to me, I greeted him with '*Namaḥ Śivāya*', i.e. 'Victory unto Śiva', as a token of respect for his particular tutelary deity. He shook his head and said solemnly; 'No, Maharaj, don't you know how *sādhūs* greet each other?' 'Of course,' I replied; 'the general salute is *Oṃ Namo Nārāyaṇāya*, but do you not object to *Nārāyaṇa* as a somewhat sectarian term?' *Nārāyaṇa* usually refers to Viṣṇu, and there is some sectarian discrimination between the Śiva and the Viṣṇu aspect of Divinity. 'Not at all,' Narsingh Baba replied, 'and even if I did object, the *Nārāyaṇa* of the *sādhū*-salute is not the *Nārāyaṇa* of the Vaiṣṇavas except by metaphysical generalization. No *sādhū*, of whatever personal predilection, should use a different salute, whatever he feels about "Nārāyaṇa".' I was amazed at this statement for, though of course there is nothing new in his metaphysical disquisition—almost all divine epithets apply equally to all gods of the Hindu pantheon, his diction was that of a critical scholar—or an Indologist, and his words gave me a thrill, the thrill of the paradox between the Nāga's wild and undisciplined appearance and the fine acumen of his mind.

The charge against anchorite nudism proferred in India, and by non-Indian critics living there, is naïve. They say that these monks are exhibitionists, that their nudeness is aggression after frustration. All these charges are childish. Everyone who is not deluded by fanaticism or by neurotic self-indulgence, and who has some commonsense, knows that displayed sanctity of any sort is exhibitionism. But why this profound respect for the terms coined by popular psychology? Let it be exhibitionism by all means and let monasticism be escapism by all means. If all human beings after Freud have to be escapists and exhibitionists 'to some extent', then let each decide the extent for himself. I accept 'exhibitionism' and 'escapism' as a charge against monastic life and I want other monks to accept them too, but without being in any way impressed by these terms. For every uniform which is worn voluntarily is the uniform of exhibitionism, be it that of the pre-Hitlerian Prussian Junkers, or the S.S., or of any one who wears uniform without having been conscripted into it: the Salvation Army's uniform, all sacerdotal garments, all monks' robes, ochre, saffron, black or white, and of course, the nudity of the 'heaven-clad' monks. But then why not the dinner jacket and 'tails'; why not the sloppy bermuda shorts of some American 'coeds'? Everyone who conforms to a conventional way of wearing his clothes, and likes wearing them to be just like those whom he wants to resemble—is an exhibitionist 'to a degree'. I can think of only one exception, the non-westernized lay Hindu, for he wears whatever he can lay his hands on when he goes out: a *dhotī*, a *cādar*, a pair of pyjamas, trousers, a shirt inside or outside the *dhotī*.

That monasticism is escapism is true, but this is no less trivial than the truth of 'exhibitionism'. It is an uninteresting truth. If it were less boring, it might be fun to be ultra-exhibitionist; and this may be a reason why some modern Hindus might join the Nāga Order. Narsingh Baba had read psychology at the university. There may be fun in exhibitionism for one who is impressed by the word, as also for one who is no longer impressed by it. I detest the occidental nudist camp, but I love the Nāga monks. The nudist colony is a church; it is neither secular nor spiritual (I regard this as the criterion of a church), its members are among the most sanctimonious puritans of the Protestant Christian world. I dislike them because the doctrine behind their nudism does not rise above *mens sana in corpore sano*. The Nāga-monks' doctrine is an elaborate theology, with all the wealth of Hindu cosmology, mythology, and speculation to support it. Their nudism is not secular, nor of course spiritual. But at least its motive is in consonance with a hoary tradition of asceticism—and of an asceticism especially worthy of attention, as it defies custom and the philistine (for presumably, people were as shocked by the Nāga monks 500 years ago as they are now). There are references to nude saints in much older texts—why, the woman-philosopher Gārgī, of the Vedic Age, appears naked in the assembly of scholars and sages and puts pretty shrewd questions to them, until one of the savants warned her that her head would fly off not because she was too nude, but because she was too loquacious.

These musings open up a problem of great importance. I have taught ever since I donned the ochre robe that everything that rests on a well-founded tradition is acceptable—I mean what rests not on hazy, indirect reference, but on direct mention. This rule—an aesthetic rule no doubt—is subject to the one provision that the practice must bring no harm to a human being. I would not condone a human or even an animal sacrifice for Kālī; no one in his senses would. But from the march of the Nāga monks through Delhi no harm accrues to any individual. If 'society' is harmed by a sense of shame, guilt and indignation among some of its spokesmen, let that not deter the Nāgas, for my exception does not apply to 'society'—it applies only to individuals. Although this concept—never refuted on a scholastic level—caused me considerable harm, I have not been able to modify it in any important aspect.

The main event was scheduled for the last day: a great procession of monks was to walk from the Gandhi Grounds and the old Company Gardens, via Chandni Chowk (the main artery of Old Delhi), past the Red Fort, through Kashmere Gate, and to the Qudsia Ghat. This was to be the first all-*sādhū* procession through the capital of India, for such processions are executed only at the three places where the periodical monastic assemblies take place. At two in the afternoon, the monks had assembled in a hall in the old Company Gardens. The doors were flung open and I walked out first—a piece of showmanship to which I took no exception. We had estimated that the crowd would be around 20,000 in the Gardens, along the route, and on the

Qudsia Ghat. In fact the crowd, at a cautious estimate, was 200,000. People squatted on the roofs, the trees were reserved for and by the urchins, and there was no square foot of empty space. It was reported that this was the largest gathering of people for decades, and that means a lot in Delhi, where people gather easily, with good reason or without. Newsreel and newspaper reporters, tourists, they all lined the roads along with pious Hindu humanity, and the air was filled with the monks' shouts, 'Hail to the ochre clad heroes' and the spectators', 'Victory, victory'. The procession lasted four hours, not because the route was long—it was barely two miles—but because of the density of the crowd. The moment any monk or group of monks came to a standstill people would flock to them and begin massaging their legs. This simple, spontaneous, but very old token of reverence, mingled no doubt with the feeling that spiritual power is transmitted from the *sādhū* to the person (think of the woman who touched the seams of Jesus' robe and was healed) is somewhat of an abomination in the eyes of the Hindu Renaissance.

It was dark when the procession—over half a mile in length—finally reached the Qudsia Ghat, and the monks settled down on the large dais. Then began the Vedic chants, there were more sermons and huge quantities of sweet food and fruit were distributed as *prasād* among the pious that filled the area. The food had been donated by some ten of the richest men in Delhi. I do not think anyone went hungry that night in the Indian capital, for about 100,000 people must have been fed along the Ghat.

The academical year was over, it was terribly hot, and I took the train to Hardvar, the monastic centre of northwestern India, and the hottest place in that region. For the Panjabi Hindus, Hardvar means about the same as Banaras for all other Hindus. The name means 'Gate of God', and it is the first major settlement along the early course of the Ganges, which is narrow and swift here, having just left its mountainous source. There is a little islet within the river, the 'Brahmākuṇḍ' ('Pond of Brahmā') fringes it off, and this is the sanctum sanctorum of Hardvar, where innumerable pilgrims take their bath by day and by night. Also, it is one of the three places where the great monastic assemblies take place, and for this reason the whole city has a more monastic ring than Banaras. There are over 1,000 monastic establishments in an area not much larger than Kensington Gardens. There is hardly any Order which has not its monastery there, and orders of the most radically disparate views, doctrinary and disciplinary, have their houses side by side.

The moment I alighted from the train the monastic atmosphere enveloped me; in fact there is no way of escaping it for anyone wearing the ochre robe. The people of Hardvar, if they are not monastics themselves, are at least attuned to the monks and everything is arranged for the monk's well-being. I put down my bundle at the Gītā-Bhavan, a fine marble building in the style of the Birla Temple at Delhi. It is a sort of rest house, but much more elegant than even the one attached to the Birla Temple. Most of the guests are well-known personalities in Hindu public life, though not necessarily monks.

The evening walk down to the Brahmākuṇḍ is a ceremony in itself. Every niche has its shrine and every house invites attention, because every building is some sort of temple or monastery. On the bank of the river, hardly a furlong from the Gītā-Bhavan, there is the Bholagiri Maṭh, one of the finest establishments of the Daśanāmī Order. Bholagiri was a Bengali *sannyāsī*, a man of tremendous insight and of considerable scholastic merit. Most of the inmates of the Maṭh are Bengali-born and a gentle discipline permeates the place. The *ārati* and other common observances take place at the right time, the monks chant in unison—which can unfortunately not be said of the majority of monasteries in India—and there is hardly one among the permanent residents who has not specialized in some particular branch of Sanskrit learning, beyond the common familiarity with the basic scriptures and commentary. Here I saw what I had badly missed in the Ramakrishna Order: the individual monks of the Bholagiri monastery really take up a specific branch of learning which albeit traditional, is wide and solid in scope. Whereas the Ramakrishna Order teaches its monastic members no more than the elements of Vedānta, and lays excessive stress on the simple, inspiring, but somewhat repetitive teachings of Ramakrishna and Vivekananda, this monastery promotes diversified studies among its members. I met a monk who had written an extensive treatise on *Navya-Nyāya*, the relatively recent, highly sophisticated school of Brahmin logic which is perhaps as formal as contemporary occidental logic, minus the latter's symbols and its mathematical perspective. There were two monks who had been studying Indian musical theory for over 20 years and there was one who had written a voluminous commentary on Bhāskara's *Līlāvatī*, an early Hindu work on mathematics.

When I passed by the Bholagiri monastery on my first evening, it was during the *ārati* to Śāṃkarācārya, and the monks stood in the main hall chanting the long hymn. They did not stand in any particular order; there was the feeling of a pleasant yet disciplined informality. I entered the shrine, and though none of the assembled monks had ever seen me before they gestured to me to join them in the chant. When the service was over some of the monks began to discuss some point of Sanskrit metre with me, without even asking my name and whence I came. This is what I call monastic etiquette. Monks, like the ancient Teutons, should not ask each others' names. Guests introduce themselves when the occasion arises, which is by no means always during the first meeting. Even then, the guru's and the *ācārya's* names are given first and one's own name may follow later, casually, as it were. This beautiful tradition is dying out in the monasteries—the rudeness of the secular world which asks names and dates of birth and which lists them in triplicate is about to enter the cloisters of Bharat. I have a feeling that the destruction of the sophisticated anonymity which dignified monastic intercourse may be one of the instruments for that total annihilation of the monastic life in India, which is bound to be completed, on a cautious estimate, within three generations from now, even if there is no radical change in the political structure of the country. Secularism just cannot accept the Indian concept of untramelled, radically individualistic monkhood.

When I left the monastery—the shrine is located right at the entrance, with an open hall facing the river—the moon was full and bright and the sounds of conchshells, the murmur of the young river, the chants from the surrounding monasteries and all the sounds and smells that go with the centres of Hindu worship struck me with immense vigour. It was here that I experienced an intense feeling derived from what I would call a consciously conceived numinous environment. I was immediately reminded of my first dip in the Ganges, a thousand miles down its course, as a young novice in the Ramakrishna Order. The term 'consciously conceived' is not negatived by the trivial fact that the Ganges is the Ganges everywhere; at other places, and in between the sacred places, it is just a river, and I have not experienced anything of the kind in dozens of baths I took elsewhere in the long river. The fact that I vividly recall only two or three instances of such intensive emotion of a perceptional kind may mean many things to the psychologist; it is not impossible that a place of such hoary antiquity, which people have visited seeking these very experiences, may engender a perceptive mind. There may be other reasons of which I am unaware.

At Hardvar hardly anyone took special notice of me: there are ochre *sādhūs*, white *sādhūs*, red *sādhūs*, and their complexions vary from the blue-black of monks hailing from some Dravidian group to the unpigmented skins of Kashmiri monks; there are berobed figures from 5 feet to 6 feet 4 inches. Not even my spectacles seemed to arouse interest or concern, for glasses have become part of the inventory of the most radically orthodox monks and orders, such as would not wear shoes or sandals unless they are made of cloth and wood.

At the entrance-bridge to the Har kī Paharī, there is a big board printed in English. It says that no persons not belonging to the Hindu religion may enter the area. To my knowledge, this is the only open space in India where such restrictions are enforced. However, when I took an American friend to the Paharī, there was no serious objection, though there were some astonished looks, but that friend wore a *dhotī* for the occasion. It seems that the objection is to the occidental dress rather than to the occidental face. I asked an officer of the municipality whether the objection to non-Hindus entering the sacred compound was based on some scriptural injunction similar to that at the Viśvanāth Temple at Banaras. No, he told me, the fear was of desecration, for it seems that some British soldiers had done real mischief over a hundred years ago and the memory of untoward incidents is tenacious around sacred places. None of the *sādhūs* would ever object to a European or an American entering the Har kī Paharī, or, for that, any Hindu shrine; and if the persons who are supposed to enforce these rules are asked for their reasons, their answer is never really definite—it is just that the custom has been to keep non-Hindus out. Only at a small number of places—among them the Viśvanāth Temple at Banaras and many of the great South Indian shrines—is the objection based on the notion of ritualistic pollution. It is never, however, directed against Europeans or Americans only; where ritualistic purity causes the restriction, any non-caste Hindu would be barred. Sir Homi Mody, Governor of Uttar Pradesh, was not admitted into the Bāṅke-Bihārī Temple at Vrindāvan, situated right in the midst of the State whose Governor he happened to be, because he was a Parsi.

I walked slowly down the Har kī Paharī, took a dip in the Brahmākuṇḍ and listened to the sermons and the litanies which were going on all around me. The picture is much the same as in Banaras, though slightly more active. I never worked out why this should be so, but it is a fact and many monks have commented on it. One theory is that the Panjabi are more vivacious, their piety more readily excited than that of people of Banaras. I personally think that the monastic density accounts for it. At Banaras, the pilgrim has *darśan* of Viśvanāth and of Mother Gaṅgā, and the monks are *darśan*-seekers themselves. But Hardvar is the monks' city; this is the place where the living deities can be seen, want to be seen and heard.

I went to the Har kī Paharī every evening and spent the days visiting various monastic institutions. This was a thoroughly professional period for me. One morning an American scholar friend drove up to the Gītā-Bhavan. He had come from Delhi and asked me if I would like to drive on up to Mussourie with him, the lovely resort in the Himalayas. I readily consented, for although Hardvar is cooler than Delhi, the thermometer went up to 100 every day. My friend said he would have to stop for half an hour at 13 Mohini Road in Dehra Doon to see M. N. Roy, orthodox Brahmin by birth, one-time communist by persuasion, who had been the only Indian member of the Cominform and was active in China. Then things went wrong; Roy proved no man of action but a theoretician. He made his escape through the Gobi desert—on trucks, which cannot usually move there. 'But', Roy told me one evening with a smile, 'believe it or not, Swamiji, God helped me: it rained, for the first time in 200 years, and our trucks got through the sand'. I certainly respect the God who helps an atheist, and it is probably the same God anyway, whom the later Roy and I both worshipped. Roy returned to India incognito, was caught and brought to trial together with Phillip Spratt on the charge of conspiracy and communist infiltration. The famous Meerut Trials ended with a severe verdict: Roy was sentenced to 15 years imprisonment, but served only 7 of them, yet in those seven years he changed as much as a human intellect can change. The communist became a humanist.

Roy had been confined in the Dehra Doon jail and, when he

was released, he stayed on in Doon and died there. Pandit Nehru visited him on his sickbed. 'We have much work to do together when you get well', Mr Nehru said. When Roy died, India's intellectuals felt a dire bereavement. His funeral was that of an orthodox Brahmin.

My friend drove up to Mohini Road, and suggested I might stay in the station waggon until he had finished his business with Roy (some publication programme I believe). It would not last more than 15 minutes and we would continue up to the delightful, cool heights of the Himalayas. I watched from the car. The American-born Mrs Roy, who wore a saree as elegantly as any Indian-born lady, welcomed my friend, and Roy joined them. After about ten minutes, M. N. Roy walked up to the car and called to me in a very pleasant, melodious, low voice, with great warmth in it: 'Well, Swamiji, won't you join us for a cup of coffee at least?' I was delighted. I had about five cups of coffee, and about five hours talk with M. N. and Ellen, and the learned American friend. Phil Singer, American anthropologist, had come straight from Gwyer Hall, Delhi, and here was a motley foursome at the feet of the master. It was late; Ellen made a delicious dinner with all the things I had been craving for in my unconscious mind—cream, coffee, bacon, cheese; and then we had drinks till late, late at night. This was the first time in my life that I enjoyed them.

Roy was heterodox on all counts: as an Indian nationalist, for he despised nationalism; as a Hindu, for he detested the social trappings of Hinduism; as a communist whose apostasy from Communism put him on to the blackest of the Communist black lists. But he had a deep love and reverence of the religious philosophers of India and he much admired my own scholastic preceptor, the founder of the Daśanāmī Order, Śaṃkarācārya (ca. A.D. 750) in spite of the great scholastics narrow casteism and apparent rigidity. Roy felt the Śaṃkarācārya had been a concealed materialist, just as his medieval contemporaries had alleged he was a crytpo-Buddhist. Materialism—not the vulgar materialism of 'eat, drink, and be merry', but the philosophical materialism taught by some humanists—was the final achievement of all philosophy in Roy's mind. On the face of it, Roy's conception of Śaṃkarācārya as a materialist sounds wrong, but chiefly because it sounds so paradoxical. Yet Roy may well have been right according to his own criteria, for as according to Śaṃkarācārya, all that exists on the physical and the mental plane is '*jaḍa*', i.e. inert, material, he thereby extends the concept of the material to cover all these things which matter to Roy and to the humanist: the human mind and its deeds, the human body and its beauty. Śaṃkarācārya teaches that all these are '*jaḍa*' and that they derive their apparent autonomy from the self-luminous Brahman. But the impersonal, absolute *spirit* of Śaṃkarācārya is totally unimportant to the humanist; the 'individual'—the only entity which interests the humanist—is really a materialistic concept. It goes without saying that Śaṃkarācārya's denigration of that 'individual' was as unacceptable to Roy as were his social ideas, his ideas of ritualistic purity and his asceticism.

Hindu friends have always been worried about my brazenness in matters of diet. Let me say that being a vegetarian in India is very easy, for the rich vegetarian food eaten by monks of good standing is a hundred times more tempting than, say, the North American high-protein cuisine. Let me also say that I am not particularly concerned about corroborating the eating of meat by adducing scriptural permission, although the Vedic seers were solid beefeaters, and even the highly orthodox lawgiver Manu, who flourished well over 1,000 years after the Vedic period and in a thoroughly vegetarian atmosphere, was quite lenient about it. Meat eating is not wrong, he taught, but those who abstain from it acquire a sort of superogatory merit. My eating meat occasionally in India and in North America is deliberate, for I object to ascribing ethical value to diet, to sex, and to other private functions of the psycho-somatic organism. In this I am not saying anything new as an occidental humanist, though I may well be saying something new as a Hindu monk. G. E. Moore's unique ethical 'good', the term understood 'in use' only, undefinable as a moral term, simply does not apply to any particular diet. I was a fanatical vegetarian as a boy and as a very young man when I became a Hindu in Europe, and for about ten years, until the day when I ate meat again with M. N. Roy at Dehra Doon, I did not touch meat, fish, fowl or eggs even under considerable duress. But I then realized—very largely, I think, under Roy's unspoken influence that I had been wrong all those years, wrong, that is, in ascribing any merit to my vegetarian diet. The protagonists of vegetarianism, Hindu, or occidental orientalizing cranks, have no arguments which will stand critical analysis. Once the learned Hindu vegetarian accepts—with a sad shrug—the historical fact that his Vedic forebears ate meat, and what is worse, beef, he usually shifts his ground and maintains that meat is an aphrodisiac which jeopardizes meditation. I admit that aphrodisiacs do jeopardize meditation, but I have not found any food, including *knīr* and mashed potatoes with salt, which are not aphrodisiacs, and fasting (for me at least) is the worst of all. I suspect, however, that vegetarianism, with the exception of the congenital variety (large sections of the Hindu population cannot stand the sight of meat because they have not had any for many generations, and they do not regard their abstention as a virtue any more than an Englishman would so regard his abstention from eating sweet-sour bat) is based on the urge to be different from other people, or—which amounts to the same—in belonging to a small circle of the elect. As for medical or quasi-medical vegetarianism and its homiletical adjuncts, they do not interest me.

The night passed, the next day and the next night, and we never got to Mussourie. I went back to Hardvar, where my American friend dropped me on his way down to Delhi.

Mr. J. K. Birla, my most loyal wellwisher and sponsor, then suggested I should go to Uttarkashi for a while. Uttarkashi means the 'Banaras of the North'—it is a very lovely place close to the Tibetan border, about a hundred odd miles up the Ganges from Hardvar. The river is narrow, cold, dangerous, and unspeakably lovely up there; Uttarkashi is the last camp for pilgrims, monastic and lay, *en route* to Gangotri, the place of 'the Descent of the Ganges'. Birla had built a fine rest house there, and that is where we put down our bundles. We lived on the mountaineers' simple diet of potatoes fried with onions and *roṭī*, of the size of a very young elephant's ear—crude food, healthy for a healthy stomach. Uttarkashi has all the traditional scholastic strife of Indian monasticism in its cloisters. The chief trend is Vedantic—and there are some of the finest scholastic brains of India among the monks who reside there, permanently or during the colder season, when their abodes in Gangotri become uninhabitable. Swami Viṣṇudevānanda, the almost elegant, extremely witty and broadminded abbot of one of the most important Daśanāmī monasteries located at Gangotri and Uttarkashi, is thought to be among the four most erudite exponents of Śaṃkarācārya's philosophy, or of the philosophy which goes by his name although most of it was written in the form of commentary and subcommentary by monks and lay scholars who flourished during the three or four centuries after his death. He permitted me to join him on his evening walks, during which he was followed by about five senior and junior monks of his institution.

Late one night, when our little party had lingered longer than usual on a small plateau overlooking the river and some mountains, the Swami asked me, 'Don't you sometimes feel all this is as unreal as our scriptures claim it is?' The first clause of this question is common monastic query, and monks ask each other this question in a somewhat rhetorical fashion. But the second clause 'as our scriptures claim' was astounding, coming from one of the pillars of orthodox Hindu scholasticism. I was flabbergasted. Did the Swami read contemporary analytical philosophy? Hardly, because he did not know any language except Sanskrit and Hindi and accounts of modern philosophy in these languages are few and quite inadequate. I expressed my surprise at the framing of his question. Then Swami Viṣṇudevānanda gave me a clue which proved to be of immense help to me as a heuristic device in all the years to come. 'We can and should assent to the Scripture and to its best commentaries', said Viṣṇudevānanda, noticing my mystification, 'but the time for a critical view is here, and we have to resist the temptation to push things down the throats of the less learned. You may think that I am influenced by your western modes of thought. But this is not so, I know nothing of them, except that they are critical or even destructive. In our own tradition, there have been masters who saw the texts critically, and whose seeing them critically did not diminish their faith in the least. But our *ādiguru*, I am sorry to say, was none of them. Study the work of Śrīharṣa some time. You do not have to go to the Buddhists, who had an easy task in refuting our doctrines, because they had rejected their canonical foundation. Criticism is easy for an outsider who rejects axioms'. These were the words of an orthodox monk, but they had the ring of modern philosophy. Swami Viṣṇudevanānda was offered the office of Śaṃkarācārya when one of the four abbots-general died a few years ago; he declined, for he valued learning above status.

It was Śrīharṣa indeed, as well as some more recent Hindu thinkers, who devised what I would call an interior critique—a critical attitude which does not disqualify its holder from being orthodox. Among the Buddhists, such had been the attitude of one of their greatest teachers, Nāgārjuna. With them, this attitude fortunately became the normal. Not so with the Hindus: Śrīharṣa and the later thinkers were exceptions and are not really accepted as exemplars in Hindu scholasticism. This important attitude can be summed up very succinctly: here is a set of canonical doctrines, which cannot be impugned without forfeiting Hinduhood. But they can be freely interpreted. And if interpretation does not suffice to make a doctrine discursively acceptable or at least plausible, then let us regard this doctrine as appertaining only to the innermost world of yoga, of meditation, and as having no bearing on our natural world (including, of course the psychical world). I accept the doctrine non-discursively, as having a purely private, incommunicable validity—of an aesthetic kind perhaps akin to some yogic vision or to a powerful, euphoric hallucinatory experience, resulting from, say, an alcaloid drug. But I do not assign discursive validity to it. Within some two years after my encounter with this learned monk, I had applied this approach to quite a few doctrines, for example, the notion of palingenesis, so intriguing and attractive to the religiously frustrated West.

The Hindu and the Buddhist never feel the need for any sort of empirical verification of rebirth, and they frown at such attempts. Why? Applying this interior critique, I would say that the notion of individual reincarnation is an ethical or even an aesthetic postulate, or a putative attempt to explain differences in ethical, intellectual or social status; it is no discursive proposition and needs no more empirical proof than, say, Kant's categorical imperative. It is simply not empirical, and the tragicomic confusion persisting among non-orientalistic admirers of Asian thought in the West arises from their desire to apply the occidental love of empirical evidence to totally non-empirical patterns of thought, such as the Indian axiom of palingenesis. Many Indian writers were confused in this matter, and profoundly so, by their respect for occidental empiricism. Vivekananda and almost all swamis in India today constantly affirm that Hinduism is a 'scientific religion', not realizing that they do enormous harm to the good repute of Hinduism in the minds of the humanist and the philosopher. A religion must be religious, not 'scientific', when 'scientific' means 'subject to empirical verification or confutation'. The pursuit of religion—through yoga and other contemplative devices—is indeed methodical, but well-meaning men both in the East and the West constantly confuse 'methodical' with 'scientific'. These terms overlap in certain contexts, but they stand distinctively apart in the universe of religious discourse. Strangely enough, a similar analysis, in a less sophisticated diction, was propounded by a very ancient Brahmin seer, Jaimini, who lived many centuries before the Buddha (assuming that Jaimini was an historical personality). He maintained that the sacred text *never* deals with mundane, objective things, or with any topic which can be dealt with and studied by the non-canonical sciences. He would say, for example, that when the word 'tree' is mentioned in a sacred text, such as the Veda, then it must not be understood to denote any physical tree, for such a one can be dealt with by botany; the scriptural 'tree' must mean some object on contemplative internalization or hypostasy, some homologization required for meditative instruction—an instruction for which only the canonical scripture is competent.

Swami Viṣṇudevānanda was the first monastic scholar who adopted this archaic, yet utterly modern attitude, never acquired by the Anglicized swamis of the Hindu Renaissance, because, I think of the attraction exerted on them by the shibboleth 'scientific religion'. Any possible translation of the phrase into Sanskrit or an Indian vernacular is hollow and without significance to the orthodox, profound scholar like Viṣṇudevānanda.

He represented the main stream of the Uttarkāśī—Gangotri monks: the orthodox, radically monistic, and highly scholastic trend of Advaita-Vedānta, not of the Advaita read in secondary, emasculated, eclecticizing literature, but in the stern original and its austere classical commentary. This is an intellectual monastic pattern, in sharp contrast to the humbler, unsophisticated monks of Uttarkāśī who practice and teach the lesser yogas—the very yogas which have made disciples *en masse* in the western world. A visitor fresh from some theo-, anthropo-, or other -sophical centre in Europe and America would feel alarmed at the dry, yet humorous and perhaps slightly sarcastic scholasticism of the Advaita monks of this place, and might well be attracted to the humble yogis and to their *āsanas* and *prāṇāyāmas*, or else to the watered-down, popularized Advaita of the Ramakrishna Mission and other Renaissance ideologies. There is a wide abyss between the Vedānta propounded in the eight volumes of Swami Vivekananda's work and the Vedānta reflected upon by the monks of Uttarkāśī.

By this time, I had lost all my enthusiasm for the popularizers of things Indian, and Viṣṇudevānanda's words were like a strong purifying breeze. In the years to come, I learnt to distinguish between the two types of monastic Hinduism—and I am bracketing the popularizers and the *haṭha-yogis* together, setting the orthodox scholastic monks apart from them not because the first two are similar to each other (there could hardly be any point of contact between, say, the Ramakrishna monks and the *haṭha-yogis* of Uttarkāśī) but because both of them avoid scholasticism with equal zeal, albeit for different reasons. Vivekananda called Hindu and other scholasticism 'logic-chopping' and 'intellectual jugglery', and the *haṭha-yogis* use similar terms. They inveigh against discursive thought, but the Hindu scholastics use discursive thought with the same relentless perseverance as the logical empiricist in the West.

On my return to Delhi I was told that the University would not further avail itself of my services. No reason was given, but it was clear that my lack of enthusiasm for separating the students of the two different sexes was partly accountable for the decision. My participation in the Monks' Conference with its rather unusual and international ramifications might also have had something to do with it, for the Indian Home Ministry is wary of aliens who wear raiments belonging to Hindu orthodoxy. India is indeed becoming secular: the orthodox view is that none but Siva Himself can say if a man wearing the robe is a real *sannyāsī* or a fraud, but I am often asked—and all *sādhūs* are asked nowadays by their profanely alarmed flock—if I believe that all who wear the robe are genuine. My own answer is perhaps more radical than can be fortified by any proof: over 90 per cent of those who wear the robes are 'frauds' in the sense the questioners would connote by 'fraud'. The idea that the monk is more perfect than the non-monk is inveterate, and it is kindled by the monks themselves. If perfection is to mean greater dedication to the search for spiritual emancipation, then there is undoubtedly more of it among the monks. But in terms of human morality and of human intellect, monks are nowhere more perfect than lay people. Yet I claim that even if many of the majority of *sādhūs* are frauds, in the generally accepted sense, these must be tolerated for the sake of the very few who are culture-bearers, especially in India where the monks have been the culture-bearers par excellence. I admit, however, that this is a matter of taste: should a mass of parasites be tolerated for the sake of a few geniuses among them? I certainly think so—and I believe that is a token of a country's culture if its rulers put up with many clowns in order to have some sages among them. Secular thinkers may differ; and if the stake is modernization, industrialization, catching up with the Jones's beyond the sea, then no parasites must be suffered, even if weeding them out means the stifling of the great whose outward demeanour is indistinguishable from theirs.

I spent a few months in complete seclusion in an old garden near Delhi, translated a manuscript, and meditated, near the city and yet far from it. Then I travelled to Pilani, the native town of the Birlas in Rajasthan, to lecture at the College—which is now one of the finest and most versatile universities in India. I fell ill—the doctor diagnosed malaria, and his argument was 'What else could it be?' It was, however, typhoid, and this about a month after I had been innoculated against typhoid. 'Without the innoculation you would have died', I was told. Dr Avalegoankar, the Head Physician and Surgeon of the Birla Hospital at Pilani, saved my life with love, devotion, and chloromycetin. I returned to Delhi very weak. There, I chanced to meet Pandit Govind Malaviya, then Vice-Chancellor of Banaras Hindu University and a Member of the Indian Parliament, which was in session. 'We want men like you', he said. 'Why don't you come and teach, and serve, and look after our students and their spiritual needs? I would like you to look into the kitchens as well as into the libraries. You should be everywhere.' I said 'Yes' immediately. It is no small thing to teach at Banaras. Every teacher in India who had anything to say, and who wanted to make himself heard, had to do so from Banaras, including the Buddha. I would teach comparative philosophy, eastern and western. As a monk I could accept no salary. I would be given quarters to live in, food, and a nominal sum for my expenses.

CHAPTER VI

PROFESSOR OF PHILOSOPHY, B.H.U.

Vidyayā amṛtam aśnute
(Through knowledge immortality is obtained)

Banaras Hindu University—whose motto heads this chapter—is one of the finest universities in Asia. The campus is huge and beautiful. The number of resident students was over 10,000 when I began my teaching there on November 17, 1951. The colleges and lecture halls, the laboratories and the library are in one long row, separated from the hostels by wide playing fields. The women's hostel and the Women's College is to the left of the main gate, behind a fairly high wall. There is no undergraduate co-education in the arts faculties; there is some co-education at the postgraduate level and—simply from financial necessity—at the undergraduate level in the applied sciences. Some departments do not accept girls—geology is one of them, I remember.

'This is Swami Agehananda Bharati, our new honorary professor of philosophy.' Thus Prof. Atreya, the Head of the Department of Philosophy, Psychology, and Indian Philosophy and Religion introduced me to the assembled students. The hall was too small and the fans were not working; they seemed to suspend their activity whenever anyone entered the room, purring beautifully at other times. There were about 150 students on about 120 chairs: about 140 men, and 10 girls shyly gathered in the far corner of the hall. I was to address them on problems of contemporary thought in the West. I adumbrated the three philosophical attitudes which seemed to me the most representative in Europe in the decade: analytical thought in the British Isles, Existentialism in France and Germany, and also in Germany nostalgic metaphysics with a tinge of what I called neo-mysticism. I spoke in English; I had suggested lecturing in Hindi, but was asked to use English as most of the philosophy and psychology textbooks were still English, and the students had to get used to hearing the language. The undergraduate classes are conducted in Hindi, even when the text is still English: the postgraduate classes are conducted in English, though with a constant Hindi commentary. South Indian or Bengali professors and lecturers, who cannot provide such a running commentary find it hard to get their thoughts across.

I noticed quite a number of blank faces in the first rows, and insisted that the questions period, or the discussions should be in Hindi. There was no question for a long time, just a somewhat painful shifting in the chairs. Then a slender, fine-featured professor with dense hair and spectacles asked me to elaborate a little on analytical *versus* mystical thought, and whether analytical thought had no hold whatever in German speaking countries? I replied that Wittgenstein and the Vienna Circle had virtually been ostracized in the place of their origin; but from that moment to the day of my departure three years later I could never get rid of the feeling that apart from my questioner (Prof. J. L. Mehta) no one in the audience had heard the names of Wittgenstein, Neurath or Mach. When they did hear them, owing to the joint efforts of Prof. Mehta and myself—and he was more active than I—our colleagues seemed to show little interest in them.

Indian university teaching is textbook-conscious and textbook-bound and there is a general feeling that textbooks should not be changed too often; in the liberal arts, that is (I do not know if this attitude prevails in the sciences, although I believe that is just as disastrous in the liberal arts and in philosophy). At the time I joined the staff of B.H.U., the philosophy department used much the same texts as most other Indian philosophy departments teaching occidental thought: metaphysics was top-heavy, idealism alone was canonical, logic was still Aristotelian, though some Indian professors of philosophy are trying to introduce multivalued-systems and symbolic logic. Prof. Mehta and I indented for the basic publications in modern and symbolic logic, but when the books arrived I found that the mathematics department drew on them with real gusto while our philosophers barely touched them.

Only those western philosophers are read who seem to teach something similar to Indian doctrine. To be more precise, Advaita Vedanta, or radical ontological monism, having become popular among intellectual Hindus since Vivekananda (largely, I feel, owing to his writings), any occidental system which can be assimilated to Advaita is welcome, and any type of western thought remote from or contrary to it will be excluded. Thus, Berkeley is popular and on every Indian philosophy graduate's lips; Bosanquet is ranked as the incontrovertible logician, and Bradley is almost a modern British patron saint—*Appearance and Reality* is a text for almost all Indian postgraduate courses on philosophy. Russell, on the other hand, was not read anywhere at the time I taught. After much persuasion, Prof. Mehta finally convinced the committees concerned that these things are no longer contemporary. Prof. S. K. Maitra, a very erudite scholar and a great admirer of Kant and Hartmann, gently opposed our plans, saying, 'In India, "contemporary" means 2,000 years old—everything is contemporary that has once been thought and taught'. Yet Mehta and I succeeded in getting some basic modern British thought on to the schedule: A. J. Ayer's *Language, Truth and Logic* was made a text and other schools in India soon followed the example. Replacing Joseph's and Jones's cumbersome logical works, Susan Stebbing's *Modern Introduction to Logic* was prescribed for the M.A. course in logic.

In short, some sort of analytical approach became more acceptable, first at B.H.U. and later at other important universities. But logical empiricism was about as much as could be introduced; it proved impossible to teach existentialist thought as representative of central European philosophical writing. I frequently spoke about the great four to my colleagues and to interested students, and some of them did read Sartre and Heidegger on their own, but it never became official reading. This puzzled me in the beginning. I had expected logical empiricism to be less acceptable to the orthodox scholastic spirit and in particular to the Advaita sentiment than the deeply introspective or even introvert existentialist thought of, say, Kierkegaard or Jaspers. Mehta held for a while that the Upaniṣads and all canonical Brahmin literature could be read from an existentialist viewpoint; he probably based this on one of the salient characteristics of Brahmin canonical lore—the complete autonomy and centripetality of the mystical quest. In later times this autonomy became tenuous: as soon as *bhakti* predominates, as soon as elements of grace and of divine trust are introduced, the radical self-reliance of the Upaniṣad(ic) seers is blurred. I did not agree with his view, for although individual autonomy is essential in choosing a path towards spiritual emancipation, the end is anything but existentialist. *Mukti*, freedom from the cycle of birth and death and the hazard of a lifelong strenuous endeavour toward this end, is a deeply essentialist notion, diametrically opposed to the existentialist; and in Brahmanism at least, it is the state of *mukti*, or liberation as an ontological state, that is important, *not* the effort.

Once I succeeded in weaning some bright students from their mental inhibitions the results were amazing. They seemed to make a huge leap forward, once they had made up their minds that philosophical thought must not be hampered by reverence for the merely old and for the great of a past age. Among Hindu scholars there is a particularly tenacious notion, pleasant to the traditionalist no doubt, but distressing to the analytical intellect, that a philosophy gathers merit with age, that what is older is also better. Thus Aristotle is better than our contemporary philosophers because he is older. I suspect that the excessive patriarchalism of official Hindudom is in part to blame for this insidious nonsense. The Hindu philosopher teaching occidental philosphy inevitably feels as a Hindu until he makes an effort not to do so at least in the pursuit of his job. But as a Hindu, he cannot easily reconcile himself to the possibility that Russell may be a more intelligent logician than Śaṃkarācārya, or that C. G. Jung may know more about the human mind than Patāñjali.

I do not know if the stuffiness of our little faculty room was at fault, but discussions between the classes, themselves strenuous, were a daily curse and added to the fatigue. The only bright spot lay in the many steaming cups of tea which were constantly brought from the nearby tea-shop on the campus. 'Any Time is Tea Time' is true of all offices in India—administrative, commercial, and scholastic alike. In the hotter seasons tea keeps one cool, in the cooler season it warms. Yet my colleagues did not see the one point which I tried to present to them over gallons of tea throughout three years: that you cannot arrange human thought in a hierarchy which has been set, once for all, by a particular school, for if any such school of thought arrogates to itself the right to establish such a hierarchy, it is not better than the 'Hearken to me or perish' of the intolerant religious teachers.

But as I have said, I did wean a handful of students from

complacent traditionalism: and this I did by convincing them of the aesthetic grandeur and uniqueness of the Hindu religion, at the same time making them disassociate religion completely from discursive philosophy. This is no easy task, for Hinduism is suspicious of aesthetics, despite the fact that it freely avails itself of aesthetic props: the gods and goddesses are not only beautiful, but their beauty is described in vividly sensuous terms—the Song of Solomon pales in comparison with the invocations and chants in which the Brahmin scriptures visualize the chosen deity and its retinue. Yet the intelligent Hindu student of comparative philosophy (meaning in India, a comparative study of Indian and occidental philosophers) can be persuaded to abandon this congenital suspicion, and I was able to demonstrate to at least four young men and to at least one bright Brahmin girl that their misgivings were not supported by the canonical scriptures themselves. *Raso vai sa* the text says, 'aesthetic sentiment indeed is He, the Universal', and hundreds —literally hundreds—of other scriptural statements prompt such an aesthetic view. Many of the very greatest of the Hindu teachers undoubtedly viewed their Hinduism aesthetically—how else could they have described the supreme being as '*satyaṃ, śivaṃ, sundaram*', as 'true, benign, beautiful', where 'beautiful' never excludes sensuous beauty, no more than in the Greek *κάλοκ'αγαθία*. I pointed out that it is the Christian and the Muslim mentality which recoils from the possibility of an aesthetic approach to religion, owing to the (partly unconscious) Christian assumption that matter and the senses that work upon and appreciate matter are fundamentally negative and sinful.

By the side of the Arts College, where our Philosophy Department occupied the lower wing, is the more recent, rather striking building of the Sanskrit University. Administered as part of B.H.U., this school is an orthodox Sanskrit institution of the highest standard. The degrees given there are the orthodox degrees and their equivalence to the 'English' degrees given by the other departments is established by decree, but I am sorry to say that the earnestness of my students did not compare with that of the Sanskrit University, in spite of the fact that the latter is restricted to orthodox and scholastic studies and does not countenance the 'comparative' approach; or perhaps for that very reason. In a way, the two 'universities' represent the two poles of divergence to which I have pointed before, a divergence which seems to permeate the cultural life of modern India. On the one hand, there is the mind which has been exposed to British ways of expression and to occidental uninhibited, discursive argument—for the student of the liberal arts at an Indian university reads and listens to very much the same things as his fellow at a British school of equal standing. This has drawn him away from the intensive indigenous scholasticism, from the vast amount of learning by rote and from the undisputed acceptance of certain scholastic axioms, which a learned man two or three generations ago would accept as a matter of course. It has made him insecure, because he is still surrounded by vestiges of that learning. If he studies philosophy, he is likely to be vociferous about Indian doctrines like Vedānta, and yet deep down he feels inferior to the pandits who master those elaborate systems in their original. He feels tempted to cast it all aside and to join the occidental philosopher in his ethnically unimpeded quest; yet he is at once proud and timid vis-à-vis the massive traditional learning of his own culture. He may ridicule the pandits as narrow and superstitious, yet he is angered by the occidental philosopher who seems to have come by his unbiased attitude, not through biting his way through the dense mazes of a tradition, but simply by jettisoning scholastic tradition. The Indian student suffers moreover from a painful dilemma. He evaluates occidental philosophy on purely discursive evidence, and yet there lingers at the back of his mind the feeling that all this is really futile and unimportant if not actually an obstacle in the quest for the highest wisdom, which is non-discursive, non-philosophical, intuitive and not accessible to the intellect.

At the other extreme stands the orthodox student. He wears a turban, he puts on his sandal mark every morning, he bathes and eats and marries and dies orthodoxly; he probably begets children orthodoxly. His daily life is somewhat cumbersome, owing to the observances which envelop every movement, every action, and a good part of his thoughts from the moment he opens his eyes, extremely early in the morning, until he closes them late at night. For the orthodox Brahman, the daily worship lasts up to three hours. He eats very little and his vegetative life requires an incredibly small portion of his time. For the rest—he studies. He reads grammar, he reads the Vedas with their 'limbs', he reads poetics, logic, philosophy, rhetoric, the art of debate, and he specializes in some particular branch of Sanskritic learning—Indian medical science, astrology, or both. The mere mass of absorbed material is enormous; the number of texts—not just verses and passages, but entire texts—which he knows by heart is fabulous.

But this passive learning does not make him a scholar qualified to teach at an institute in the category of the Sanskrit University, that attractive large building by the side of our B.H.U. Arts College, separated by a paved road and by a radically different approach to all things of the intellect. In order to be a teacher at this institute or a similar one (there are at least a dozen if not more of its quality spread out over Bharat), he has to have written prolific commentaries in chaste Sanskrit on any one or more of the branches of traditional learning in which he has specialized. But it is *only* commentary and subcommentary that he writes. Were he to refute Vedic wisdom as nonsense, he would have to found his own religion, as did Buddha. He is free to interpret the Vedic word as he pleases, but he pays overt loyalty to it. On this he has no scruples: and that he has none is part of his being on the other pole of learning. He is perfectly secure. He does not suffer any feelings of inferiority. He is humble when facing a man of learning outside his own discipline, extremely haughty, at times, when among his own and on a rostrum of debate. Of late, some of these titans of the tradition have evinced deep interest in occidental thought: Pandit Ramachandra Dixitar, Head of the Philosophy Department of the Sanskrit University, who spoke only Sanskrit, Tamil and English (but *not* Hindi, despite 30 years residence in Banaras) studied English in order to read Kant in Norman Kemp Smith's translation. Pandit Laxman Shastri Tarkatirtha, one of the must erudite pandits of India and a devotee of M. N. Roy, studied English in order to read Hegel and Marx! Now this sort of profoundly scholastic interest in occidental thought is on the increase among the very best of the orthodox Hindu savants. There is a deep humility in their approach; they recognize that the human intellect is capable of probing into all aspects of wisdom, even where it happens to be ensconced in a barbarian body. Only twenty years ago the Brahmin pandit would have thought it beneath his dignity to study what the *mlechha* had thought and speculated.

The orthodox pandit, being completely certain about the

truth of the Brahmin doctrine, sees nothing wrong in occasionally considering radically atheistic views. His most ancient ancestors did it and the spiritual heirs of that breathtaking ancient Indian freedom of the speculative intellect, the pandits who teach at the Sanskrit University, love to learn about Kant, but also about Russell and Wittgenstein. I gave the gist of Russell's ideas on logical fictions or logical constructions to two of the finest pandits: 'A marvellous insight!' they exclaimed. Then I gave them the gist of Russell's ideas on marriage and morals. They were silent for a while and then the senior of them said thoughtfully: 'If the mind stands by its own decree after having argued it, it is the right thing to act upon that decree. We do not feel inclined to accept what the English scholar says, but he might not feel inclined to accept what Ramachandra did to Śitā.' (Ramachandra, the most beloved divine hero of Hinduism, rejected his spouse Sītā when told that a washerman and the people in general had cast aspersions on her chastity during her imprisonment at the hands of the King of Laṅkā—in spite of the fact that Ramachandra had proof and was wholly convinced of her innocence.)

There had always been much 'politicking' at B.H.U. The main currents seem to be Hindu chauvinism and regional parochialism—'U.P.ism' as a colleague used to call it. One can understand Hindu nationalism in a university founded by Pandit Malaviya, and 'U.P.ism' in any university in Uttar Pradesh which, by reason of its scholastic merit, was becoming increasingly exposed to non-local influences (B.H.U. is one of the few Indian universities—there were only four of the kind at that time—which is directly coordinated to New Delhi, the President of India being the 'Visitor' to B.H.U.) There was however, also quite a bit of communism among the students—of a less informed variety than, say, at Calcutta or Madras, yet of a particularly angry brand, owing to the fact that the 'opium of the people' was so pervasively evident at B.H.U. Young communists, both among students and staff, were constantly vexed by the fact that their friends and colleagues, equally poor and equally brilliant, should nevertheless accept the opiate of Hinduism. And yet the young communist of orthodox Hindu origin retains his Hindu Renaissance morality. Bad to the young B.H.U. communist is what is bad to the B.H.U. Hindu, in matters of personal character. An instance: on United Nations

Day there was a meeting of students of all faculties in the Arts College Hall and I was one of the speakers. Describing the Declaration of Human Rights, I emphasized the need of humanistic individualism, which I defined as the attitude which emphasizes the value of the human individual alone, and which is constantly aware that 'nation', 'people', 'mankind', etc. are convenient abbreviations, but not larger individuals; that these abbreviations are but names, and that they must not be conceded the right to subjugate what alone is real—the human individual. This tallied with my conception of humanism in general, which I had just then propounded in a lengthy contribution to a felicitation volume for Dr Radhakrishnan. Individualism as the attitude that takes the human being seriously only as an individual, not as a member of a class ('mankind', 'nation', 'the people', 'children of god'—these are classes, and the humanist is not interested in them); rationalism (in the sense of knowing which issues in life should be decided by discursive reasoning and which by emotional decree); and cosmopolitanism (vanquishing the idea that the site of one's own cradle is in any way more important than that of anyone else's cradle)—these three, again, constitute what I call humanism.

After the talk, two young men followed me on my way from the Arts Hall to my Hostel, about half a mile away. It was quite dark, and I felt there was something fishy about them. True enough, after a while they caught up with me and stopped me. 'Sir', one of them said in a hoarse, angry whisper, 'we have put up with your dangerous ways long enough; you are not getting away with it this time!' 'With what?' I demanded. 'With your anti-people, anti-Indian, anti-decent perorations.' What had I said that was wrong? Both of them reeled off their charge-sheet: I had been consistently trying to deflate the needs of the people, trying to steep them more and more in their past superstitions; this Hindu University, with its superstitious background provided a good ground for me. But they knew better: I had put on the ochre robe to make the people listen more attentively and to fall back deeper and deeper into their intellectual turpitude; I was denigrating the Russians and the Chinese, and also Hitler and my own background; I was praising the British; I was disregarding the growing demand of the young people for something new, for the great light shown by the people of Russia and China.

The harangue must have lasted well over ten minutes. Then,

as I did not interrupt their effusions, they came to a sudden halt—the reel was at its end. 'Do you suspect', I asked them, 'that I am teaching anything else but what the philosophers of the West and of India have taught and are teaching? Can you show me where I have said or written something which is my own concoction?' 'No, not that', they said, 'everyone knows that you are an *intellectual giant*' I had heard this phrase before and from very different people; it can mean 'very intelligent, very learned, but dangerous, because standing against our deepest intuitions', I now learnt that these intuitions do not necessarily have to be Hindu—mystical—doctrinary—yogic; my attitude could be equally repugnant to the gospel of the Kremlin. 'But we know more about you and what you are hiding.' 'What is it, you young idiots?' I demanded in some exasperation, 'either you speak up or you clear out!' Then they blurted out: 'You are an American agent! You want to spread the American way of life! You use your Hindu robe to divert people's attention from your true purpose. You insult our great friends, the Russians and the Chinese, you insult the great giant Hitler, you call out the names of the Hindu gods and teachers, but in reality you are a lover of women and of comforts, you are an imperialist, you are a capitalist pretending cleverly to be poor, you want to enslave us again, you drink and go to women, we will kill you one day!'

Now the cat was out of the bag: if a man thinks and teaches what conflicts with any established orthodoxy (whether communism or any other religion) in the India of the Renaissance he will be charged with two things: first, that he has some sinister political motive; second, that he is a libertine, and the second is the worse offence. When B.H.U. was closed down in 1958 for a considerable length of time, when 'U.P.ism', nepotism, strife and irregularity had been exposed, the majority of commentators in India were particularly indignant about the moral laxity that had crept in. And these two young communists shared the same outlook.

'You may kill me some day, brothers', I said, 'but now, if you don't clear out, I shall be obliged to knock you out.' I don't know whether I should actually have struck out had they shown violence, but they whispered something to each other, and I caught only the words 'very strong . . . much food . . . yogic exercises . . . *pahlvān*. . . .' Then they muttered a not too literary phrase and vanished into the dark. I never found out who they were, nor did I try to. But I made a point of mentioning the incident in public lectures at B.H.U. and then later at other places. The usual reaction was, 'What *goondas* our young men have become'. The cause lies deeper.

Ninety-nine per cent of the B.H.U. staff were married. One per cent were widowers. In this they did not differ from any other group in India. People are married; so much so that monks are virtually the only bachelors. But what rather saddened me was the quality of their converse with their wives. Woman is honoured in the Hindu scriptures, of this there is no doubt. Her place by the side of the husband's altar is instituted by the Vedas—the Vedic word for wife is *sahadharminī*, 'she who shares the *dharma*', the ritual performed by her husband. But with the decay of classical India the status of woman has declined. Hindu men praise wives in principle, but not any specific wife. There are of course exceptions, but when some sort of tenderness or affection are shown to the wife in society, it is noticed with a frown, and it is rare. Only once in my long travels did I see a husband pay attention to his wife. He spoke tenderly and politely to her; they conversed as equals in spite of their three children travelling with them. Then again, I saw a young couple holding hands as they walked through a village among the Santhals in Bihar. But Hindus today are shocked by even that much display: if affection is shown between husband and wife, especially by the husband to his wife, it is considered crude or barbarian. At B.H.U. a colleague of mine, a very brilliant young South Indian Brahmin philosopher, was rebuked by his father and some other male relatives because he went into his wife's room to look after her when she was ill. Young men at B.H.U., as at other places, walk arm in arm, giggling at each other and grabbing each other by the neck, nobody objects to that. A highly frustrated, highly intelligent Panjabi woman, who had been returned to her parents by her husband because she did not conceive after three years of marriage, once gave me unasked some explanation of this particular display: 'Those two lads over the street hugging each other, do you know Maharaj why they do it?' I confessed that I had been wanting to know for quite some time. 'It is a vicarious hug, you see; I am said to be a fairly good-looking woman. They cannot in any way give evidence that they are noticing it, yet they want to. So they hug each other in the manner you have seen.' 'And do you approve of it, Devī?' I asked her. 'Approve of it?' she repeated with a frown. 'What can I do? If they even hinted their appreciation directly to me, I should hit them over the head with my *chappals*.'

One day I went to Pandit Omkarnath, Principal of the College of Music and the Fine Arts, and asked whether he would permit me to sit in to learn the elements of Indian vocal music. He was enthusiastic and for almost three years I sat on the hard floor of the roof of the Ruya Hostel, together with young students who took music for the love of it, although they did get some credit in their undergraduate work. At least two of my youthful colleagues were determined to make singing their life work. One of them had been my student in the M.A. class in Logic, of all things. He constantly fell asleep, which would not have bothered me over much, but for the fact that he began to snore melodiously the moment his head touched the desk. He failed twice consecutively, and then switched over to music as his full-time study. He sounds like Omkarnath, and he consciously imitated every gesture, every modulation, everything the great Pandit does, including all the mannerisms which are perfectly acceptable in Indian vocal music performance. He also imitated me exceedingly well, for sometimes I let loose a loud operatic tone in the midst of gentle Indian music practice.

It took me a long time to adapt my voice to the demands of Indian music. My *messa voce* training under Uncle Harry at Vienna was not only of no avail, but proved a definite handicap. There is no such thing as voice-training in the European sense; the voice is the extended speaking voice, and as Indian music is purely melodious, homophonous, and extremely subtle in its scales, it is the quantitative training that counts. The full course offered at the B.H.U. is one of ten years and is pretty close to the traditional methods of music teaching. Orthodox training however, is far more intensive: Omkarnath had been singing for 13 hours every day for over 20 years before he was recognized as an authority equal to his deceased guru. During the first four months or so all the boys and girls laughed aloud whenever I started off—there is no such thing as tactful reticence in Indian critical expression, and I learnt that this uninhibited reaction is amusing rather than painful, and certainly less exacerbating than the polite commendations of bad musical performance in an occidental audience!

In less than six months however, I had turned my mind completely to Indian music. The question I was often asked by non-Indians, whether I enjoyed Indian music as much as Beethoven, began to sound rather silly to me. Somehow, the notion in the West seems to be that Indian music is a different sort of noise and not just music: the question is no less jejune than such small talk as 'Do you prefer Italian to German music?' a question which can be asked only by a person who is not interested in music of another person equally uninterested. There is only good and bad Indian music, just as there is only good and bad western music.

It was the pentatonic scales which delighted me particularly. They have a strange, haunting quality; there is a very archaic, very classic and among music lovers very well-known mode called *mālkosh*, c – ♭e – f – ♭a ♭b – c, usually sung and played in slow rhythms and late at night (in fact, it is the midnight mode par excellence); all '*rāgas*' or melody types have a time of the day or the night when they are sung. After Prof. Balwant Rai had taught his scale to his class, it occupied my mind for about six weeks, day and night, giving a *mālkosh* flavour to everything I did and wrote and spoke.

At least once a week the peon of Clarks Hotel or of the Hotel de Paris came over to me with a letter and a request: would I be good enough to honour some illustrious guests by showing them Banaras? Ivory vendors and snake-charmers converge on both of these establishments, for here are their prospective customers. But it is different with the fabulous Banarasi brocades: the hotel-owners have their own brocade-shop and factory, but the visitors have also learnt to see brocades displayed in scores of beautiful shops in the city centre, for Banaras silks are the most gorgeous and expensive in India. Parents aspire to wrap their daughters in a Banaras fabric on the day of her marriage, although this may be the only occasion in her life on which she will wear those heavy, heavenly garments, with gold, silver, flowers, peacocks, elephants, damsels, hunters, and rich ornaments woven into them, between their broad golden borders of exasperating variety. The wealthy shopkeepers need little psychology to sell their goods: the customer is made to sit in the shop, and the things are simply rolled out before him—or her. I have never seen anv woman resist the temptation to purchase more than she had sworn to herself that she would—

ambassadors' wives, ambassadorial attachés' wives, and wealthy Hindu ladies from all over the country. I recall a rather touching scene: I was taking the kindly, charming, and enormously popular West German Ambassador, Professor E. W. Meyer, and Mrs Meyer to my most favoured shop. The veils and shawls and sarees were being rolled out for her. At the other end of the table similar goods were being aimed at a very charming, silent middle-aged Hindu lady who had obviously come to buy a saree for her daughter's wedding. The lady knew no word of English and yet, what a rapport between those two women! They glanced at each other, sighed over the prices, and held a discourse in that wordless, purely feminine medium which language-analysts have not yet studied.

What really led me—despite my more orthodox colleagues' frowns—to guide friends to the sights of Banaras? I felt that these occasions gave me something by way of a needed distance, a view from outside into the things with which I had identified myself. Hitherto, I had not felt that I was becoming enclosed in any ethnic *Weltanschauung*. I still felt that I had to emulate everything Indian and the greatest compliment anyone could pay me—and there were many who did, wittingly or otherwise—was to think I was Indian and Hindu by birth. It was during the months preceding my appointment at B.H.U., but well after my pilgrimage through India, that I began to feel the triviality of that ambition. Not that I ever reverted to 'being European'—heaven forbid!—for that would only have been to exchange one ethnocentricity for another. From then on until today I have been trying to be whatever I am, with no racial allegiance: a Hindu, yes, but not an Indian; a philosopher, but not a British nor an Austrian, neither a European nor an Indian philosopher; a humanist, but not a European humanist; a man mildly fond of comfort, but not dependent on American standards of plumbing. These not infrequent encounters with people from the other side of the world, scholars, diplomats, plain globetrotters, who identified themselves with some area or some culture, or who unconsciously appealed to some national origin, did much to check my increasing enthnocentricity. For without hair, with the ochre robe, with *pān* in my mouth, with Hindi and Sanskrit on my lips and in my thoughts, I was becoming a Banarasi, and the idea of being sized up as a *pukka Banarasi bhayyā* is about as nauseating to me as that of being an *echter Wiener*—a typical Viennese.

CHAPTER VII

PASTORAL EXPERIMENT

Et Nos Inducas in Tentationem—Ad Maiorem Dei Gloriam

If two modified Christian mottoes quoted together can form an orthodox heathen proposition, it is these two. The Hindu seeks temptation in order to overcome it, and he may also blaspheme in order to get nearer to the Deity. Rāvaṇa insulted Rāma in order to be killed by the latter and to find the liberation he sought.

The 'Circle of Holy Company' invited an American friend and myself to visit the city of Ambala in the Panjab; a wealthy, quite sophisticated city, an old British Cantonment. The City proper is purely Panjabi in language and culture, and Sikhism is the majority religion there; the Cantonment has U.P. population, mostly speaking Hindi, though since partition the 'Panjabification' of all the cities of northwestern India, including the capital, is progressing rapidly. Panjabis make money and spend money; they eat real food and drink real fruit-juice; their bulls and cows are the biggest and the best in India. Their women are vivacious, their townsfolk well-dressed and fond of parties. But I must say that I was never enamoured by that area, despite its fabulous hospitality to the sādhūs, and the reason is that Punjabi Hinduism somehow lacks the imagination of the Hinduism of the central, eastern, and southern parts of India. The Arya Samaj (Society of Aryans) is iconoclastic and hence anti-intellectual and Sikhism is a creed for active men and soldiers. The joys of speculation and scholastic argument, and the zest for experimentation with the mind and with morality is somehow lacking in the cities of the Panjab. The Sikhs are martial people; a great percentage of the Victoria Crosses of the last two wars went to them. This alone would suffice to keep me away, yet the simple enthusiasm of the Panjabi Hindus in courting the Hindu monk from within or from outside the Panjab does a lot to compensate for those shortcomings.

The 'Circle of Holy Company' (*Satsaṅg Maṇḍalī*) was founded by an Inspector of Police, a C.I.D. officer. He had converted his large house into a place of worship and litany, and a motley crowd came to listen to religious discourse every day, starting in the earliest morning hours. Affluent merchants joined the Circle and famous Hindu monks and laymen were invited to address the meetings. There are hundreds of circles of this kind all over Hindu India—I must have addressed scores of them. This one was typical, and in presenting it I am describing a common pattern. Those who attend it, those who give quite lavishly to its upkeep, the organizers and the well-wishers, all become a little monotonous after a time, not because there is something particularly boring about the Circle of the Holy *per se*, but because typical people and situations tend to weary. I often feel tempted to regard 'boring' and 'typical' as synonyms, just as I would like to equate 'interesting' with 'untypical'.

We were welcomed at the station by a group of men dressed in white with a little band of drummers and trumpeters, the same who play at weddings and funerals. As we alighted, the usual garlands were hung around our necks and each of the gentlemen greeted me by respectfully touching my feet—by that time I was no longer embarrassed by this general expression of respect to the ochre robe. We then mounted an open carriage with two horses and the procession started, to involuntary variations on 'Tales from the Vienna Woods' and 'Valencia' from the band walking in front. We meandered through the main bazaar and the main streets, halting at every corner while a loudspeaker mounted on a jeep ahead of us announced to the curious: 'Brothers and Gentlemen, today is a great festive day for Ambala. You will have the great joy and honour of listening to the words of a famous yogi and *sannyāsī*, who has come all the way from Germany to speak to you! Bring your friends and the pious members of your family to the "Circle of Holy Company" at our dear Police-Inspector's assembly house!' By the time we had reached the vicinity of the house, a huge crowd had gathered and was blocking the roads; some busy policemen were trying to keep order, and they too greeted us devoutly as we passed. The usual shouts of '*bolo swāmījī kī jai*!' (Victory to the Swami), initiated by the organizers and their friends, were taken up lustily by the crowd.

The house had been charmingly decorated with flowers and the proprietor's family strewed petals over us as we entered the little archway erected for the occasion. We were immediately shown to our rooms, plain, large and comfortable, with white-washed walls and the inevitable 'photos' of Viṣṇu, Śiva, some less important members of the pantheon, Gandhi, Nehru, and Bose on the walls (all these millions of multicoloured glossy prints are referred to as 'photos', regardless of whether the portrayed figures are mythological, dead or alive). Tea, some rich sweets and luscious fruit were brought and we were asked to help ourselves, while the host fanned us with a hand-fan—a supererogatory action, as two brand new electric fans blew plenty of pleasant air on us from the ceiling.

The meeting was to commence around 7 p.m., it was now about four, and the host suggested we might rest awhile: one of the genuinely pleasant and considerate features of Indian hospitality, for great care is taken that the guest, between his commitments, of whatever kind they may be, holy or mundane, should eat and sleep—not just sit and rest, but sleep. The climate of the Indian cities of the North is conducive to this and I always found the towns of the Punjab peculiarly soporific.

A little window allowed us to peep straight into the assembly hall. We noticed that it was completely filled by 6.30 p.m. and after a while the host announced some of the preliminary speakers, local pandits and saints. A few minutes after seven we two were conducted into the hall, which had almost been converted into a temple, the men sitting on one side of the dais, the women on the other, with the children commuting between them, as always in pious Hindu assemblies. We were seated side by side, some little girls sang a Panjabi song composed in our honour and the host introduced us: 'Here, sisters and brothers, are the two famous scholars and saints from far away. Of Swami Agehananda you have heard, his name has spread all over India. He belongs to the heroic German nation, which fought the British, which joined with Netaji Subhas Bose to drive out the foreigners from here—that German nation which speaks Sanskrit and which for its victories had recourse to the Veda, whose use we have forgotten. Worldly attachment does not defile the Swami, he is an eternal *brahmacārī;* lust and women and wealth mean nothing to him. He could easily earn Rs. 500 to 800, perhaps even 1,100 per month, but he does not care for this filth. He has come to tell us how we can live in this world and yet have *bhakti* and see God! Men like him are indeed the treasure of Bharat. And by his side you see that healthy, strong friend of his, a famous American scholar. He took a B.A., and then, brothers, he took an M.A.! And although he is so learned and famous, he has come to our humble place to see how we unlearned, worldly people take the name of God!'

Now there is nothing unusual in such an introduction. To equate an academic degree with great scholarship and that in turn with a high potential income (as erroneously in India as elsewhere) is an illusion shared by all but the sophisticated. To this the Hindu Renaissance also adds the equation: 'academic degree—renunciation of potential affluence—sanctity and spiritual power'.

I had been planning to give this audience some general bread and butter advice, but somehow, I drifted into Vedantic monistic jargon and spoke on the rather technical level of monistic dialectic for over an hour. There was silence and close attention and more questions from the audience after that than after more general sermons. Thereafter, I did not exclude Hindu metaphysical doctrine from my range of themes for such occasions. Brahmin philosophy can be 'brought to the masses' without losing its value in the process of popularization, in a way which is denied to western philosophy. All Indian philosophy is finally intuitive and touches human, non-scholastic interests in spite of its scholastic jargon (which is indeed a formidable barrier to the simple Hindu). I am no longer impressed by the fact that most occidental teachers of philosophy deny the label 'philosophy' to Indian thought for this very reason. Until quite recently I myself criticized Dr Radhakrishnan for styling Indian thought 'philosophy', but I have now practically abandoned the view that Indian thought is no philosophy just because it is not ultimately interested in discursive reasoning, in truth-functions and truth-tables, and I begin to sympathize more than I did then with the late R. G. Collingwood. He defined metaphysics as statements of *what* the axiomatic sentences in a particular philosophy were, not *how* those axioms came about or whether they were correct or false. Thus I no longer deny that 'I am the Brahman', the great dictum of the Upaniṣad, is a philosophical statement. It is metaphysical, and if Collingwood meant—although he did not say so—that metaphysics is the historical discipline in philosophy, filing the history of philosophy in the files of History rather than of Philosophy, then 'I am the

Brahman' is a metaphysical or an historical statement, but in any case a philosophical one.

This is to re-admit Indian thought into 'philosophy' in my own terminological tool-box; it is not to accept Indian thought as 'philosophy' *par excellence,* in the sense in which I had accepted it before I became Agehananda. For then I accepted the Indian and debarred contemporary western philosophy from the appellation, partly because I knew little about the latter, but mainly because my critical faculties were suspended in a phase of conversion and enthusiasm—a sacrifice of the factual and scientific at the altar of aesthetics and religious exultation. It was not that Russell and Wittgenstein and Moore came to me first and were superseded by the Upaniṣad and its prolix adjuncts in East and West: no, the Upaniṣad came first (via the Hindusthan Academical Association of Vienna, via Vivekananda, and Subhas Bose and others). Then came Wittgenstein and Analysis—and about this time the Upaniṣads, the Buddhist Dharma, and Analysis began to form a pattern in my mind to which I give the name 'philosophy', regardless of the possibility of estranging both logicians and aesthetes. The only charge I really fear is that of eclecticism and it may appear as though my present attitude were eclectic. But this is not so, for an eclectic uses the pieces obtained from here and there either to build a system or to fit them into a preconceived system. I am not doing this, because I abhor systems of thought. I do not think 'eclecticism' denotes method; but if it did, I would not object to my *method* being called eclectic, or better, syncretistic. Many people and dictionaries use 'eclecticism' and 'syncretism' as synonyms, and there has been no ruling on whether this is permissible. I will suggest a terminological barrier: 'eclecticism' is patchwork for a system; 'syncretism' is methodology deriving from various sources. It is not possible to explain this to the Hindu pundit, because semantics has not yet entered his mind. (Although the Buddhist heretic developed rudimentary semantics as early as in the 4th century A.D.; heretics can be freer in their pursuit of philosophy of any kind.)

Until that sermon at Ambala, I had been embarrassed by my very special dilemma. I knew the logical shortcomings of Vedānta; I appreciated the analysts' work in dealing with religious propositions, but I also admired the Brahmin thinker of all schools who knew how dangerous logic might be to his ontology or theory of the essence of things, who nevertheless studied it with the same intensity as the logician aiming to attack ontology, but who rejected logic with a shrug when it arrogated to itself more than the right to arbitrate between various schools of ontology, for the Brahmin philosopher reserved for himself the final judgement as to what was more important in a total, albeit intellectual world view. Here, the Brahmin is right, and the logician—Aristotelian or Indian or modern—is wrong: if the human being and its welfare is at stake (which means its spiritual welfare), then paradoxical, illogical, Vedāntic or other non-discursive speculation and meditation are more important than the syllogism or the truth-table. Until this meeting, I had also pitied the *satsaṅg*-audiences, and this intellectual pity, which you are free to call snobbery, added to my embarrassment and restricted my topics to naïve moralizing and edifying sermon. On that day, however, I realized that the *satsaṅg*-audience is as interested, and perhaps more attentive, when Vedānta and other Hindu 'philosophy' is brought to it by the sādhū or the pundit, if only the latter can avoid scholastic jargon.

It was from this Ambala sermon onward that I acquired some name for putting over the more sophisticated topics of Hindu thought to humble audiences. There is a great pedagogical stimulus inherent in Indian thought: unlike academic western philosophers, Indian thinkers have never fought shy of simile which appeals to commonsense, even when the doctrine supported by the simile is anything but commonsense, as in the case of Vedanta. In the canonical texts themselves, and in classical commentary, not only are similes in constant use, but they are repeated literally again and again, to the exclusion of equally plausible analogues. Thus, in explaining the absoluteness of the Brahman and the relativity of the world, the phenomenality of objects, the analogy of the snake and the rope, plus two equally simple analogies, have been used without modification from the Upaniṣad down to the present day. A man sees what he thinks is a snake, and he acts accordingly—he hits it, or he gets afraid, he may even die with terror; but if a clever person directs a light towards the object and makes the man realize that it was only a piece of rope, this particular illusion disappears, and questions like 'when and where did the snake originate?' are no longer asked, or asked in a facetious manner. The 'snake' is the phenomenal world, the 'rope' the absolute Brahman.

I cannot say whether the tedious repetitiveness of these analogies derives from naiveté in the Indian scholastic, or whether it is deliberate—in which latter case it may well be a formidable instrument of indoctrination. I found among all strata of Hindu laity in pursuit of some religious problem that a persuasive analogue tends to have a greater effect than even a well-reasoned argument when unsupported by a simile or an analogue. The 'snake' and the 'rope' seemed to convince the Police Inspector and his guests just as they have been convincing learned pundits for many centuries.

We could not leave the dais before midnight, as many other speakers were yet to address the hall, and it would have been bad manners to leave. But just after midnight, after the *ārati*, my American friend and I were taken to the kitchen and fed sumptuously. The succulent vegetarian food given to sādhūs in the houses where they speak draws on the resources of the Indian cuisine: it is drenched in *ghee*, exasperatingly tasty, completely fried and starchy and very unwholesome when taken late at night. But gluttony is no sin for the *sādhū*, provided it is vegetarian; in fact a *sādhū* who cannot eat a thorough meal of this sort is viewed with some suspicion. There is a lot of joking about the *sādhūs*' and the brahmins' delight in large quantities of rich, especially sweet food. This is the only field in which monks and pandits may poke fun at themselves and this for several reasons. To the pious Hindu the holy man is healthy through his holiness, therefore he must have good food, can digest it and deserves it. He is a great person, hence his appetite for this permissible pleasure is also great. The explanation offered by common sense is that pure food, given in love and respect, is morally pure, and its enjoyment should be conceded to the ascetic who has foregone all other ordinary pleasures. To this the psychologist's explanation adds: the sādhū has subdued the erotic element in his personality and this permits a smiling approval of gustatory enjoyment.

Swami Hari Giri, a bulky, fair-looking Panjabi Hindu saint, member of the Congress Party, presides over a beautiful monastery in Bakalo near Dalhousie, in the ravishingly lovely Himalayan foothills of the Panjab. He is an orthodox Daśanāmī, but nevertheless shares the secular outlook of the Congress Party. How this works I have never quite understood, but probably everything works through goodwill. Hari Giri had a way of popularizing the teaching of monistic Vedānta by using down-to-earth analogies and by interspersing his sermon with delightful village tales in a Panjabi setting. He wore an ochre cap designed by himself. It looked exactly like that of a French chéf in action and started something of a fashion among the assembled monks; I for one obtained an identical cap from him and have been cherishing it ever since.

Hari Giri, like many or perhaps even most sādhūs was a great admirer of Hitler. This is one thing of which those outside India seem unaware: the active Hindu loves Hitler, just as he loves Bose, loved Stalin, and would have continued loving Mao had the Chinese behaved differently in Tibet and along the Indian border. Hero-worship is in the Hindu tradition, and unless the hero is considered a direct enemy of the Indian cause—like Churchill—every dictator has the sympathy of many orthodox Hindus. This is a phenomenon of some complexity, but not really hard to explain. There is the *avatāra* idea—in every powerful man there is a segment of the cosmic power which manifested itself in the god-kings and heroes of the epic and of mythology. Hitler was particularly popular, especially with the politically aggressive, for he trounced the British, at least in the beginning; he proclaimed the superiority of the Aryan (this being a Sanskrit word denoting the Hindu as he sees himself), and he was a leader of the Sanskrit-knowing Germans! I argued against this enthusiasm, and have asked enthusiasts, both monastic and lay, how they thought Hitler's deeds and attitudes compatible with *ahiṃsa*, and how they explained the dislike of Gandhi and Nehru for Hitler? The answers were always in the same jargon: when honour is threatened, when silence could be interpreted as cowardice, and when the inner spirit tells the leader to act, then *ahiṃsa* takes on a different meaning. As in Kṛṣṇa's counsel to Arjuna, there is a higher sort of *ahiṃsa*, such that there is no killing even in killing, that is, when the spirit has realized its oneness with the Supreme—and so forth. Basically, of course, this uncritical acceptance of Hitler derives from the total lack of objective information. Yet I must blame those of intelligence who are in a position to know better.

Near Amṛtsar, when the monks were assembled for a Vedānta Conference, I came upon a government-sponsored team of doctors and nurses attempting to instruct people on the desirability and possibility of birth-control. Now monastic attitudes on this important matter differ widely in India. The old-timers are against it. As elsewhere when religion is asked its opinion, the argument is, 'Let the souls that seek expression have their chance to find bodies in which to work out their fate'. Younger monks, and I among them, are seeking valid religious arguments in favour of planned parenthood and this is not so difficult owing to the variegation of scriptural texts which permit mutually contrary interpretations. I never quite found an orthodoxically convincing formula, but got near to one: give the souls that seek a body the chance to find good and healthful bodies; if they must become incarnate, and if parenthood can be planned so that people will be wealthier and healthier, then the only bodies available for incarnation will be healthier, and their surroundings more affluent. Perhaps this sounds fatuous, but it is important when the problem is how to adapt the idea of planned parenthood to a deep-rooted, albeit flexible religious code of behaviour. There was much discussion following the visit of the government team and that evening a very saintly and revered lady came to preside over a meeting for the women, conducted by some female ascetics; the monks were requested to sit as observers and advisers. She was over 70 and belonged to one of the most aristocratic Kashmere families settled in the plains. A lady-teacher, from the rather lovely girls' college across the road from the monks' camp, mentioned that children were born out of wedlock, that the mothers were then ostracized; would it not be better if young people were taught birth-control? I hardly think the young lady meant to condone pre-marital relations between young people, but she may have become confused between the two issues most exasperatingly present to the minds of Indian educators in this decade—that of co-education and its bearing on romance, and that of overpopulation and its effects on the spread of higher education in the country. The old lady flared up and said sharply: 'No children are born out of wedlock!' There was embarrassed silence and even the benevolent faces of the older sādhūs showed some dismay. Then the old lady elaborated, 'Out of wedlock, no children are born, but only goats'. In Urdu, over which the old lady had a chaste command, this sounds more compelling, as there is a pun on the two nouns: *bacce nahīṇ balkih bakre; 'bacce'* meaning 'children' and *'bakre'* 'goats'. There was no answer, and the young college teacher looked as though she wished the platform would swallow her up. I felt very sorry for her and suggested mildly but very firmly: 'Goats have to be cared for, too, Mātājī; or do you wish to sacrifice them all to some bloodthirsty god?' I do not know how the old lady took it, for her face retained the imperturbability of age, but I doubted whether her cruel punning doctrine would come quite so readily to her lips in future.

I now turn to another world. South India is different; and South India became to me the quintessence of that cultural sophistication which constitutes a large part of my very own, private India. I never learnt its languages very well (and one of the reasons for this shortcoming was, perhaps, a slight fear lest I should hear and read the trivialities and hackneyed religious idiom which irked me so much in the North whose languages I knew so well). Southern Indian music has been immensely dear to me, more than North Indian music which I had studied—and maybe I did not want to risk being annoyed by sentimental effusions of village saints, no doubt comparable to their northern colleagues, to Kabir and Nānak. I do not say Kabir and Nānak and the whole host of low-brow saint-poets in medieval North India were bad poets; quite the contrary, but they happened to write and believe in themes which I consider stale and mediocre, such as the struggle against the beauty of the senses and the resultant hatred of woman as the eternal seductress. I realized very soon that many South Indian poet-saints wrote in a similar vein; but intellectual knowledge of an aesthetic shortcoming does not interfere with enjoyment when this shortcoming is not apperceived, and a song may be enjoyed in spite of its silly words, when the words are not understood. I also knew that many South Indian poet-saints wrote in a different vein, that they used sensuous language in the tradition of mysticism, even though disparagingly like the great poet Bhartṛhari in much earlier days, whose 'Century of Renunciation' has been to me more of a literary aphrodisiac than the *kāmasūtra* with all its disenthusing pedantry, or that same Bhartṛhari's own 'Century of Dalliance'. So whenever I became steeped in South Indian classical music—which is always religious in diction and purpose—I set aside my worries, assuming that the particular poem being sung belonged to the pleasant category, and certain loaded key-words added to the rapture—they are heavy Sanskrit, their pronunciation is closer to the classical language than the identical words in Northern languages which omit the final short vowel 'a', which has a wildly charismatic effect on my ears.

The dance and the sculpture of Southern India seem to be

functions of its music—the sounds and the delightful movements of a host of mythological damsels and their male adjuncts are frozen into the friezes and frescoes of the beautiful South Indian temples. Here dance has been—until recently at least—part of the temple worship, the temple and not the brothel being the natural habitat of the dancer and the musician.

In Kerala, or rather in the two States which preceded it, in Travancore and Cochin, there is a government office which looks after the temples with great efficiency. The Devaswom Board is managed by the most pious and the most learned, and it was inaugurated and sponsored by the Prince. I had an audience with the Maharaja of Travancore at the Kaudiyar Palace in Trivandrum: a modest, small and charming man, who stood with folded palms and barefoot as he spoke to the monks. A patron of the arts and of scholastic learning, like all the princes of the South in the last decade of the decaying rajadom, he and Maharaja Jaya Chamaraja Wadiyar of Mysore are the only two princes who still embody that unique tradition of feudal learning and active scholarliness which was once the hallmark of India's many rulers.

Near Palghat in South Malabar, I spent a few weeks at a Gandhian Ashram. Its founder and head had been a student at B.H.U., a nice young man, married to a nice girl who was an LL.B. and an M.A.—her husband had been so active in living the Gandhian way of life that he failed in most of his university exams. At his Ashram there was all the daily ceremony approved by the Mahatma: religious spinning, semi-professional weaving, the care of cows and kine, instructions on cottage industry and lectures on basic science. 'Basic' in this context is a technical term and means a number of things taught by the Mahatma. Thus, 'basic education' means getting the children and students away from such bookish knowledge as saying that a circle has a periphery of $2 \pi r$ and an area of πr^2.

'This is unimportant and means nothing to the villagers, when you want to teach them science', my host informed me. 'But take a rod, fix a cord to it, draw a circle, and plant cotton in the circle. In this way the villagers will learn about a circle, not if you teach them $2\pi r$ and πr^2.' 'But', I remarked, 'don't you see that these two ways of teaching do not conflict, because they are really different subjects? The circle on which you grow cotton or in which your cow grazes is something completely different from the circle which is πr^2. Both have to be taught, although you may be justified in thinking that the πr^2 circle doesn't matter to the villager.' 'No, you are wrong,' he exclaimed. 'It is this dry book-learning that has killed our nation. Basic education teaches the same circle, but its method is correct, and your bookish method is wrong.' There were numerous discussions in this strain. 'Basic education' is contrasted to all kinds of education as conceived and used by pedagogues in India and elsewhere. There is much opposition to it, and it has not been accepted on any official level but the Gandhian Ashrams perpetuate it with fervour.

At the end of my sojourn at the Peoples Service Ashram, Achuthan and his spouse Laxmikutty Amma accompanied me to my next port of call in the southernmost area of the country. The southern tip of India is presided over by a lovely goddess, Kanyā Kumārī, which means 'Virgin Princess'. She was to be wedded to Śiva, but the gods disliked the prospect, fearing it would endanger their power, so as the divine groom's procession set out to fetch the bride, the God Indra assumed the guise of a rooster and crowed in the road as the procession came by; duped, they thought they had missed the auspicious moment and returned to the bridegroom's palace. The Virgin Goddess has been waiting ever since and if she is impatient, she does not show it. There is no more beautiful and serene idol anywhere in India than this chaste, divinely feminine, small Kanyā Kumārī. Her numinous beauty is unclouded even by the fact that the Belgian nuns who have their convent less than a mile from the temple have called her 'Kanyā Mary' and 'Kumārī' became corrupted on western lips into 'Comorin'—hence the name of the Cape forming the tip of the triangle. She has a big diamond on her forehead and she faces the south, the sea, the spot where three oceans meet in three different colours—green, blue, and not exactly bluegreen. The sacred, fragrant air that pervades Dravidian shrines—a blend of incense, austerely reticent bats, old sandstone and continuous worship, through the centuries, with coconuts, plantains, flowers, and deep piety—is more fragrant and thicker here, for it is enriched by the humidity of the ocean. The pilgrims take their bath in the warm sea fifty yards from the shrine in clean if brackish water, fenced off from the more risky depths by an iron chain. I sat in the small, dark, central shrine throughout a day and a night, as a monastic guest, and witnessed the six regular daily rituals. Only the acting Nambuthiri priest approaches the Goddess, but monks and

Brahmins sit outside the little gate through which the whole small figure is visible. When the head priest bathes the goddess—in a mixture of milk, incense and rose water, together with some *ghee* and other precious ingredients—he pats her body in a motion that suggests an oil-massage. Here is reason to be annoyed with Freud: there is powerful libido in this bath for the goddess, but it works on a level to which the good Doctor had no access; perhaps Jung has, and perhaps this bars him from academic respectability.

After this initial sojourn at the feet of the Virgin Goddess, I came every year for a week or more. If the dispenser of future births asked me if in my next life I would prefer to be the Head Brahmin for Kanyā Kumārī, Professor at Harvard, or the Master of Trinity, Oxford, I would find the choice more difficult than that between the latter two alone. Yet, this is an idle thought, for monks are not reborn anyway.

The journey by bus and steam launch from Palghat to Trivandrum is fraught with toil and beauty. The voyage along the lagoons of Kerala is the most enchanting I have ever made. The launch wends its cumbersome way between coconut palms, through the green, tropical, feverish water, dotted with hundreds of little islets. Everywhere are the clean Nyeṛ houses of red brick and wood, and even the fairly frequent big red and white brick churches do not spoil the scene. A lovely little village, Kālaḍī, (now entirely Christian) was the birthplace of Śaṃkarācārya, the preceptor of my Order and Hinduism's greatest scholar, and I visited Kālaḍī in two consecutive years. On this occasion, accompanied by my two friends, I had come to stay at the Ramakrishna Mission Centre as Swami Agamananda's guest—and this was quite an event, for it was the first time that a House of the Order that had sent me away had asked me to speak.

Swami Agamananda is a constant source of fear to the Christians around for he is very learned, has a fine mastery of philosophical Sanskrit, and speaks beautiful English. A Christian missionary—or so it is related—wanted to heckle him one day many years ago. 'Swamiji', he said, 'if you say that God is everything, or everything God, that means he is in the lavatory as well, or maybe he is also the lavatory?' 'Yes, of course', Agamananda replied, 'and if you put a Cross in there, then he is in the Cross, and he is that Cross, too'. The more sophisticated Christian minister in India has abandoned the older missionary's notion that Hinduism is polytheistic, but is as nervous about the Brahmin quasi-pantheistic, monistic Absolutism as were the early Christians, St. Augustine foremost among them. For the earliest spiritual struggle within intelligent Christianity was that against the monism or pantheism which filled the cultivated pagan atmosphere around, perturbing Origen, Basilides and many another early teacher.

Swami Agamananda himself was a strange conglomeration of orthodoxy and of the Renaissance. By training he belonged to the finest Brahmin tradition; by choice he had become a Ramakrishna-Vivekananda monk. To him Ramakrishna and Śaṃkarācārya were preceptors in a single tradition, Ramakrishna being the fulfiller of Śaṃkarācārya, with a hint perhaps of being the latter's more recent incarnation. Moreover, Agamanandaji had found out that the two teachers, though 1,200 years apart, were born on the same day of the year, a revelation which enabled the Centre to pay homage to the two great teachers at the same time in a ceremony purporting to show the people of Kerala that there was no fundamental distinction between the teachings of their great Śaṃkarācārya and of the Bengali Paramahaṃsa. Agamananda is amongst the well-meaning, but perhaps somewhat depressing savants who believe that all the really good teaching of the world is basically identical. In opposition to this I doggedly adduce the simile that Christianity and Hinduism are 'basically the same', the teachings of Śaṃkarācārya and of Ramakrishna and Vivekananda are 'basically the same', because all of them are 'religion', just as 'boiled Brussels sprouts' and 'deep-fried lamb curry' are 'basically the same' because they are both 'food'. This is true, but not very interesting. The absolutist, impersonal, aristocratic, highly dialectical teachings of Śaṃkarācārya and the devotional, highly personal, popular, anti-intellectual words of Ramakrishna are as different from one another as Brussels sprouts and chicken curry, although they have many things in common—precisely the things that sprouts and curry have in common; they are both 'nourishing', each in its own way.

On that Ramakrishna-cum-Śaṃkarācārya birthday festival at Kālaḍī I saw with delight and apprehension some of the senior Ramakrishna monks whom I had met years earlier as a novice in their fold. Moreover, Swami Sambuddhananda of the Ramakrishna Monastery at Bombay, my very first monastic host on my arrival in India was now the guest of honour. It was my turn to speak first, so I compared Śaṃkarācārya and Ramakrishna as Agamananda had asked me to. I pointed out what I thought were the main similarities—deep and irrefragable commitment to their spiritual vocation, powerful personality, uncompromising loyalty to the Hindu tradition; and I showed their differences, in personality and in approach. The one was a scholar and intellectual, a man of scholastic genius like Thomas Aquinas (this for the Christians who must have been in the audience, here in Kerala, where one third of the population is Christian), a man of tremendous intellectual acumen, at once a mystic and a logician, the preceptor of monistic monkhood, the great Śaṃkarācārya, born on this very spot in Kālaḍī, 1,200 years ago. The 'very spot' was on Swami Agamananda's authority, for he had assured me that Śaṃkarācārya had been born just where the Ramakrishna Ashrama was now located. The other, the Bengali Paramahaṃsa of the last century, a mystic, a devotee of probably unmatched intensity and vigour, a yogic teacher by nature, fervent lover of his disciples, a saint of signal personal courage and foresight, a simple man, a naïve man, not an intellectual. All these differences were as evident, to the student of Indian hagiography at least, as the similarities which I had adumbrated at the beginning of my speech. I had been asked to speak for about an hour, but after less than 30 minutes a pencilled note was sent up to me from Swami Agamananda: 'Speak about Śaṃkarācārya—don't criticize here'. I had not been aware that I was criticizing and continued with some bewilderment. Hardly five minutes passed, when a *brahmacārī* handed me another slip, which said 'Don't mention Ramakrishna any more today'. This at least was clear; in the pursuit of objectivity, I had been treading on the swamijis' toes. It was not quite as clear which points had offended, but it became so when Swami Sambuddhananda spoke, for I was abruptly shaken out of a spell of somnolent reflection induced by the humid heat of the evening when the speaker unexpectedly raised his voice to declare: 'Who can say, who dares to say that Ramakrishna was no intellectual? When all the intellectual giants of his time, all the seers and philosophers of Calcutta and India came to his feet for instruction, when the great intellectuals, men and women, of the whole world pay homage to him? Who can say that such a man was not intellectual? Is it not preposterous to say such a thing?'

I hoped that the two swamijis would have discussed our

difference in outlook privately with me that evening, but Agamanandaji gave me a wide berth until the next day when I left for Trivandrum, and Sambuddhanandaji had already left before I could make my obeisance to him. I then swore to myself—after a fashion (for 'swearing' belongs to the kind of intensity which I detest)—that one day I would find an opportunity to present my simple, logical argument in a manner which could not be overlooked. Now this day has come, after the traditional seven years: That intellectuals, and perhaps some giants amongst them, went to Ramakrishna is a fact. But they did not go to him to see an intellectual; they went to see a non-intellectual, for of intellectuals they had a surfeit. Many went to him, shrugged, laughed, and left—among them, too, were some intellectuals. But I am interested in those who stayed: they stayed and admired, and paid their homage to the naïve, non-intellectual saint, because they hungered after a man who was naïve, non-intellectual, at one with himself, convinced. The intellectuals went to him because he was *not* of them.

A year later, I attended a function at the temple built by the Śringeri Maṭha. Chembai Vaidyanatha Iyer, the famous vocalist, had come to sing and to offer his devotion to Śaṃkarācārya at the shrine. Here was orthodox, genial, most beautiful Hinduism, untouched by the Renaissance. A panel of monks discussed the self-sufficiency of Vedānta—the system that had out-argued all other systems, had disqualified scholastic Buddhism, and was now attracting the Western world. The music was pure, the architecture exquisite, the Renaissance far away. I was given something of a send-off. Maestro Chembai insisted I should sing a classical German song—I did so, and in the pillared hall of the Goddess Śāradā, tutelary deity of wisdom and of the Śaṃkarācārya Head Maṭh of Śringeri, I sang *Dies Bildnis ist bezaubernd schön*, folding my palms towards the lovely icon of the Goddess. Everyone laughed with glee, for Mozart does seem funny to the Indian ear, at least at a first hearing, though less of a tonal or atonal travesty than things written after 1800.

The bus to Thiruvalla, on the way to Kavyoor, was filled with a motley crowd. There were about half a dozen drunk villagers singing Christian songs in Malayalam (the region was not 'dry' at that time); there were two of the sannyāsins who had attended the celebrations at Kālaḍī, and there was myself. A young student sat beside me, returning to College at Trivandrum. He was a Nambuthiri Brahmin lad, very intelligent, and he spoke fluent English, though with a heavy accent. 'My elder brother could not go to College,' he confided to us. 'He is 15 years older than I, and prejudices against modern education are only now breaking down, to some extent, in our community.' Changing the topic abruptly, he added 'I wish I knew the Brahman like you or Swami Vivekananda or other sages, for then I would not have to study so hard for my exams!' It did not take me long to get at the root of this baffling reasoning. Here was a young victim of an age-old fallacy, for there is a term in the scriptures which literally means 'omniscient', *sarvajña*, and it is averred that a person who has intuited the Absolute becomes a *sarvajña*, literally one who knows everything. But the trouble is that '*sarvajña*' is a purely technical term used in Vedāntic literature, and is synonymous with '*brahmajña*', a 'knower of Brahman', which again means one who has realized his oneness with the Absolute—for the Absolute cannot be known objectively, it being the subject of the knower, never his object. So I asked the young Brahmin if he was aware of this specific meaning of 'omniscient'. 'What do you mean, sir?' he retorted with some indignation. 'We have been told that those who successfully meditate on the Brahman will be omniscient.' 'But do you realize, friend,' I continued, 'that this was never meant to imply that you will know objective things like botany and mathematics; that it referred to the state of mind which is *ānanda*, supreme beatitude?' He shook his head violently: 'No, sir, you must be wrong. Sages who have realized the Brahman know everything. Sages like Śaṃkarācārya, Ramakrishna Paramahaṃsa. . . .' 'Do you then believe,' I asked, 'that Ramakrishna Paramahaṃsa knew mathematics, atomic physics, English literature, and all that?' 'Most decidedly, sir,' he said, and I knew he meant it. 'Then why did people say that he was illiterate, why did he himself affirm it?' 'Because,' the young Brahmin said, 'he wanted to set an example to the vain intellectuals of his day, and to us who would become vain with our bookish learning, and our college degrees; for though he knew everything, though he was *sarvajña*, he pretended he knew nothing. This is real greatness.'

Inspired words, no doubt, but not well-informed words. In the Hindu mind, inspiration tends to eschew information. A Hindu of intelligence and integrity may be well informed, for instance, about the imbecility and cruelty of a leader X, but that leader is a hero, or perhaps a concealed *avatāra* who wears the guise of cruelty to achieve a higher purpose, then this mystical possibility exonerates the despot and inspires the Hindu; and inspiration supersedes information. . . .

In my travels in the South, I was often confronted with the problem of Christian conversion, and with Hindu reactions to it. With the Syrian Christians, or with any of the old Christians in India I have no quarrel. Nor for that matter with the converts, but I was distressed to realize that the majority of the Indian Christian clergy and many of the more primitive western missionaries ascribe their success in proselytizing to the intrinsically greater spiritual merit of Christianity. This is disturbing because Hinduism has no weapon to counter this arrogance: Hinduism does not and cannot proselytize; it is not a world religion, one cannot become a Hindu as one can become a Christian or a Muslim, or even a Buddhist. I am myself not fully accepted as a Hindu by very many learned, orthodox Hindus—I cannot be a Hindu by orthodox definition for a Hindu is one who is born into a Hindu caste, high or low. Hindu doctrine does not claim that its teachings are in any way superior to those of other religions, in fact it never addresses people of other faiths in whom it has no interest. But the Christian missionary has the Preceptor's own injunction to back him: 'go ye into all lands'. When the Christian missionary goes to the Hindu and tells him, 'what I bring you is the truth, because Christ said so', the Hindu has no call to counter the Christian by a similar device, because no one ever told him to go into the world and preach. Hinduism is non-historical; it does not seek, nor possess, any historical founders. The Christian missionary has been standing in the middle of the road, crying, 'You who are going to worship Śiva and Viṣṇu and the Goddess, you will go to Hell!' The Hindu cannot answer, 'You who worship the triune God will go to hell', because Hinduism teaches the very opposite. It teaches that he who worships God in any form, as the triune Father-Son-Paraclite, or as Śiva, or as Viṣṇu, or Allah, will be the better for it.

There is a band of devoted Hindus in the extreme South, laymen most of them and intelligent men, who feel deeply humiliated at the way in which Christian missionaries have penetrated into their villages. Sri Velayudhan Pillay, proprietor of a small, fairly affluent bank, was their moving spirit. He was no great Sanskrit scholar, but he had none of the childish 'we are spiritual in India, you are materialistic in the West, hence accept our guidance unless you want to perish', which lies behind the more vociferous of the spiritual children of Vivekananda and his compeers. Velayudhan just deplored what seemed to him the unchecked intrusion of a foreign tradition. 'See what happens, Swamiji', he complained with tears in his voice; 'the Christians have much of the money of Travancore. Had it not been for the valiant skill of some of our Hindu politicians in the last fifty years, Christians would have taken over and converted our shrines into churches.' I tried to suggest that he might be exaggerating. 'No, no, Swamiji, see for yourself. They will buy a little bit of land, perhaps an acre, in the midst of a Hindu village. That is cheap, and they offer more than Hindu buyers. Then they will erect a large cross in the centre. Then they will build a little wooden church around it. Then there will be a big church one day, and our simple village Hindus will nod and say: "God is with the powerful, perhaps the padres are right and we should cease worshipping our gods?" What shall we do, Swamiji, to counter these tricks?' I had an idea, and I think I was not being facetious when I suggested to him: 'Can you buy a bit of land in a predominantly Christian village?' 'That is possible, but why?' 'Well,' I said, 'buy an acre, and build a huge, beautiful *liṅga* (Śiva's phallic symbol) on it, of stone or wood. The *liṅga*, you know, is an abomination to all good Christians, and you will not even have to build a temple around it to scare them away.' But Velayudhan shook his head sadly; such a thing could not be thought of—because it was not good to give offence to people, not even to Christians.

However, just at that time a call reached Velayudhan from a place nearby. In a little locality quite close to Nagercoil, there was a huge church—the place was called 'little Rome' by the local people on account of the influence it wielded over the Christian communities around. Now it seems that the people of Vaḍakaṅgulam had for some reason fallen out with the clergy and had made up their minds to revert to Hinduism, which until a generation ago would have been impossible for converts to Christianity or to Islam. There are several Hindu sects of medieval origin in the South which observe little or no caste-restrictions. A zealous preacher from one of them—it was a Śivite group—had taken it upon himself to see those Nāḍas back into their ancestral fold. He was anxious to convince them that the caste Hindus around them would not resent their forebears' apostasy, although they had been Christians, of sorts, for about three generations. Aramugan Śāstriar, the preacher, approached Velayudhan, and when he saw me he asked my host who I was. His eyes lit up when he was told; he turned to me and said: 'You are sent by God, Swamiji. Why don't you come and give my Nāḍas the necessary *saṃskāras* to make them Hindus again?' I was rather moved, but I refused. I tried to explain that I did not believe in any sort of proselytization, and that I opposed Hindus trying to make converts, or even re-converts, as I felt that such action was counter to the spirit of their tradition. Aramugan listened with rapt attention, but then he insisted that I should at least accompany him and Velayudhan and address the Nāḍas. To this I consented.

When we reached Vaḍakaṅgulam, late in the evening, there was a crowd of at least 5,000, including some monks who were intoning Hindu *bhajans* in Tamil. Aramugan had made me up for the occasion: he had me remove my upper garment, so as to be sartorially thoroughly orthodox, and then he painted me with sandal and other fragrant ingredients, the *tripundram* (the parallel white stripes) being applied on my forehead, arms, and chest, indicating the worship of Śiva. If I am permitted a plagiarism, I looked like a leopard all over (Vivekananda used this description for this sort of orthodox paint). I had also had an all-over shave that morning, for the sannyāsī either shaves his whole head or he does not shave at all—there is no such thing as partial shaving. He then led me on to the little dais that had been erected for us and introduced me to the expectant crowd in a fiery harangue. A pure *brahmacārī*, he said, the very manifestation of the Vedic splendour, a man, who, learned in all sciences, having travelled all over the universe, has renounced the teachings which he thought unfitting, to become a Hindu. He then gave me a sign, and I spoke—in English, as I could not lecture in Tamil and neither Velayudhan nor Aramugan could speak in Hindi or Sanskrit. I spoke, and Aramugan translated. Or at least I hope he did. It is quite possible that what he said was something entirely different, because it seemed to me that there were many local references in his translation, and names were mentioned by him which I had never heard before.

The gist of my own lecture was simple enough: 'The point is this, sisters and brothers. No one wants to impose anything on you; you are aware that there are social strictures in Hinduism which are not present in Christianity. (Not so much the caste system, for South Indian Christendom has a caste-system of its own, an almost exact replica of the Hindu system. There are Brahmin Christian churches and there are non-Brahmin assemblies.) As for the teachings of Christianity, they are good, no doubt, but I for one think they do not blend with genuine Indian traditions. Christianity makes claim to universality; it claims "we alone are right, all others are wrong". Hinduism does not. Whether the Hindu or the Christian concept of the Supreme is to be chosen, depends solely on the kind of individual the chooser is, but my plea for Hinduism is one of greater beauty—the Saviour on the cross conflicts with the whole gamut of beauty which the Hindu teachers have proclaimed as steps toward the divine. The Christian teacher declares body and soul separate from each other: he regards God as separate from man; and when he speaks of the 'oneness' of God and the soul, it is oneness through an act of faith, of faith in the words of a personal teacher. He claims that there is but one son of God, but the Hindu masters teach that each of you is Christ, each of you is the son of God, is God, you must only remember it. Worst of all, the Christian harps on sin, on the smallness of man; his God is so good and great, his man so wicked and small. There is no such teaching in Hinduism—the human being is not belittled in order to exalt God. God's greatness cannot be bought at the expense of the human being—at least in the Hindu view. If you make the step and revert to the *dharma* of your ancestors, it will be a step of great courage, for as I said, there are immense social strictures in Hinduism, more than in Christianity. But there is freedom of the spirit, freedom of the intellect in Hinduism, which Christianity cannot give. It is up to you. You must choose. I am neither encouraging nor dissuading you.'

Velayudhan whisked me off, back to Nagercoil, before I could see the reaction. But I learnt a short while after that the Hinduization of the Nāḍa community at Vaḍakaṅgulam maintained its progress. Now it may seem to some of my less perspicacious readers that the above episode was an act of conversion. That is not so. In the first place, it does not seem likely that my single appearance could in about 5,000 souls have changed a way of life established for about three generations. At the most, it is conceivable that my going to Vaḍakaṅgulam gave some impetus to the endeavours of local Hindu leaders who believed, like Velayudhan and Aramugan, that the Hindu *dharma* should have the respect it deserves, among its own people. I do not condone conversion of any kind and my purpose in accepting that invitation—it was the only one of its kind during my pastoral career—was simply to see how much truth lay in the claim of the Indian Christian clergy that Christianity could convert Hindus owing to its intrinsic merit, and how much justification lay in their somewhat brazen assumption that Hindus did not convert Christians because of the intrinsic inferiority of the Hindu doctrine. It is perhaps a good thing that scholastic Hinduism does not have to make a pretext of humility. Christian proselytism has often been in an almost pitiable predicament: even when it was in a position to use the stake and the rack, it had to use them with a humble mien. Hinduism never used any such means for the greater glory of God, because it did not really care for his greater glory.

At Tirukelikundram, quite close to the famous Mahabalipuram caves, two white eagles come to partake daily of the sacrificial morsel at about the same hour. The place is called 'Birds' Sanctuary', and the phenomenon has been mentioned in texts which are at least 400 years old. The white birds are *ṛṣis*, seers, and they come every day from Banaras, 1,500 miles to the North. Let us follow them back to the North.

Once in 12 years, all the monks, many Brahmins, and all the actively devout among the Hindus converge on Allahabad for their great congress, the *Kumbhamela*. It is mentioned in ancient scriptures, the Buddha knew about it. There is little organization and hardly any systematic exchange of views between the learned Hindus, lay and monastic, for Hinduism defies organization. Its means of communication are not ecclesiastical. But during the six days of the great *Kumbhamela*, the yogic and scholastic labour of 12 years is brought to a forum: day and night, the monks and the pandits sit together in a profound contemplation and discussion; they address the masses of the pious; and the monks take part in the most gigantic procession of the thousands of processions which are part of the Indian scene.

The great *Kumbhamela* of 1954 occurred during my last year at B.H.U. The roads to Allahabad were jammed with streams of pilgrims; rickshaw pullers from as far as Patna—about 160 miles from Allahabad—had loaded their families on to their vehicles, pedalling them all the way. The more affluent rode in cars; there were special air services—all the motley means of transport, animal or mechanical, which India has at her disposal filled the thoroughfares in casteless unison. Friends from the German Embassy at New Delhi had come to see Banaras, and they drove me to the Kumbhamela. As our somewhat incongruous new Opel rolled along the highway, past the pilgrims and the ox carts, we sang a few *Lieder* in four parts for a change (the wives were in the car, too), and we soon sighted the Phaphamau Bridge leading into Allahabad. In India there is no such thing as too large a crowd, yet what I saw here filled me with some fear. The municipality of Allahabad had ruled that all participants were to be inoculated against typhoid and cholera. Had this order been upheld, about one-third of the pilgrims would have stayed at home, for the hypodermic needle is a considerable deterrent to many a good villager. But just four days before the commencement, the order was rescinded—I never found out why and I myself had already taken the innoculations which I loathe.

I was put in the tent of the Abbot of the Daśanāmī Monastery at Bile Parla in Bombay, one of India's most revered monks and scholars. A man of about 50, husky, strong, fair-complexioned, spectacled, impressive, he spoke with a loud, clear, and yet rather soft voice. There was no trace of sanctimoniousness in his speech, and we recognized each other, for we had met in the lovely shrine of Kanyā Kumārī. 'You will ride in the car with me and Swami Brahmanandaji', he ruled. I had actually been looking forward to marching in the two-mile long procession and taking the holy dip from a running start, as it were, but Maheśvarānanda was firm. The proceedings began at 4.30 the next morning, with the sun still a mere streak of red on the eastern horizon. The procession emerged from the mile-long expanse of tents while the spectators—pilgrims, men, women and children, all ages, all castes—filled the dry and half-dry space along the processional route, looking like a beehive not yet on the move. The slogans and chants began—the monks called their exhortations in Sanskrit, the crowd lustily repeated them, adding its less-learned chorus to the controlled bedlam. The Nāga monks, whom we had already met at Delhi, marched in front, clad only in the four directions, smeared with sacred ashes, with matted hair, huge beads covering their chests. Aged between 11 and 90, they presented an impressive array, in A.D. 1954 as in the days of antiquity. Our own group followed; then the Udāsins, another highly respected ascetic order, more recent in origin, but of a similar type; then the Nirmalis, the only Sikh monastic group (the founders of the Sikh religion were against monasticism, and this order is considered unorthodox by the most orthodox Sikhs, for whom family life is a *sine qua non*); then some Vaiṣṇava groups, and then a host of other monastic and semi-monastic groups. The monks in procession totalled about 20,000, the lay spectators half a million; the space around the sacred confluence was sufficient for about 150,000 all told.

Our car crept forward. There were some heavily bedizened elephants in front of us and more than 300 Nāgas and *sannyāsīs* around us, marching slowly, step for step, chanting their hymns and stanzas. We approached the confluence and alighted from the cars. His Holiness the Śamkarācārya of Govardhana Maṭha, Puri, entered the river first; then followed our group. I must have been among the first two dozen to step into the water and the brief immersion was wild, unmitigated rapture.

Almost immediately thereafter, so it seems, some of the less considerate monks began pushing their way through the crowd and it was reported that some actually used their tridents. Exactly what happened was never clear, in spite of official enquiry, but some people—probably children and older women in the front rows—slipped into the water, and as others kept pressing forward from behind, there was an immediate stampede. Within 20 minutes death took a heavy toll on what should have been so auspicious an occasion: some 300 people were killed—trampled upon, or perhaps drowned—and about 900 injured. By that time the senior monks and I were already back in our cars, returning by a circular route to the camp. Everything came to a stop, but it was about half an hour before we became aware of what had happened, for although the site was only about 200 yards behind us, hundreds of thousands of people blocked our view. A young monk came up to me and screamed: 'Maharaj, I have lost my nerve!' (a statement unthinkable from a Hindu monk save under excessive strain). He clung to the running board of our open car and began to tear at my *cādar*, crying like a child. 'What can I do brother, what do you want me to do?' I shouted at him. 'Do something, protect me, protect these wretched people, Maharaj. You have the power to do it!' As he said it, I had the power, and I jumped out of the car, making my way back to the site of terror. How I did it I do not know, for there did not appear to be space enough for a mouse to pass through the stagnant, petrified throng, yet somehow, a path opened up before me, and I stood on the spot. The young monk had followed me, screaming, 'He is the leader, he must save, he must bless!' I had never before realized so intensively how accidental a growth charisma is: once a person is placed at the focus of eminence, is physically present where leadership is expected, he acquires all the strength that is needed to fulfil the expectation, momentary though this may be —and in this phenomenon I see the main clue to the miraculous, for if miracles are ever performed, this is surely the explanation.

There was madness in the air around me, screams of anguish and agonized frenzy, yet under the influence of the situation my instructions sounded as calm as though I was a referee at a football match. Simple, commonsense instructions: 'Be quiet, calm down, sit still where you are, sit down until the stretchers are brought, don't scream, nothing has happened, stop behaving like madmen'. All these things must already have been said dozens of times, shouted at the victims and their loved ones, but the secular voices of help had remained unheeded. The moment I spoke, there was hushed silence. Those within earshot sat down, amidst the corpses, amidst their kin writhing in pain. Then, as soon as there was order, kind hands could begin to help. . . . Monks and lay volunteers worked together the whole day and half the night, cremating the dead, or what remained of them. There was not a hundredth part of the fuel needed to cremate the corpses, for no one had thought of such a calamity, but we struck upon some ingenious, if rather unpalatable devices to complete the obsequies. Nevertheless dead matter continued to float down the river, clogging the area around the Naini Bridge, for about two months after the kumbhamela.

At one public lecture the speaker before me, a young monk, began his address: 'My own self, in the form of you sisters and brothers' (a monastic opening phrase much favoured by the Hindu Renaissance, threadbare, but doubtless new each time to quite a few persons in an audience of twenty thousand), 'and you by my side, Forest of Ascetics (a traditional address), what do we mean by the fame of purity? By it, we mean adherence to the traditions of India. When Vijayalakshmi Pandit, our beloved Prime Minister's sister, was Ambassador in Moscow, Stalin did not receive her. When our Vice-President became Ambassador to the great country of Russia after her, Śri Stalin immediately received him with great honour. And why?

Because, so the great Stalin said: "I will not speak to women who do not cover their heads with the saree." ' The sermon lasted for well over an hour, but my wrath did not subside. When my turn came, I did not make a long preamble, but went *medias in res*. 'Do you know, sisters and brothers, and Forest of Ascetics, what we mean by imbecility? By that we mean broadcasting things which are manifestly stupid in themselves. What my good fellow-sādhū told you was well-meant, but utterly false. Please listen, and listen carefully: Śrī Stalin, in the first place, does not know that women in some parts of India cover their heads, with their saree or with anything else; had he known it, in the second place, he would rather have received a woman who did not cover her head, because she was about to break a bourgeois tradition by uncovering it (this required a longish paraphrase—but that was no longer a problem for me by that time); in the third place, women in most parts of the world do not cover their heads. Even in India, only North Indian women do so, and that is perhaps due to the influence of Islam, which made the Hindus alert or which contaminated their customs with slavery, for in ancient India women did not cover their heads. And in India to-day, South Indian Hindu ladies never cover their heads, not from Madras down to Kanya Kumari, and not again from Kanya Kumari up to Hyderabad. Only prostitutes cover their heads in some regions in the South. . . .'

In another public lecture on the day after the procession I tried to show—in mild and popular terms—that the Hindu tradition did not envisage asceticism as the only way to achieve liberation; that many great seers and many schools of religious discipline had taught that killing the senses was but one of the ways, and that harnessing them, using all their strength toward the supreme goal was another alternative. The audience looked calm to me, but there was some commotion on the platform. As soon as I had finished, a bearded Vaiṣṇava monk, clad in the yellow garment of his order, jumped to his feet (an unusual procedure, as monks generally address a meeting sitting cross-legged, even when using a microphone) and cried: 'Swami Agehananda teaches that there is no need of sense-control, that one must indulge in sensual pleasures in order to achieve *mukti*, that the ascetic life is misconceived' and so on. I was distressed by this gross misrepresentation, particularly as the procedure on these occasions gives an earlier speaker no opportunity of speaking again—in fact the last speaker can with impunity contradict, criticize, refute and distort almost everything which has gone before.

That same evening, a young monk came to my tent and asked me to present myself at the camp of His Holiness the Jagadguru Śaṃkarācārya Bhāratī Kṛṣṇa Tīrtha of Govardhanapīṭha, who had expressed his desire to see me. I was worried, as I felt sure this was a summons in connection with that morning's incident. As I entered the Supreme Patriarch's camp with considerable apprehension, I noticed that some of the most senior abbots were already assembled in a room behind which His Holiness had his private quarters during the festival. They nodded to me in a cordial way and began a conversation on general, mildly scholastic matters, as is the etiquette of monastic conversation. Very soon a curtain parted and His Holiness the Śaṃkarācārya entered. I stood up and prostrated myself before him, doing the 'obeisance with the eight limbs' (which means touching the floor with the forehead, the nose, the palms of the hands, the knees, and the toes), completing the salutation with the 'rod-like obeisance' into which the earlier one merges when a monk greets the supreme master of his Order. There are four Śaṃkarācāryas in India, in the four corners of the subcontinent. The Śaṃkarācārya of the South had refused to see me; the Śaṃkarācārya of the East now called me to see him.

The other senior monks had evidently arrived earlier, as they did not repeat any obeisance. His Holiness sat down and joined in the talk, without so much as a hint of any forthcoming censure. After a while, however, the conversation became more technical, and I could see that I was being tested by a most elegant method: I was made to state my views in commenting on the scriptural themes under discussion. His Holiness, assisted by a second monk of his own advanced age, built up the questions unobtrusively, and when they finally asked, 'Do you consider asceticism essential to achieve *mukti* and *jñānam* (supreme wisdom through non-discursive intuition)?' the transition had been so gradual that the question caused no surprise.

I began to explain my viewpoint, and as none of the monks, nor His Holiness himself, interrupted me, I elaborated. I paused to see their reaction, but there were only encouraging, friendly faces around me—and I may even have noticed an approving smile now and then. The Śaṃkarācārya himself was serious, though not unfriendly. He did not smile once during the next three hours—the three hours in which I gave testimony of my beliefs to the supreme ones of my Order—but he looked at me with a deep, probing, interested gaze, not devoid of intellectual excitement. He had been a professor of mathematics many decades earlier, before he became a monk and before his spiritual and scholastic excellence carried him to the summit of the most revered hierarchy of the Indian realm.

I said that I did think asceticism was essential for the achievement of *mukti* and *jñāna*, but that there were different types of aspirants. Some have to sustain the ascetic life up to their last moment in the living body; others have to train themselves in ascetic disciplines, but once they have reached the poise that asceticism yields they must desist from further asceticism, because instead of advancing them, it harms them; it harms them because it creates such passions as it is thought to eschew —sloth, misanthropism, moodiness, frustration; and all these are passions, even if they are not shown in the doctrinary lists of human passions. Yet, abandoning practices does not imply changing from a monastic to a mundane way of life; rather, it means pursuing those activities and thinking those thoughts for which the thus-trained individual is best equipped—if he was a scholar, he must be a scholar again; if he was an artist, he must resume the practice of art.

'How then, Agehananda, can one distinguish a monk from an ordinary scholar, or artist, or from any good man in the world—certainly not just because he wears the ochre robe?' There is no sign, nor any combination of signs by which a monk can be recognized by anyone, I averred. 'Not even by his *guru!*' That I did not know. In fact, I added, 'Looking like a true monk or "appearing" or "acting" like a true monk implies not *being* one, for such appearance panders to the criteria of the mundane.' 'That is true, Agehananda. There are many scriptural passages corroborating your view. Sages act like ordinary people, sometimes like madmen, sometimes like kings and ministers—no one can know their ways.' 'I have often been asked, venerable Sirs,' I continued, 'why, if such is my view, I do not disrobe and dress in white, in ordinary clothes, as an ordinary citizen of the world, yet remain a *sannyāsī* within myself. Why do I make a show of the ochre robe, why do I surround myself in that ochre smokescreen? It makes people suspicious; it makes lay scholars think I am a scholastic fraud, trying to buttress my inadequate knowledge of Hindu doctrine by the robe symbolizing that doctrine.' 'Don't they read what you write and publish, don't they hear what you speak, don't they challenge your knowledge?' 'No, venerable Sirs, colleagues never read what one writes; they seldom attend one's classes, because their students would then think that they also went to learn from one. And as for challenging one's knowledge, they are too polite. Furthermore,' I said, 'policemen, from the betel-chewing police-sergeant to the Tennyson-quoting official in the Home Ministry, all think I wear the smokescreen of ochre hue in order to disguise sinister motives and interests in vicious things.' 'What things, Agehananda?' 'Politics, fornication, disruption of young minds, and deliberate denigration of the Hindu lore.'

'You do antagonize monks and laymen, Agehananda', said the South Indian monk after a short silence. 'I do say, and say repeatedly, what I hold to be both important and excellent in our tradition.' 'Do you preach that it is not important to believe in a Being, a Supreme God?' 'I certainly did preach that at times, for, as I understand the texts, we are free to see a Supreme Being in them, or to deny it, or to suspend judgement, according to our interpretation of the Scriptures. When the Scriptures speak of the Brahman, of various Divine Manifestations, gods and *avatāras*, of the Witness and of the Prompter, I regard all these statements as being in the category of yogic experience. Is that wrong?' 'It is not wrong, Maharaj, it is compatible with Scriptures. Jaimini did not attach any importance to a Supreme Being; Kapila's Sāṃkhya philosophy is often said to be *nirīśvara*, without God. But you do know that there is the rule of *adhikārabheda*, that you must not divulge things too subtle to the unsubtle, lest they should be confused?' I did know that. But as a man with pedagogic experience, I think it is wrong to pamper the 'unsubtle', especially when they come for instruction. Shock-therapy, much in the manner of the Chan Buddhists of China, or the Zen Buddhists of Japan, and even of some extinct Indian schools—I did believe there was much good in that. 'We do not necessarily agree with that view, but we cannot say that you are wrong. Try it out, by all means, but be prepared for dangerous risks.'

'I believe in the merit of the ochre robe,' I then said. 'It is a uniform that sets us apart from the rest of society—it warns people not to take us lightly. It warns them also not to tempt us, or not to tempt us too severely. With the ochre robe draped over my body, I feel I can face temptation, just as a man, skilled in arms, feels readier for the fight when he puts on a military uniform. Psychological, no doubt, self-suggestion; but what is not? To me the ochre garment gives a strange quasi-canonical confidence. Its cool, austere, rough contact with my skin makes me alert, and more susceptible to things and persons around me. Perhaps this is because it helps me to identify myself with the culture I have chosen for my own? Would the Venerable Sirs object to this idea about the ochre robe, in my particular case?'

'There is no objection, because your case is unprecedented. None of the others who have worn the ochre robe had to *choose* this culture, as they were born into it. But we do not see why it should not prove an additional asset in your case, in the manner you have indicated. As for your "canonical confidence", Agehananda, that may well be so; we, who have worn the garment twice as long as you have lived, cannot pronounce upon this, for we do not remember how it feels to don any other. But, don't you think that this very garment marks you out as one who must preach in the tradition? And as this tradition has in the main postulated a Supreme Being—regardless of the fact that the Hindu *dharma* permits, or even at times suggests, in some of its teachers, non-acceptance of a personal God, or agnosticism—regardless of that fact, does not this robe enjoin on you a more literal pursuit of the homiletic conventions?'

'Indeed it does,' I mused. 'But should we not try to exhibit the profoundness of this tradition by teaching without, or with less compromise? This is my point, and it is very close to my heart, and I welcome this opportunity of putting it to you, venerable Sirs. Whether God is or is not—this has to be experienced, else it has no meaning. But suppose I experience God? Suppose I am completely convinced, through my own experience, that the Being of the Upaniṣads, the Brahman, is, and that I am It in essence? Nothing, venerable Sirs, follows from my experience either for the existence of such a Being, or against it.'

'But don't you think, Agehananda, that this view of yours is more Buddhist than Hindu? Is it not saying as much as "all things are only perceived and have no existence outside perception"?' I did not think it was more Buddhist than Hindu, nor even idealistic in the sense of occidental philosophy—suspending my judgement on such epistemological distinctions as 'idealism' and 'realism', because I am not really interested in epistemology. 'No, venerable Sirs, my attitude about the "existence" of God, as compared with my attitude about the "existence" of things, is more committed, and I think it is closer to Hindu than to Buddhist thought, though some very late schools of Buddhism propounded somewhat similar ideas. My thoughts and feelings about the existence of God are private commitments; my attitude about *things* and their existence is a public commitment. I am unwilling to share with anyone my feelings and thoughts about the existence or non-existence of God, because I am deeply convinced that teaching a way to conceive the "existence of God" is fraught with disaster—it creates prophets, it creates fanatics. Prophets are fanatics; seers and mystics remain silent. Both in Greek and Sanskrit, venerable Sirs, the word "mystic" means "one who keeps silent", silent about his experiences. The prophet is convinced that what he sees, what he feels, what he experiences is true in the same sense that the existence of his garment or his staff is true and he preaches it as truth; and that is a fallacy, for he cannot infer any such truth from his own, private experience. And (here I spoke in English, as this specific formulation cannot be unequivocally given in Sanskrit without an elaborate paraphrase, which would have deflected my main exposition) *private experience of an object of the religious sort does not confer existential status on the object* or more simply (here I resumed in Sanskrit) from the fact that a saint sees God, or the Goddess, or Kṛṣṇa, or Rāma, or identifies himself with the Brahman, the existence of God, of the Goddess, of Kṛṣṇa, or Rāma, or the Brahman *does not follow*.'

'*Vākyamidaṃ navīnayuktiḥ*, this proposition entails a novel reasoning,' one of the monks, hitherto silent, exclaimed in genuine surprise, focusing me intensely with what I thought was a condoning frown. 'Novel, but not inadmissible for, Agehananda Svāmin, there have been thinkers in the Brahmin tradition who propounded views which do not clash with yours. There was Śrīharṣa, who said "every proposition can be shown to be absurd, I have no proposition to make myself, because that could also be refuted. My own knowledge about that Brahman and the Universe and myself I do have, but I cannot formulate them because they are no one's concern". This teacher in our own tradition, Agehananda, was similar to the

Buddhist teachers, except that he accepted Brahman by implication. I take it you do the same. But don't affirm or negate it. Say nothing.'

I did not, and would not have, even if the Swami had not enjoined silence. Instead, I took up the thread where I had left it a few minutes earlier: my feelings and attitudes about the existence or non-existence of God are deeply committing to me, hence not communicable—for I hold that what is totally committing is totally incommunicable (this, I have come to believe in later days, is the only possible humanist interpretation of *Advaita*-monism). My feelings and attitudes about persons and material things, about the universe and bodies and souls and minds, however, are public, and hence not committing —and therefore they are communicable. 'What are these feelings and attitudes of yours about the world, then?' 'To the layman, venerable Sirs, these feelings and attitudes of mine do not commend themselves, because he thinks they are abstruse. But they are not, and I have been trying to expound them on every platform, among scholars and saints just as much as among the *bhaktas*, though of course in different dictions—about the existence or non-existence of things (which includes material things, scriptural things, minds, human beings, stars, world systems, scriptures, physical laws, moral laws—in short, everything of which it can either be said that it exists or that can be described; like tables and the Ganges which exist, or like the moral law which can be described). About these I suspend my judgement, and I suspend it for no philosophical reasons, but for reasons of intellectual humility. As very great thinkers, equally great thinkers, have propounded and have lived or died for diametrically opposed views on each of these "things", I feel it is not meet that I should decide one way or the other. If I were to be a martyr one day, venerable Sirs, then I would choose martyrdom for the truth whose name is "Suspension of Judgement on all things on which philosophers and saints through 3000 years have held mutually contradictory views"—a novel cause for martyrdom, but to my feeling the only worthy one. This is communicable, and if I am asked to give a set of values which can be emulated through active allegiance and described in the clear language of academic philosophy without sanctimoniousness; if I am asked "show us the road, Maharaj", then my only advice (adumbrated by sundry similes or by terse ratiocination according to the audience) is this: suspend your judgement on things. As to God, who is not a thing (neither material, nor spiritual, not anything that 'exists' or that 'can be described'), if that interests you, try to make your own experience, for the only God of value to you is the one you experience, and whether or not he exists apart from your experience is none of your concern, nor does it concern anyone else.

As to how to make God's experience—or, in other words, as to how to make God—it is here only that the actual instruction in meditative practices can set in. 'Most of my *gurubhāīs*, venerable Sirs (I said that tongue-in-cheek), seem to me to be putting the cart before the horse; they first talk to their disciples about God, and then they tell them how to meditate and practice yoga of all sorts, or *bhakti*, or discrimination. They create an image in their disciple's mind, to which his experience should presumably conform. But the result is that, instead of giving the seeking mind a chance to find what can be found, the old images are perpetuated, firmly lodged in the minds of the aspirants before they even start to experiment themselves.'

'Do you then mean to say, Agehananda, that we should not talk about the Brahman, nor about the qualified Deity as Rāma, Kṛṣṇa, the Devī, Śiva, etc., at all, and begin giving instructions on how to meditate before even mentioning what the Scriptures have said about the Supreme?' Yes, I certainly did mean to say that. 'In that case, Agehananda, you will make many enemies, and this also explains why you have already antagonized so many, for the lay pandit and the monk, they both want to elaborate first on the scripture, because they feel that this elaboration—through parables and *purāṇic* tales, through similes, or through straight scholastic sermon will create a taste, a desire for achievement in their audience. Then, when this desire is created, they will begin instruction, or give *dīkṣā*, and teach how to accomplish meditation. This is the traditional way. If you don't follow it, you will have trouble. Yet, if you think you have something new, you must take a risk. It would be wrong for you to act upon convention if that is against your persuasion.'

'There is another reason, venerable Swamijis,' I resumed, 'and one which I think is very close to the spirit of Hinduism. Is not spiritual austerity one of the stipulations of the *dharma*?' 'It is indeed: "through *tapas* (austerity, asceticism, including mental austerity) everything is obtained," that is the word of the text.' 'Then,' I continued, 'is it not more austere to renounce generalization on the basis of one's private mystical experience instead of talking about it? And furthermore, is not the suspension of judgement more austere than conferring upon the experience of the Supreme the status of objective existence and then preaching that objective existence? On embracing a woman, is it not more difficult to restrain one's sperm than to ejaculate? And yet, yogic teachers teach us to restrain it. I take this as the best analogue, because it is so pungent: I may know the agonizing urge of the mystic to teach the God he has seen, to go out and teach all the people after his experience—and yet I must control the urge and keep the experience to myself. This is a piece of asceticism as well as good logic.'

'Why is it, Agehananda, that you so often bring similes from the sensuous sphere into your argument and speeches?' Did not most of the *ācāryas* do that? Was not erotic symbolism common coin in canonical and exegetical literature? 'That is true, Agehananda, but it appears to people that you flaunt this symbolism in order to annoy them; you use it, it seems, with a vengeance. Why?' In the first place, in order to exhibit the delicate intimacy of spiritual experiences—what a yogi sees or otherwise experiences in pursuit of his meditations is private not only in the logical sense in which a toothache is a private experience that cannot be shared, but it is private also in a charientic sense: it is private just as the rapture of two lovers is private between them. The Scriptures and the teachers use the sensuous analogue after depersonalizing it. In the same way, the poet speaks about his experience of love with his lady, but it is no longer the Miss or Mrs So-and-So to whom he made love; it is a depersonalized woman. It is in order to speak of 'God' and the 'Divine Light' and the 'Eternal Spark in us' and to use the many other accepted mystical terms as the Scriptures do, for then these experiences have become depersonalized. If I say, 'In a particular yogic state, the devotee saw the Goddess of the Universe enter his body'—these are the words of a particular text, then there can be no objection; it is like a poet's description of his lady's embrace. But if I say, 'In my yogic state, and, if you follow my instructions, then eventually in your yogic state, I see, and you will see, the Goddess enter your body, or you entering Hers,' then this is bad taste, in the same way as it would be bad taste for a poet to write, 'When I embraced Mrs X., of 1120 Marine Drive'.

There was a long silence—both consent and disapproval were in the air, but judgement was held in abeyance. I felt that I had been too close to the core, so I resumed after a while, although no questions had been asked. I said that I also felt very strongly about certain things which had nothing directly to do with the monastic life; things concerning my own person and other persons as human beings. I had very strong dislikes, and I tried to communicate them: hero-worship, cultural and national chauvinism, sanctimoniousness—in fact all the things which, under different names, are thought praiseworthy and worth striving for by the Hindus of our day. I had been sarcastic about them and felt I would be in future—and this no doubt has made enemies, and would make them. Above all, a specific form of intellectual dishonesty is abomination to me: the idea that the culture or the achievements of the place in which one chanced to be born have to be extolled above those of other regions. 'Let us do away with the idea that Aryans and Dravidians had a different culture, *because* this notion has caused harm to India's unity', instead of 'Let us do away with it, *if* their cultures can be proved, on archaeological, linguistic, and other verifiable evidence to be identical'—I deplore also such attitudes as the former and they are legion in Hindu India.

'The mystic, yogic life, symbolized by the robe, and the humanistic, intellectual, aesthetically rich life, symbolized by a non-conformist, uninhibited, taboo-free way of speaking do not clash even if they are found in one person. And it is here that I may be creating, or suggesting something new. Hitherto, venerated Sirs, our monks could not be humanists, because humanism involves the use of the human being *per se*, not as a paradigm of the Absolute. But I declare that one can be both a monk and a humanist, because these two ways of being do not clash. Being a monk is a private affair—the mystical life is delicate, not communicable—it is *doing* something, practising something. Being a humanist is delicate too, but communicable —it is *thinking* in a particular way. The two do not clash, because thinking and doing are not two activities on the same plane, however much sanctimonious gibberish has gone into the solemn affirmation of the unity of thought and deed. The two do not clash. The error of all our *ācāryas*—and I must risk your considering this insolence—lay in considering that a particular *Weltanschauung* follow from a particular sort of mystic or yogic practice; and conversely also, that a particular view of the universe promotes the yogic effort. But this just is not so: for one can practise yoga and be a mystic, while holding any conceivable world view—nihilism, Advaita, Buddhism, communism or materialism. Or one may hold the most austerely ascetic philosophy; one may feel convinced by Advaita or by some Buddhist doctrine, or else by logical analysis and existentialism, and neither of these "follow" from or prompt yogic practice, or the mystical life. Yoga and the monastic life—in short, the mystical world view—are ways of doing, of practising certain things; philosophies, eastern and western alike, are ways of thinking of things.'

'What you have now said, Agehananda Bharati, does not seem to be in accordance with the tradition. How can you say that thinking and doing have nothing to do with each other? Do you then mean to imply that one could be an *advaitin* and yet indulge in low sensual pleasures? This is the difference between the materialist philosophy of the West and the spiritual philosophy of India. (*Et tu, Brute,* I thought.) The western philosopher believes that he can think high ideals and yet roll in the mud of the senses. Our teachers have seen that this is not possible. Do you then side with the European and American way of philosophy, or do you share our view?'

'I am trying not to categorize philosophy according to parts of the world, venerable Sir. My view on this matter is quite firm at this moment, and I can abandon it only when my argument is defeated. The teachers of yore did not teach us to accept their argument because they were senior and more revered—they asked us to reason for ourselves. Yes, a person may conceivably be an *advaitin,* and yet not averse to the senses. If he happens to be an *advaita* monk, then it is his monastic vows alone that must restrain him from sensual pleasures. He will see nothing wrong in them; he will not speak disparagingly about the senses and their objects of beauty, but he will not indulge them himself, pledged as he is to his monastic discipline. If he feels that the monastic life gives him more than would a lay life, he, after striking the balance, will renounce the senses, with an apology to them, but not with a sneer. He will not say: You ugly, low, mean senses, preventing the seeker from finding oneness with the Absolute, I spit on you, I kick you, I will have nothing to do with you, and will teach as many as I can to have nothing to do with you. He will say: You beautiful objects, and you lovely senses that grasp those beautiful objects, I cherish you, sentient and inert alike. But I have taken a pledge which obliges me to say good-bye to you forever, because I am interested in something which you could not give me. But I shall teach others to see and appreciate your loveliness. . . .'

There was a long, but not a tense silence. Then His Holiness resumed the conversation on a general level, much in the way the talk had begun when I had sat down with the monks, hours earlier. As he was about to retire, he rose and after I had prostrated before him, he said in English: 'You are a rather extraordinary monk; be it permissible that you hold rather extraordinary views. I do not say at all that they are incompatible with the tradition; they are just a rather extraordinary way of seeing the tradition.'

The theme of harnessing instead of suppressing the senses for the sake of the higher life is one of the most delicate and, to my mind, also one of the most important in the religious traditions of Asia. This was the theme which had given rise to the Śaṃkarācārya's summons. It would not be helpful for me to discuss any personal experiences of my own, but the tradition of this school of yogic experimentation is at least as ancient as the Veda and autochthonous. For many reasons, the tradition has fallen on evil days and its few votaries are silent or apologetic. It is bound to die out, as puritanism waxes stronger every year, and it is necessary that it should die if modernization, industrialization, and de-individualization are to be the objectives of modern India, for esoteric disciplines have indeed weakened the zest for a successful and extravert, that is, a spiritually mediocre life. The nuns and monks who still practice and study within this tradition are few. It is a tradition shared by both Hinduism and Buddhism; it has become the standard lore of Tibetan Buddhism, but is less known to the West, because it was Hīnayāṇa Buddhism, whose sources were more easily accessible and digestible, which obtained a western audience.

I am talking about the *tāntric* tradition. The *Tantras* are an immense body of Hindu and Buddhist literature, written in Sanskrit, medieval North Indian vernaculars, Tibetan and Chinese. Their origin is no doubt purely Indian. They are special forms of yogic instruction and like all yogic texts, they eventually deal with spiritual emancipation; their frame is esoteric and redemptive. Their methods, however, are diametrically opposed to those of the canonical exoteric Brahmins and Buddhists, who teach that asceticism is essential to the achievement of the state of *Nirvāṇa*, or of *Kaivalya*, its Hindu equivalent—the state, which is the *summum bonum* in all Indian religions. The followers of the *tāntric* tradition, on the other hand, believe that it is not the eradication of the senses and the sensuous powers that lead to that supremely blissful state from which there is no return into new births and new deaths, but that the senses must be harnessed and utilized toward that goal. Among the senses, the sexual impulse is the most powerful, and it is precisely this immense force which has to be skilfully employed. Both these diametrically opposed approaches assume what Freud assumed in more recent days: that the libido is the most potent factor in the individual. Each school drew a different conclusion: the one, that the sensuous self must be killed before the phoenix of redemption can arise—this school has always been the canonically accepted, the more respectable, and the more highly scholastic in India. Its suspicion of the senses, and its inherent dislike for their concupiscent manifestations is the one facet of the classical Brahmin lore which modern India has taken over without the least modification. A Buddhist tantric text says: 'By the very deeds which take ordinary people into the most terrible hells, the wise accomplished yogi is delivered into the supreme freedom'. Such sentences—and they abound in both Buddhist and Hindu tāntric literature—are anathema to the modern Hindu. They were anathema to the Brahmin scholar centuries ago, but for different, and more palatable reasons, for he doubted the authenticity of the texts, which claimed to be on an equal footing with the Veda.

Now one of the greatest visual delights of India's visible past is the pageant of its temples and shrines. Both foreign tourists without Christian prejudice and Indian lovers of art and of tradition are enchanted, in growing measure, by the abundant erotic sculpture and bas-relief which penetrates temple-India from one end to the other. The Renaissance Hindu, however, loathes these images. Swami Vivekananda was the first who, fighting the Christian missionary, adopted the latter's denigration of Eros, and began to unsex the Hindu pantheon—a process which is now almost complete in the temples built after 1910. The Birla Temple in New Delhi has a rather philistine looking

Śiva instead of the prescribed *liṅgam*. In accordance with ritualistic injunction, Śiva must never be formally worshipped through any other symbol than the *liṅga*—of all the deities, this divine form alone must not be anthropomorphized. This is not a facetious statement, for the *liṅgam* is *not* anthropomorphic, Indian symbolic thought inverts the analogy: the *liṅga* stands for Śiva, who is the god of asceticism, of renunciation, the tutelary god of all monks. The *liṅga* is not priapic; its erect shape indicates complete control, retention, not emission. Every mental control, every state of yogic concentration is a replica of the *liṅga*. Desirelessness is supreme beautitude. *Nirvāṇa* is desireless, *kaivalya* is desireless—in the life of sentient beings, only the state of total sexual consummation is desireless, hence again the symbolism of the *liṅga*. The Hindu Renaissance feels apologetic for Śiva—it humanizes him, it removes the numinous from Him, it makes Him a good citizen. There could hardly be a greater blasphemy from an esoteric viewpoint.

It was at one of the numerous gatherings to which monks are constantly being invited that I met a most interesting ascetic, a most uncommon figure. She was about 35, though she looked younger, and of fair complexion; her buxom figure was draped in a deep red robe, with a leopard-skin around the upper portion. The nun's hair hung loose and very black; it was mat and dry, but it gave the impression that she had some trouble in preventing it from shining lustrously. It hung down to her waist, its lowest part showing beneath the leopard skin. She wore a huge, large-bead rosary around her neck and held a crude, iron trident, the emblem of Śakti, the divine feminine primeval power, the dynamic of the universe. 'Who is that striking female ascetic?' I asked my neighbour. 'Do you then not know of Siddhimātā?' he asked with some astonishment. Siddhimātā is known all over Northern India as one of the most learned and spiritually advanced women saints of the day. Born as the daughter of one of the small feudal houses of Uttar Pradesh, some 50 miles North of Muradabad, the little Rājeśvarī—that had been her name—showed deep mystical inclinations by the age of 7. The Raja, her father, was proud and worried: an age-old pattern in pious India. It is rumoured that she participated in scholastic disputes among the pandits of her father's court when a girl of 12 and that she was thought to be a *jātismara*—a person who can elucidate subtle philosophical and mystical doctrines without ever having studied them, the supposition being that of rebirth (a *jātismara*, in particular, remembers his or her previous births).

When she was 13 a husband was selected for her, some neighbouring prince, but on the wedding morning, when the bridegroom came on his horse, bedecked with ornaments beyond recognition, the little bride could not be found. There was a frantic search for a day, a month, a year, involving the police, and even the British authorities, but she was not found.

About 12 years later, a beautiful young nun appeared in Almora, close to the Nepalese border (and presumably within 20 miles of Mayavati, where I had been a novice). She was seen roaming the wild forests, defying the tigers and the dangers of the jungle night, living on roots and fruits and water, sleeping under trees, dressed in the bark of a tree. She did not speak with anyone, as she had taken a vow of silence for 10 years. She broke her silence and emerged into the monastic world during the *Kumbhamela* at Hardvar. Siddhimātā soon acquired fame for three things, disparate in a way, but fitly juxtaposed in the Hindu tradition: for her learning, for her spiritual powers, and for her beauty. To the first and the last, I was witness on this first meeting; the second I could only infer from what both her devotees and her opponents said and from my own observations, for there are codified criteria by which a person who has these powers can be recognized. 'Spiritual powers' is a generic phrase, both in English and its Indian equivalent. It covers at once communion with the divine and the possession of certain occult powers. I say 'occult' powers with my tongue in cheek: I mean by that dangerous adjective the ability to accomplish things which cannot yet be explained by any rational statement, and I refuse to omit the 'yet' in this definition, because it is silly to claim that certain events will 'never' be explained. Statements like 'this was accomplished by yogic concentration or supernatural control of the mind' are tautologies, for yoga is control of the mind and nothing else.

At this gathering Siddhimātā spoke after me. She chanted in perfect Vedic Sanskrit for at least five minutes, and this was the first time I heard a woman chant, for nuns usually do not address large audiences, and even if they do, they just do not know Sanskrit. And then she spoke for one hour and a half, in a melodious, but stressless voice. There was absolute silence, a thing which I had never before encountered in pious meetings of this size. The strange thing, however, was this: it was unthinkable that the majority of the people understood what Siddhimātā was talking about. For in the first place, she used such a highly Sanskritized Hindi that even the schoolmasters of the place would find it hard to follow. And in addition her theme was well over the heads of all the laymen present. I remember her particular topic—it was the place of discursive reasoning in ritualistic pursuits; the classical theme of a speculative vindication for liturgical proliferation. I noticed her *śākta* slant: here was a teacher who did not feel apologetic about her *tāntric* background. She brought it out almost aggressively, although the scholastic formulation toned down her vehemence.

There were two more speakers after Siddhimātā, and when it was over the monks and Siddhimātā were invited to partake of refreshments in the wealthiest man's house. As we sat and ate the numerous dainties served by affluent piety, Siddhimātā addressed me and asked if I agreed with the points she had made. I did, for by that time I had become suffused with the *śākta* principle. Our conversation was held in Sanskrit, which is a way to keep it on a formally scholastic level, but then our hosts and their lay friends insisted with folded palms that we should condescend to speak in Hindi, so that all could benefit from our discourse. I do not know whether they did, for the discussion was immensely technical: was the position of a simile an integral part of a syllogistic argument? Some ancient teachers, both Hindu and Buddhist, had thought it was, some did not. With modern logic at the back of my mind, I tried to back the schools which denied simile its claim to a status equal to the other elements of a valid syllogism. Siddhimātā insisted on the contrary. The simile is as important as the statement of the major and the minor term. I could not convince her, and she did not convince me. 'We shall continue this debate some time', she said when the host came in to inform us that our transport had arrived.

Up in Uttarkashi and Gangotri, where the Ganges leaves its Himalayan womb, where the air is as austere as the monks that live in its perpetual chill, Siddhimātā stayed for a few weeks every year. All the learned abbots and monks knew her and respected her. And I thought it was rather charming to see how they all waited in patience and silence before they settled down to their alms-food, until Siddhimātā had emerged from her ablutions and from her much more elaborate preparatory worship, after which she joined us for our meal. There was more than mere connivance at her delay; the Vedāntic monks were thus paying a gentle, unobtrusive homage to a tradition which was not their own, but which they respected profoundly. For even Śaṃkarācārya, the preceptor of all the illustrious monks up here, had been a worshipper of Śakti, and had sung her praise in eloquent poetry.

The Himalayan range is long, and the meditations along its valleys have been variegated. But all the systems and methods of contemplation have had their place of origin somewhere in these valleys. Over 1,500 miles to the East of Uttarkashi and Gangotri, on the easternmost slopes of the Himalaya, lies the luxurious land of Assam, only partly Indian in ethnical and linguistic constitution, tropical, wild, moist, and always very warm. Assam has been the home of magic, and the home of *tantric* practice from times immemorial. It is not impossible that the *tantric* tradition, not Indo-Aryan by any reckoning, might have had its origin here. Assam's tutelary deity is the Goddess, the Magna Mater. Bloody sacrifices were offered to her in earlier days. They have long ceased, but Assam has remained one of the centres of esoteric initiation up to this day, although it is not likely to retain this status much longer; there will be no esoteric initiation once the country has progressed and fallen in with the modern world. The *tantric* initiates of India meet here in Assam during the season when the Goddess menstruates. They learn supreme self-control, not through giving a wide berth to woman, but through her company. The *tāntric* learns control through the senses, not against them. There is much theory behind his practice, and much practice behind his theory: that the breath, the thoughts, and the sperm have to be kept motionless, and that this equilibrium is the key to complete freedom, complete wisdom, full emancipation—not only from temporal affliction, but from the great disease of life and death. The woman who can help in this supreme realization is Śakti incarnate. Some call her the *Mudrā*, the great gesture, the great pose which opens the gate to the truth of which the Scriptures have spoken. The Buddhist *tantrics* call her Wisdom, *Prajñā*. In union with the Method, *Upāya*, which is the Great Compassion (and whose part is played by the male in the yogic replica of the universe), oneness is attained. It is for this reason that the deity is represented as male and female in close embrace, not only in India, but in Tibet and Mongolia—wherever the *tāntric* tradition went.

Assam was the centre of both Hindu and Buddhist tantrisms. Whatever vestige of that powerful, but to the philistine necessarily uncanny school of meditation remains, is to be found here in Assam. It was here that I saw Siddhimātā the last time. 'How did you come here, Mātājī?' I exclaimed. 'I come here every year. Didn't you know?' 'I should have known it,' I said, 'but I didn't'.

CHAPTER VIII

INDIA BEYOND BHARAT

'. . . *qui trans mare currunt*'

My interest in India's spiritual exports was first aroused at Nalanda. Buddhism, like Christianity, proved to be an export religion only, neither surviving in the country of its origin. For well over 400 years of India's early middle-ages Nalanda was her foremost Buddhist academy. To its gates came monks and scholars from Tibet, China, Mongolia and other parts of Central Asia; they learnt Sanskrit and Pali; they studied Buddhist tradition and philosophy; and they carried loads of sacred literature back to their own lands. They also translated hundreds of holy tomes into Tibetan, Chinese, Kuchan, Sogdian and other languages now no longer spoken. It was from Nalanda that it spread into the other parts of Asia. Ask a pious lama at the Galdan or Shigatse Monastery in Tibet whether he has heard of Delhi, Calcutta, London, New York? No, but he has heard of Nalanda, and this name conjures up in his mind all that is both sacred and learned.

There came a Mohammedan chieftain called Bakhtiar Khalji. He ravaged the Indian countryside, his soldiers raped, and his divines burnt the books and the libraries of the pagan whenever they could lay hands on them—a thing no Hindu or Buddhist, whether king or petty chieftain has ever done, for books are revered, even those of the barbarian. Bakhtiar Khalji will have seen a group of beautiful buildings, with wells around and inside, and thousands of strong saffron-clad men, Indian and foreign. He will have seen some beautiful women amongst or near them, for at that time Nalanda also taught tantric Buddhism, requiring the presence of *mudrās*, i.e. trained women, close to those monks who underwent the dangerous tantric disciplines. It is not impossible that systematized tantric ritual and meditation had its origin in Buddhism, and if so then it will most certainly have been practised at Nalanda. Khalji looted, burned and put over 5,000 monks to the sword, but hundreds of books had fortunately been taken to Tibet and China, in the course of the four preceeding centuries of peaceful study. Thus in India there is very little extant Sanskrit and Indic literature on later Buddhism but we have almost everything the Buddhist scholars wrote as commentaries on the Buddha's teachings, in Tibetan and in Chinese translations; and quite a few texts were preserved in the Sanskrit original in some Tibetan monasteries.

I was called to Nalanda when my teaching at B.H.U. came to an end. Nalanda had been in ruins for 800 years, but the Government of Bihar, aided by the federal Government at Delhi, built the 'New Monastery' by the ruins of the ancient one. I taught there for several months, and I began to study Tibetan—among the monk-scholars, there was a brilliant young Tibetan Lama, who picked up both Hindi and English in no time. There were also about six monks from Thailand, six from Ceylon, and a lay scholar from Japan, Professor Kajiyama, later my host and guide in his own country. There were some Burmese monks, and there were a very few Indian students and teachers; one of them a Hindu novice of the Daśanāmī Order, studying Buddhist logic and Tibetan. The senior Indian Buddhist monk, the Rev. Kashyapa Mahathera, had conceived the idea of reviving the ancient glory of Nalanda, and it was he who invited me to teach; in return, I could read Pali literature and learn whatever the 'Nalanda Institute of Pali and Buddhist Studies' could offer me.

There is much speculation as to why Buddhism has not remained one of the Indian religions. Some point to the Buddha's absolute rejection of the caste-system; others think Buddhism too dry and austere to have a wide appeal in the long run, despite the fact that for at least three centuries after the Buddha's death, monasteries were crowded like revivalist centres in our day—and crowded with a similar social range; for two centuries rich and poor, kings and merchants, learned and illiterate, thronged to become Buddhist monks. I believe the main reason for the disappearance of Buddhism from India may have been accidental, for it was never really divorced from Hinduism, except in pure doctrine—there had always been heretical sects within the Hindu tradition and to the laity this was just another one, arousing scant interest. In course of time, the Hindu pandits absorbed the figure of the Buddha into their own pantheon; Buddha is the generally accepted ninth incarnation of Viṣṇu, preceded by Kṛṣṇa, to be followed by the apocalyptic Kalki who will usher in the end of the world. The Hindu of the Renaissance will not admit that the Buddha taught something essentially different, and much argument has resulted. Gandhi simply refused to credit that the Buddha did not believe in any supreme being. In fact, no modern Hindu will believe this, except those who study the two religions from primary source material. These—the monks and lay scholars of the Hindu scholastic tradition—are not only aware that the teaching of the Buddha and of his disciples is radically opposed to their own, but they are constantly concerned to refute the Buddhist argument, yet this in a queer sort of vacuum, there being no Buddhist pandits to argue with them.

No doubt, the non-theistic nature of the Buddhist teaching could have been a partial reason for its decline in India, in spite of the fact that later Buddhism introduced its own type of absolutist philosophy which, in style at least, is very close to the monistic Vedānta. On the criterion of doctrine alone Buddhism differs from Hinduism as much as any teaching can, but if considerations of culture and outlook are allowed, then the distinction between the two does indeed become somewhat tenuous. With this, however, I make no concession to the facile assertion that the two religions are the same, because that assertion rests on the jejune idea that all good people and all great teachers have taught essentially the same thing.

Now in the last twenty years some Hindu intellectuals have embraced Buddhism; not many, but their number is on the increase. Strangely, however, these conversions are to one form of Buddhism alone, to the old Theravāda school, more popularly known as Hīnayāṇa. Strange, because it was precisely this form which gave way to the more familiar idiom of Mahāyāṇa and other later schools of Buddhism in early medieval India, Theravāda being too austere and too colourless for Indian feeling on the whole, at least after the initial rush into the Buddhist order around the time of Aśoka (second century B.C.). And yet, the contemporary sympathy of Hindu intellectuals for Theravāda Buddhism rather than for its more familiar Mahāyāṇa forms is explicable from the viewpoint of psychological paradox: Mahāyāṇa, with its Vedānta-like absolutism, its surreptitiously reintroduced pantheon, its eclectic proclivities, and its connivance at ritual, is too akin to the Hinduism from which the Hindu intellectual may wish to escape without thereby forfeiting his traditional Indian values. What lies behind these recent conversions is no doubt the commendable desire to achieve a degree of religious emancipation without having to burn one's cultural boats. And let us face it: the Buddha, even in the Hīnayāṇa interpretation, which is aesthetically one-sided and excessively austere, is a more pleasant choice as an instrument of emancipation than most of the alternatives offering themselves to the frustrated Hindu intellect: Tennyson, Carlyle, Tolstoy, Marx and Lenin.

Of all the inmates, it was with the Siamese group of monks that I became most friendly, and that within 48 hours of my arrival. What jolly, uninhibited, amiable young people they were! One of them, Phramaha Manas Chittadama Phunglamchiak, is now on his way to the supreme hierarchy in Buddhist Thailand. He was then the best of the Siamese students. He took his Master's degree in Buddhist studies, and his English was excellent. At that time he was only about 25 and he and the younger monks were much fun. They were not appalled by any reference to the other sex; in fact, they gave me some interesting information on beauty contests in Thailand. It was through them that I learnt to my great dismay that Siamese ladies, with the exception of remote villagers and royalty on festive occasions, have taken to occidental dress. Then I fell in love with the Siamese script; I could see at the first glance that it was an Indian script, adapted to their very un-Indian phonemes. We played 'mouse mouse little mouse'—a game I invented to lessen the tedium of solitary study, something like a monastic blind-man's buff, with a lot of colloquial English vocabulary thrown in; for English was a much greater problem to the Thai than to the Ceylonese, Indian, Burmese, or even Tibetan and Japanese students. And I decided, my enthusiasm warmed by theirs, to visit Thailand to see how the Buddha's teaching and the other lore of India's past had taken root among very different people.

I booked a passage on Thai Airways, and took off from Calcutta's impressive airport—a somewhat shaggy Dakota, no doubt, but tidy and clean and all decorated in blue silk on the inside. A quite lovely, smiling little Siamese air hostess withdrew hastily from my side as she came to offer the passengers tea and snacks: she withdrew, because Thai women keep a prescribed distance from the monk. Although the rules of the order are in many ways more lenient than those of the Hindu cloisters, the etiquette between monks and women is very strict. When tea or other refreshments have to be offered to a monk by a Siamese woman, she kneels down with the cup; the monk lowers a part of his saffron haversack or the corner of the upper part of his robe, or a kerchief, placing it on a table or another flat surface; on that the woman deposits the cup or the food—the monk then takes it from there, thus avoiding any direct contact through simultaneously touching the same object.

It was late in the evening and the sun had set in the bay of Siam when our Dakota touched down in Bangkok. It was warm and sultry as in Calcutta, but things looked different. Smiling, quiet, friendly people, who looked efficient. An Indian of about fifty greeted me with a formal salutation: he was Pandit Raghunath Sharma, Director of the Thai-Bharat Cultural Lodge where I was to teach and study. This is a spacious compound with a school for Indian, Chinese, and Siamese children attached to it. To me it was always psychologically extraterritorial—it was purely Indian, for the Siamese and Chinese children did not detract from the Indian atmosphere of the compound. The male servants were Hindus, but the cook engaged for me was a gentle, humorous little Siamese woman of about 40 years, who tried to cook Indian food for me, although it never tasted right.

Siamese people are indeed less inhibited in their general demeanour than other Asian people I have observed. They are good Buddhists, to be sure. They visit temples, they regard the Buddha and his teaching as indisputably the greatest and most benign objects of veneration and their veneration is unquestioned, absolute. There are no 'sceptics' as in Hindu India, for the simple reason that Buddhism itself is a sceptical religion, if religion you can call it. By the time a Siamese has reached that degree of sophistication which might lead him to break from his ancestral tradition, he realizes that it already fulfils all the sceptic's needs, for Siam is a Theravāda country—not a shadow of a supernatural being, no apotheosized Buddha, no Buddha Principle lending itself to virtual or actual deification as it does in the Mahāyāṇa countries, but only the cool, benign, impersonal, yet deeply committing doctrine of momentariness, of the impermanence of everything from stone to the gods and to men, the doctrine of dependent origination, and of the great compassion of the Buddha. I vividly recall two young Siamese monks, on a pilgrimage to the Buddhist reliquaries in India, whom I observed in the Birla Temple of New Delhi. When they stood before the images of the main deities, Lakṣmī and Nārāyaṇa (Viṣṇu and his spouse Śrī or Lakṣmī), they had to stifle their laughter in their saffron haversacks—a human couple, each with four arms, being worshipped by the crowd was too much for them. No notion of a personal God has ever intruded upon Siamese Buddhism. The Buddha's image is worshipped in all homes and in all temples, but he is a human teacher, the greatest of all, meriting all the veneration of which a human being can be worthy. It seems to me that the Siamese worshipper, in this respect, is subtler and practices a sounder psychology than the Hindu. Of course, we prostrate ourselves before the deity as we do before the *guru*, who is the incarnate deity, and so we do when we worship divinity in the temple. Yet, there is the feeling that a god merits more veneration than a human teacher, although this is not corroborated by scripture: *gurur brahmā gurur viṣṇur gururdevo maheśvaraḥ, gurureva sākṣādbrahma tasmai śrīgurave namaḥ*, 'the *guru* is the demiurg Brahmā, the *guru* is Viṣṇu, the *guru* is Śiva, verily, the *guru* is the Absolute made visible, obeisance to that *guru*'—but then, the scripture is one thing, the devotee's feelings are another. The Siamese worshipper, however emotional, has no such qualms: for in prostrating himself before the Buddha's image, he shows his veneration for a human teacher, albeit for the greatest human teacher. The numinous is drawn into the human sphere.

A misconception of the working of the numinous was revealed to me by the new Indian Ambassador to Thailand, who was appointed while I was there. He had just attended his daughter's wedding back home in India. 'Swamiji', he said, 'although the ceremony was Vedic all right, I believe we must move with the times. That pandit chanted everything in Sanskrit! No one understood a word of it. So I said to him: "My dear Sir, will you please say what you have to say in Hindi, or at least translate everything into Hindi, so that all of us can understand it?" ' This was to me another facet of the Renaissance. Some of its protagonists in Hindu India believe that magic can be translated into the domestic vernacular; but it cannot. Of course, almost all of the Vedic chants used at a wedding or any other Hindu ceremony can and have been translated into other languages, including English, German and French, and there are scores of manuals in Indian vernaculars which give either full translations or excerpts. Yet the idea that a translation can stand for the original is fatuous and I was taken aback by the Ambassador's remark; for I had thought it was only the more philistine among the Protestants in Europe and America who regard the use of Latin by the Roman Church as a basis of valid criticism. I had met an Indonesian nationalist who grumbled that his people's prayers were in Arabic, a language hardly anyone understood, but among Hindus, intellectual or otherwise, I had not so far encountered any objection to the ceremonies being conducted in the language of ritual, or any idea that the meaning of the texts is important. It is not. On the contrary, complete literary understanding of sacred texts is often disturbing—it may jeopardize the numinous which is what the text has to convey. Moreover, the literary meaning of most of the texts is naive and trivial owing to their extreme age. It is the chant that counts.

Four times a week I delivered a sermon in Urdu mixed with Panjabi—the only kind of mixture the Panjabi settlers in South-east Asia will readily understand, apart from village Panjabi which I can no longer speak. I decided to break the homiletic convention, for hitherto the Hindus in Bangkok had mostly had the Sikh holy book interpreted to them, owing to the preponderance of Sikhs and also owing to the rather disheartening fact that the Panjabi Hindu does not seem fully aware that originality lies within his scriptural ken, not in that of the Sikhs. The occasional stray Hindu pandit had spoken on the Purāṇas, narrating Hindu mythology and its somewhat hackneyed proverbial lore, and of course on the Bhagavadgītā. I announced to the Hindu community that I would hold my sermons on the actual canonical text, the Upaniṣhad. During the first week, the Hall was crammed with people, rich and poor, men and women. I plunged *medias in res*, and without compromise I took up the four great dicta establishing identity of the individual with the cosmic soul—the central teaching of the Upaniṣhads. No Kṛṣṇa, no Rāma, no Guru Nānak and no Kabīr, but for a change clear, solid Vedānta. There was interest and excitement, but it did not last long. Within three weeks the number had dwindled from about 300 to 20, and after two months there were only five ladies who attended regularly. Middle-aged or elderly women they were, and barely literate. And yet they did pick up the thread. In the end, they felt that they had realized what was important in the tenets of Hinduism. But the others reverted to their local Panjabi brand of Hinduism—plenty of village saints, plenty of Sikh quotations, and a nodding acquaintance with the Hindu *avatāras*.

After some reconnaissance I came to know where my own specific knowledge and experience could be of service. There are two Buddhist monastic universities in Bangkok, belonging to the two only slightly differing Siamese sects of Buddhism. The monks at Nalanda had mostly graduated from the Mahachulalongkorn Academy. The other Academy functions under the auspices of the Dhammayut sect, the smaller, allegedly more scholastically inclined, and certainly more austere sect, founded by King Mahamongkut (badly caricatured for the West in a famous musical.) He himself had been a monk for over twenty years before he ascended the throne, and he founded the Mahāmukuṭa Buddhist Academy, to which I was appointed as a Guest Professor of Comparative Religion. My students were all graduates from the Academy, and my medium was English, as my Thai was not good enough for academic instruction.

Teaching comparative religion and philosophy meant teaching the Hindu, Buddhist and Jaina religions in their essence, and reflecting on the salient similarities and differences between them. I began with a survey of the world's religions in general, pointing out the fundamental distinction between the historical, mediterranean and the unhistorical or anti-historical Indian religions. I then made a wide sweep over Athens and Rome, showing that element in secular philosophy which (in my own considered opinion) is alone pertinent for the study of comparative religion: the two possible views of the universe as a static entity *or* as a dynamic, fluctuating pseudo-entity, as mere flux. For her religious and secular thinkers of all ages and climes have but two alternatives for choice: they can conceive of *being* or of *becoming*, the two conceptions being more rigidly distinct in the religious than in the philosophical approach. In the West Parmenides, Plato, Aristotle, the German and British Idealists, and Christian thinkers teach a static universe, i.e. the existence of a Being, as does in India the Vedic, Brahmin, Hindu tradition. In the West, Heracleitus, Antisthenes, the Empiricists, Russell and all Anglo-American philosophers who could call themselves 'analysts' envisage, in one way or another, a flux; in Asia, it is the Buddhists who take this view—of flux, of constant becoming, of momentary arising and momentary decay.

In the attempt to get these fundamental notions across to my

Siamese Buddhist brother-monks, I encountered a difficulty which I had anticipated only in theory, but which is of enormous systematic importance. I found that it is virtually impossible to convey to them the notion of a Being, of a static universe, of a 'Thing' in the philosophical sense, and *a fortiori*, of a Supreme Being, a God. They have never heard anything but the pristine, austere, strictly essence-less views of the Buddhist teachers. The Buddha broke down the Brahmin notion of a 'Thing'; a Being, God—but he and his Indian followers after him were always surrounded by thousands who held theistic and absolutist views—they could compare and exchange notes. Not so the Siamese, the Burmese and other South-east-Asian Theravāda Buddhists. For many generations they have heard nothing but the non-essentialist views of primitive Buddhism, and there was no one around them who held other views. This is why evangelizing is a heartbreaking affair for the Christian missions in Thailand; the Hindu at least knows what the Christian is talking about, but the Siamese honestly does not. The occidental idea that the human mind grasps a 'thing' better than 'no-thing' is clearly wrong, and I state this on the basis of my Siamese professorial experience: there is no common human proclivity toward the one or the other alternative—it is wholly an acquired attitude. This has wider analogies. The famous notion that human beings somehow believe in a supernatural being, some God, just as they somehow believe that food will appease their hunger is disproved by this one example—the Buddhist, at least of the Theravāda tradition, does *not* feel this way. True, any person born and bred in any of the occidental traditions understands the notion of 'being' much more readily than the notion of 'not-being', of 'momentariness' and of the other concepts which are axiomatic in the Buddhist doctrine. Unless he studies academic philosophy, the notion of 'being' gradually becomes ingrained in his mind as the obvious one. Observing him, the theologian and the absolutist philosopher of the West draws the conclusion that men 'naturally' believe in being rather than in momentariness. The occidental traditionalist thus uses his unsophisticated neighbour as a guinea-pig to establish the 'naturalness' of his fundamental doctrines—the doctrines of 'being', of 'God' and a host of kindred things. Were he sent to the Buddhist Academy at Bangkok, he would soon realize that the notion of being etc. is anything but 'natural'—it has to be learnt, and it is harder to teach it to the Siamese Buddhist than it is to teach the Buddhist doctrine of non-being, of non-self, and of momentariness to the occidental, for the simple reason that the latter has been exposed to similar teachings ever since the days of Heracleitus who said, 'All is in a flux. You cannot step into the same river twice'.

However, I did succeed in teaching the Buddhist monks how the notion of a Being, and *mutatis mutandis*, of a God, may come about. I realized in the teaching process, that the Siamese Buddhist monk at first harbours the idea that entertaining such strange notions as 'Being' and 'God' is something pathological—and this is the exact parallel to the occidental student's feeling about Buddhist doctrine when he first encounters it. 'Negative' 'sick', etc.: these are the epithets the less polite occidental student tends to give to the Buddhist doctrine until he becomes better acquainted with it. I succeeded by putting myself in the Buddha's own position: whom and what did he refute?—the notion of a Self, the notion of permanence, and all kindred notions. By juxtaposing in pairs such correlative terms as 'momentary', 'lasting', 'becoming without end', 'being unchangeable without beginning and end', in other words, by contrasting terms connoting ideas familiar to the Buddhist way of thinking with their opposites, I succeeded in creating a conception so far unknown to these monks. Their reluctance to accept anything the Buddha refuted, even for purely hypothetic purposes, was a great obstacle to understanding and their antagonism to other schools of Buddhism (the Mahāyāṇa schools, of which they knew little except that it was doctrinarily closer to the Brahmin teachings which the Buddha had criticized throughout his life) was strong and inveterate. I had to keep reassuring them in a running commentary which constantly confirmed that I had not come to convert them to different ideas, and that in the non-discursive field conversion from one set of views to another was taboo to me.

I believe that in the end there emerged from my class a batch of brilliant young Buddhist monks, who knew pretty well what it was the teaching of their Master had been opposing: the Brahmin notion of a Being, of a cosmic entity, of the *Brahman*, and of the related or identical Self. I do not think that the Siamese Buddhists mean the same as Indian students of religion when they use the term *anātmavāda*, i.e. the 'doctrine of non-self', which is the key doctrine of Theravāda Buddhism. The Hindu, when he hears the term 'non-self', immediately thinks of the Absolute with which the Self is identified. Not so the Siamese—for he has never really heard about an Absolute. For him, *anātmavāda* simply means 'doctrine of non-self', where *atma* (self) refers solely to his own ego, his particular individuality, which Buddhism denies as a fiction. The facile manner in which Hindu and Siamese Buddhist scholars aver a mutual understanding of the key-term *ātmavāda* misleads them: the term 'self' (*ātman*) is a loaded term for the Indian, but a very simple one for the Siamese, and probably for all other Theravāda Buddhists. This seems a case where intelligent and even erudite people have been using the same words, the same idioms, but with totally different meanings of which they are mutually unaware.

Siam is a wonderful country for a scholar in cultural lore, for unlike India and China, Siam *can* be studied comprehensively. India and China cannot: a serious scholar of Indica or Sinica has to specialize sooner or later in classical literature, religion and philosophy, history, grammar, polity—and in each of them he will have to seek his further subsection. Not so in Siamica: Siam's history is not very old, its claims to cultural universality are sparse, its literature is quantitatively limited. I am not being facetious when I say that a scholar can read *all* of Siamese traditional literature in a lifetime. He can also study all its dances, its sculpture and architecture, and its music. The arts derive from Indian sources, but the Indian sources are vastly more intricate and diversified, and they demand so much more from the student. When observing Indian classical dance of the southern schools, I am constantly worried that I am missing some special message, that I am overlooking some cryptic hint, that some gateway to supreme wisdom and salvation is being opened before me and that I fail to perceive it. The same feeling bothers me as I circumambulate the great temples of Southern India, but I have no such fears when I watch the guileless though by no means unsophisticated Siamese children of the Indian Muse. The Siamese classical dancers dance their masked *kon* and their ballet-like *lakorn* epics, but I can enjoy them as dance and music, without the least metaphysical scruple or numinous awe.

As a people which you meet, the Siamese have some virtues that Indians you meet seem to lack. In the first place, the Siamese I met never displayed the faintest feeling of inferiority, whereas in India this feeling is deep-rooted and strong. Perhaps the political past of the two countries has something to do with it, for Siam has been independent for many centuries. Yet I think this is too easy an explanation. India has had long periods of partial freedom and of splendour, and political dependence did not touch the people at large any more than political freedom touched the Siamese people at large. No, I think rather that the personality image of the Indian differs from that of the Thai, and I could trace one part of that image—the religious image. There is nothing in Buddhism which is sufficiently different from Hinduism to account for the difference in the Siamese and the Indian personality image—the way they view themselves, ideally and factually. The Indian worships the hero and the ascetic, and both these types merge in the image of the supremely realized soul. The Siamese no doubt respects the hero and the ascetic, but he takes neither of them too seriously, or more precisely, he does not let them encroach on his secular world. The Hindu goes to a saint, or he goes to have *darśan* in a temple, or he goes on a pilgrimage: on his return, he is so deeply affected by the experience, that the accustomed world seems trivial and polluting to him—he wants to emulate the saint or the godly teachers whose images he has seen on the bas reliefs in the shrine. He feels that whatever he has done up to this point has been a waste of time—he has lain with woman, his wife, and she has deprived him of the precious fluid whose preservation alone grants eternal bliss and mastery of both the self and the universe. 'Women are the snakes', an affluent Sindhi merchant said to me, 'they are truly the snakes, Swamiji. They want our virility and they will not let us reach the supreme. You are happy. You have nothing to do with them and they must keep away from you. You can preserve and purify your sperm by not letting it flow. You are blessed. We are cursed.'

In the beautiful, comfortable mansion of that same Sindhi merchant at Bangkok, he conducted a weekly *satsaṅg*. He belonged to the *sahajdhārī* Sikhs, i.e. the people of Sindh who follow Guru Nānak and the *Guru Granth Sāhib* but who do not wear beards and turbans. There was pleasant *bhajan*, and then he himself gave a sermon, which was stereotyped. 'These houses, these cars, these children, this wealth—they are all a waste of time, nothing but a waste of time', he cried with passion in each sermon, and the equally affluent merchants around him nodded their guilty assent. They all had houses and cars and children and money—but it was all a waste of time. What then, for them, would be good use of time? My merchant-sermonist himself would provide the answer: 'Take the name of the Lord, the name of the Guru, the True Name, day and night and night and day. Do nothing else, immerse yourself in His sweet name'—this alone is no waste of time.

Such was a typical example of how the personality image of the Hindu (and Sikh and Jain, and in earlier times no doubt of the Indian Buddhist as well) affects his attitude toward life. It is different with the Siamese, and the difference dawned upon me when I commuted between Siamese Buddhist and Hindu or Sikh households in Bangkok. For there are thousands of men who feel and speak like this particular Sindhi Sikh merchant—you will find them in the rich mansions and the poor hovels of India. The formal theologian might say: the Buddhist does not have to take the numinous seriously, he does not have to create an image nor to strive for a merger with that image, as there is no image, nor anything to merge in; there is in the Buddhist doctrine no *ātman*, no *Brahman*, no super-self wherewith to establish or to realize identity. This is true, but it has no bearing upon the believer's attitude towards life. The Ceylonese are Buddhists, and there are also some Buddhist groups of Indic background in East Pakistan, in and around Chittagong. Yet both of them display the Indian outlook which I have just described. (I cannot say anything about the Burmese.) The Thai are Buddhist, too, but they separate the religious and the mundane life in a most wholesome manner. The temples are crammed with devout visitors on holy days, and full even during the week. Well dressed in western style clothing (in the cities of Siam), laughing and smiling, they enter the shrine, prostrate themselves before the Buddha's serene image, listen to the monks' sermons and exhortations and bring their offerings. They hear and read and know that everything is momentary, that nothing is permanent, that salvation lies in denying the senses their play, and that *nirvāṇa* is total cessation of all that is impermanent and of all misery—that is, of the known and loved world with all the living and inert objects in it. And yet, when they emerge from the temple, they are as jovial and cheerful as they were both in the temple and before they entered it. The experience does not upset their balance. Hindu friends in Siam to whom I pointed this out gave me the one answer I knew they would: the Siamese just do not take their religion seriously, whereas we do. But my Hindu friends do not know that there are different ways of taking a religion seriously.

Young lovers exchange tender glances even as they worship together in the temple—an atrocity to the Hindu mind, for affection between men and women, legal or illicit, may not be shown. Here lies the difference. Both the Hindu and the Buddhist religion offer a gamut of gifts: asceticism, compassion, mercy, love, austerity, gentle indulgence, devotion, serenity, keen meditation, self-torture, wild saints and mild saints. It all depends on the choice among these gifts, on the stress laid upon one or the other of them. I am wary of such notions as 'national character' but I have seen that the Hindus choose asceticism first, the other gifts afterwards. The Thai choose love, compassion, and the Buddha's indulgence in the first place, the canonical austerities in the second. There is but one Buddha Śakyamuni and he has all things to offer—asceticism and austerity, compassion and tenderness, stern justice as a monastic disciplinarian, and mild indulgence when things have gone wrong. The Thai have chosen the pleasant aspects, those that make for extraversion.

The Asia Foundation is one of those rich American bodies which the Hindu sages might have likened to the wish-granting tree or the wish-fulfilling cow of mythological fame. It sponsors studies in Asian humanities, and it has its offices all over free Asia, its headquarters in San Francisco. It gave much aid to the Mahāmukuta Buddhist Academy, and it was through the Academy that I became known to the Foundation. It was suggested that I should go on a lecture tour to Japan and I was very pleased with the suggestion. As Japan is halfway between India and the New World, I thought this would be the time to see North America, and to see what can be learnt and done there about what I might call the cultural and intellectual (*not* spiritual and religious) rapprochement between India and America, and the countries that lie between the two, to the East of India that is, and to the West of America.

Kyoto is one of the very few places where I would stay for the rest of my life if anyone gave me the opportunity. It has a simple, deeply classical sophistication, or sophisticated classicality, I do not know which, that kept me spellbound for three months. I was lodged at the Rakuyukaikan, a sort of hotel-like dwelling affiliated to Kyoto (Imperial) University and I lectured on Indian and western philosophy, on the evaluation of Indian philosophical axioms and western analytical methods. It is not known to occidental non-orientalists, that Japanese scholarship in the field of Indic studies ranks first in bulk, and possibly first in quality, in international orientalistic scholarship. The number of publications in these subjects is enormous, but it is not accessible to anyone who does not read Japanese. I thought it irritating that so much valuable material on every aspect of Indology, and particularly on Buddhism, should not become known to the West, and above all that there is inevitably a vast amount of duplication.

Now over 90 per cent of the indologists of Japan are Buddhologists, and devout Buddhists. Many of them are ordained priests in one or the other of the many Japanese schools of Mahāyāṇa Buddhism. Professor Gajin Nagao, Head of the Department at the University of Kyoto, is an ordained monk-priest and lives in a temple. Celibacy is not in effect incumbent on Japanese Buddhist monks, and Professor Nagao lives with his charming silent wife and his children as do other scholar-monks. Neither have they too many scruples about alcohol. *Saké* is freely enjoyed, and little if any opprobrium attaches to the enjoyment of alcoholic drinks among priests. (Buddhist facetious jargon has indeed rechristened *saké 'hanyato'*, which is the Japanese transcription of the Sanskrit-Buddhist term for intuitive wisdom and complete analytical understanding!) The same holds good for food: it seems that among Buddhist monks, it is only the Chinese who are strict vegetarian. The question of what to eat and what not to eat simply does not arise for the Japanese monk.

My talks were all followed by long 'specialist' discussions—American administrative terminology had now made its appearance. In the large seminar room of the Faculty of Letters, some of Japan's most eminent indologists and thinkers sat around me and around the tape-recorder (this was the first time that I really faced that admirable gadget.) The argument was long-winded and difficult. At first it seemed to me that the language barrier was to blame for the slowness of the procedure but this was not entirely true, for almost all of the scholars have an excellent passive understanding of English scholastic language. No, it became evident to me that quick repartee is not considered good style. This is very different from learned argument amongst Hindu savants, where presence of mind and quick wit are not only permissible, but a canonically sanctioned asset in theological and philosophical discourse. All of the people around me were profound scholars of Mahāyāṇa Buddhist doctrine—all of them knew primary material in Chinese and Japanese, Tibetan, and Sanskrit. Some of them were also conversant with contemporary and traditional western philosophy. Professor Nishitani glowed with intensive, controlled, and slowly mounting excitement as the argument progressed:—are the intuitive, non-discursive methods of Indian, and Buddhist thought in general inferior to western analytical methods, or can there be no mutual criticism at all between these two fundamentally different approaches to knowledge? I pointed out in my introductory address (which was translated sentence for sentence) that many Indic terms had been completely misunderstood by occidental scholars, because they had tried to impose the function of western dictionary equivalents on the Indic term. For instance the root *jñā*, 'to know', in Sanskrit, does not mean objective knowledge when used in philosophical parlance, though it does mean simply to 'know' in common speech, just as the occidental term 'idealism' has two totally different meanings when used in popular and in philosophically learned discourse.

The professors were keenly curious to find out my view on the question: which kind of truth was more desirable, the one arrived at by discursive means, or the one reached by analytical or scientific investigation? And it was here that I spoke my heart perhaps for the first time in a learned assembly, for the pressure of Indian scholastic fashion no longer weighed on me in this different environment. Though I regard discursive truth, i.e. the knowledge of facts, as alone valid in an objective sense, as also more important for the world at large and as a directive for seekers of higher education or for those who build universities and libraries, I personally regard intuitive, or mystical knowledge, the type of intuition and detached apprehension reached through meditative processes, yogic or otherwise, as more interesting—albeit less austere—and certainly more important for myself. I do not know whether I made my point, which, as I told the audience, was primarily a declaration of faith, because I could not tell whether I made myself clear in a medium which was unfamiliar to them except in the written word. But if their kind and friendly nod signified agreement I should be happy.

I left Japan with a very heavy heart. I have been searching my heart ever since, but I find in it no single complaint against this country. I had promised old friends in Europe that I would return to Asia from America via Europe. Yet I am almost sure I will break that promise when the day comes and travel westward again into Asia, via those islands of indefatigable form.

CHAPTER IX

MONKISH GLIMPSES OF THE NEW WORLD

Aurean Trans Portam

swami: Hindu idol; Hindu religious teacher . . .
Oxford English Dictionary

swami: . . . often equivalent to *yogi*, *fakir*, *wonder-worker*, etc.
Webster's New International Dictionary

THERE came to America and Europe, at the turn of the century, that unique Hindu monk Vivekananda, and it was largely due to him that serious minds in the West turned to Indian lore with keen interest and with some intellectual excitement. But unfortunately the seekers of spurious mystery, the devotees of non-existent Masters levitating on Tibetan heights, also attached themselves to the Swami, and although he realized the situation soon enough, he did not try sufficiently hard to disengage himself from their interests. They then fell easy prey to scores of swamis and other self-appointed exponents of India's wisdom, partly Indian by birth, partly claiming some Indian origin—physical or by previous incarnation—and in part western but 'imbued with the Spirit of the East'. These swamis travelled the two continents, collecting followers and money, reaping where Vivekananda had sown. There are, of course, the Ramakrishna-Vivekananda-Vedanta Centres, run by monks of the Order and they are genuine, if not over-exciting institutes. Some have glamour: the Southern Californian Center in Hollywood is under Swami Prabhavananda, whose translation of the Gita has sold over a million copies. Aldous Huxley, Christopher Isherwood, Gerald Herd, Greta Garbo, and other serious proponents of truth or beauty frequent the place. Three young American women obtained their initiation from the Swami; at the Kumbhamela they dipped into the River and had their bath together with thousands of Hindu-born monks and nuns. Swami Ashokananda in San Francisco is a serious Sanskrit scholar, and he maintains a strict regiment over his American monastic disciples and the inmates of his *āśrama*. Swami Nikhilananda in New York is well-known to serious occidental readers; his translations and interpretations of canonical Brahmin literature and of Ramakrishna's Gospel have brought him and the Mission well-deserved literary fame. There are many more of this admirable type, but alas, there is also a much larger number of people sailing under the same colours whose characteristics extend from the misguided through the fraudulent to the almost lunatic.

The University of Washington has a large, exquisite Far Eastern Institute, rapidly climbing to the highest American reputation in the field. Here I found a scholastic haven after very little knocking. As Indian studies have not so far been introduced at this school on an official level, I was included by an act of courtesy, as it were—the 'Inner Asia Project' (for at American universities it is the projects that count) deals with Inner Asia, but as Inner Asia has derived much of its cultural lore from its southern neighbour, an indologist's work could be used as a 'feeder-service'. (I coined the term myself, but it was accepted so unquestionably that I prided myself on having acquired some American academic jargon when I had but just entered the premises.)

I am now writing a book on *Indian Tantra and its Relation to Tibetan Buddhism;* and it is only in this land that a man is paid for writing a book, without any further stipulation. Along with it I have been smuggling Sanskrit and Hindi into the Institute by way of informal courses, and I shared the astonishment of my colleagues when the Hindi course attracted 98 students, the Sanskrit course 28. Each course dropped to about 7 per cent of its original roll—amazing nevertheless, that the Pacific North-west, regarded as a wild and risky region by the less informed of the Eastern seaboard, and as a cultural vacuum by all Eastern schools, should evince interest in such abstruse things as Indic languages. Not only are such subjects admittedly abstruse, but to many good citizens they are almost subversive because so directly contrary to the solid, material, extravert interests which are basic to the American scene—the car, the television and the dishwasher; the muscular pastimes of hunting and fishing (both of which I abhor), climbing, camping, ball-games and building one's own house.

All this, however, is atoned for a hundredfold by what is unique and what must remain the scholar's dream for decades to come: the fabulous research facilities provided in the United States, once a scholar, or a set of scholars has succeeded in convincing the administration and, indirectly, the taxpayer, that his research will pay off in terms of the general advancement of the people. I can only speak for my own discipline, but this I do with gusto: the bibliographical apparatus, books, manuscripts, journals, which I failed to assemble in seven years' hard effort in India, I obtained for my desk at the University of Washington in Seattle within one year. The school lavishly orders whatever book I want; works which are not available are microfilmed and flown over; there is the Inter-Library loan service, which makes available to the scholar all the books and rare items obtainable from any library or university on the North American continent—at no cost, for the mailing charges are carried by the University post-office. Instead of having to persuade or bribe the recalcitrant minor Brahmin in charge of a temple-library, and then squat in a damp, hot, fly and mosquito infested corner copying out passages, I have the blown-up microfilm copies on my huge, comfortable desk in an air-conditioned office, with powerful indirect light from the ceiling.

All this would be a veritable paradise, were it not for certain inner agonies which beset the scholar. There is, in the first place, an enormous dilemma for the student of the antiquities. American foundations, American educational authorities, and American university administrations are, so far as the humanities are concerned, extremely contemporary-minded. This is perfect for the sciences, for after all the sciences dictate their latest achievements to the audience of the people, its legislators, and its financiers. Historians and anthropologists do not experience any particular qualm, I believe, for their interests are always also contemporary—it does not require much persuasion to show that, say, modern Greece cannot be properly understood until Pericles' and Alcibiades' ideologies have been throughly investigated. Anthropology in America is a real epitome of the contemporary, for it preserves human groups from ever becoming objects of antiquarian study. But the difficulty is acute with philology and the study of ideas, especially when the latter are unrelated or even antagonistic to what is officially acceptable. This may be a secular campus, religion must be no part of any of its schedules and activities, yet a Christian value system is somehow presupposed. Licence is granted to the established native genius whose non-Christian ideas are fitfully admired, but then his ideas fall into another acceptable pattern, that of humanism as a substitute for unacceptable religious dogma, well-informed mild flirtation with things behind the curtains, or non-conformist individualism. But I somehow do not fit into any of these patterns, or only partially so. Non-Christian, anti-Christian perhaps in matters of doctrine, humanist—all that would be all right. But this 'Swami' is a pest because—see the definition in Webster's Dictionary—he may be little better than a fakir.

Yet it is not this that worries me so much as my realization that the philologist, the antiquarian and student of ideas has to practice a sort of double-think two decades before 1984. The foundations and the taxpayer stipulate some sort of cash-value for what they give to the scholar. But the Orientalist scholar, who is not interested in contemporary political science and in international relations, has little cash-value to offer. He is not really interested in the things the foundations and the taxpayer expect him to be, and what he produces in fulfilment of their stipulation is not his best—because he is just not interested in the possible applications of his studies to contemporary political and economic relations. The American economist, or the teacher of political science specializing on India is immensely better off vis-à-vis the foundations and the taxpayer, for he really supplies much of what they want. In addition, the Government of India and its information services abroad want people to know about indigenous manufacture of clinical thermometers, electricity meters and cylindrical grinding machines, about a steel-foundry to be set up at Chittaranjan, and about an Indian pharmacologist's recovery of edible oil from rice-bran. Official India is highly suspicious of such interests as the Indian antiquarian outside India may pursue: collating medieval texts on secret, possibly immoral rituals in Assam and Bengal, or on disputes between some ancient Indian logician and his mystico-theological opponent. The official Indian attitude is that we have had enough of it; it has brought about our weakness and our disinclination to work; let people abroad not constantly direct their attention to the things we no longer really want.

But how does the academic world take the message of the Indian sages? It does not, and in a way its refusal is justified. The point is that the 'interesting', that is to say, the great and hallowed things about Indian lore have been banalized and man-handled beyond recognition by the faddists of the land, by the scores of people in every city who, in some form or other are suffering from the disease of the mysterious and esoteric. It is clear and necessary that the academic must have no commerce with the mystical clubs around town. Solid scholarship stipulates that research proceed laboriously, with painstaking exactitude, and only on primary sources. Secondary sources created in academic pursuit of the primary sources (the journals of oriental studies, that is, and the richly annotated critical editions and translations) must be taken into account, and I do not object to their being used as 'ponies'. But there is all the difference between say, a critical study of the Bhagavadgītā, collating many manuscripts, conforming to the present-day model of textual apparatus, indexed, with attempts at chronology and at dating on stylistic and textual evidence, etc., and one of the numerous and, I am sorry to say, still continuing pompous renditions of the book.

Ever since I came to America, seekers of all age-groups have come to me for spiritual solace. They have heard a swami was there and they come to me, or came to me in the beginning, for exactly the same type of instruction as they found in that disastrous string of literature which exploits the poor, sadly torn western heart's hot desire for eastern balm. If I gave them such counsel, then all my academic colleagues' misgivings about the meaning of my swamihood would be justified. But it is not for this reason that I send them away. When I tell them to go and study Sanskrit and Pali before they talk about yoga, Buddhism and reincarnation, or to learn Chinese (not Japanese) before they talk about Zen, and to leave me alone until they have read these primary languages for two or three years, I act on the true behest of my Order: the difficulty of access is no excuse, for if that were allowed, it would imply that achieving yogic powers and nirvāṇa and wisdom are *easier* than learning Sanskrit and Tibetan. But they are not.

What then am I bringing to America, and what can I take from here back to India? Yogis and swamis in plenty have come to this hospitable land, and good doctors and engineers have gone from here to India, all of them, presumably, with a genuine desire to serve. In my attempt to find something which is helpful even though it be new, I think I have found something which I can use, and whose use I can recommend to others, something which is both an import and an export commodity; something which neither the swamis before me, nor the doctors and engineers have carried with them. I call it cultural criticism.

What I mean is this. If a person—scholar, journalist, or plain tourist—complains, about the bad roads or the bad hygiene or even the corrupt officials in India, he may perhaps be frowned upon, but he will make no contribution and no enemies. Indeed many of the best and most influential Indians will support his charges and corroborate them. On this side of the ocean, similarly, if an alien visitor or a new settler criticizes the slot-machines or the medicated meats on the supermarkets, he will encounter some frowns, but also much apologetic confirmation. But these are not cultural criticism. This book on the other hand has been mainly cultural criticism. If Gandhi is criticized, say, for his eclectic views on religion, for his deliberate or involuntary mis-statement of some doctrine (as for instance his claim that the Buddha believed in God), or for his deprecation of sexual love, this is cultural criticism, and it is deeply resented by the votaries of the Hindu Renaissance. Similarly in America, if I were to criticize Mr Eisenhower for ostentatious churchgoing, maintained during his successful State visit to India, I should evoke pungent rejoinders in the Press, for this is cultural criticism. But such criticism can be validly countered only by refuting its contents on objective grounds, by disproving that Gandhi ever asserted the Buddha's belief in God, or by showing conclusively that there is no element whatever of bowing to the *mores* of his country, to the American way of life, nothing whatever beyond private piety which I readily acknowledge in the President's public church-going.

Or again, I have taken exception to Pandit M. M. Malaviya's dictum to students: 'Drink milk, do physical exercise, and take the name of the Lord'. A rejoinder to my criticism which accuses me of not understanding the spirit of Hinduism, of not seeing that the Pandit was right in his advice to Hindu students because it rested on the experience of ancient Hindu sages, misses the mark. The rejoinder would be valid if it could be shown that Malaviya never said it, or that he said it casually as a piece of advice to some loggers and miners. But he said it to the assembled students of B.H.U., which was his creation, and he meant it to be the essence of student-counselling. My criticism is directed against the ubiquitous Hindu notion that milk-drinking, gymnastics, and prayers are essential for the better academic knowledge. Also I criticize the idea implicit in the Hindu notion that building the saintly man is as important in a university as it is in a forest hermitage—in other words, I am criticizing a facet of Hindu culture.

Take another example. The late Russian scholar Professor Stcherbatsky (he died of starvation during the Nazi siege of Leningrad) was the world's leading authority on Buddhist logic and on Mahāyāṇa Buddhism in general. I mentioned some aspect of his work to one of India's outstanding Sanskritists, a scholar who writes most of his books in chaste, modern English. When I referred to the late Russian savant with the awe due to his memory, the learned pandit made a disdainful gesture: Stcherbatsky was no scholar, he said. No scholar? I marvelled. What about his pioneering works in the Bibliotheca Buddhica, his philological acumen, his doctrinary insights into Buddhism? The Brahmin professor remained adamant: Stcherbatsky visited night-clubs and drank wine in Paris. A man who leads such an impure life is not a scholar. Now when I point out the stupendous fallacies involved in this judgement then my procedure again is cultural criticism. In criticizing the Hindu doctor, I must try to show that there is no necessary connexion between scholarship and a way of life—neither psychological nor philosophical; that the connexion derives solely from a particular way of using language, in this case, from the Hindu conjunction of 'behaving according to a set of standards traditionally connected with a genuine pandit's behaviour' on the one hand and 'scholarly achievement and status' on the other.

Just after I arrived in North America, I heard the President deliver a nation-wide broadcast on the situation in the Near East. Towards the end of his talk, he said something like this: '. . . such loyalties and scruples cannot be expected from a people that is ruled by atheistic despots'. Now here, I object by way of cultural criticism and also—though this is incidental—for reasons of expediency, for such a statement is potentially harmful. The connexion between 'atheistic' and 'despotic', and between 'atheistic' and the 'lack of loyalties and (moral) scruples' is not a necessary one, though in the case of the Russians and the Chinese there is such a connexion. The statement confuses a particular with a generic rule, for 'atheism' and 'unscrupulous despotism' are indeed found together in these two colossi, but their togetherness is akin to the connexion between 'blue sky' and 'Monday' in the proposition 'we had a blue sky last Monday'. Just as there is no generic rule about bright Mondays, so there is no generic rule about despotic atheists. For if the world were ruled by Russell and other atheists of his kind, it would probably be neither an unscruplous nor a despotic rule. But I criticize the North American majority attitude which links the two terms together in a generic fashion, and which does not object to such linkage. As to the matter of expediency, if the Supreme Patriarch of Thailand listened to the broadcast he would be saddened and estranged by such a statement from the President of the country that is his own country's best friend, for Theravāda Buddhism is rigidly atheistic and the linking of 'atheism' with 'despotism' must cause the Buddhist pontifex considerable discomfort.

I put forward this claim, opening myself to all the criticism—cultural criticism I hope—which it will no doubt evoke, as the very special message of this book. I contend that cultural criticism is not only wholesome, but that it is the only possible intercultural contribution which can be made on the communicatory, discursive level. Panegyrics are easy, for they require no knowledge of the other's culture. If I praise Gandhi's teachings, I will have many friends in India and no Indian will oppose me even if my eulogy rests on a concatenation of vague notions, scant knowledge of the philosophical background and purely subjective enthusiasm—even though I may be saying the right things for the wrong reasons. On the other hand, if I criticize, I have to arm myself with detailed knowledge, for the spirit is weak though the flesh may be strong: human beings however civilized, connive at pleasant things said about them or about their kin, even when they know them to be untrue.

I will then submit this advice, that instead of ignoring doctrinal or ethical discrepancies and differences with a benign smile, let us instead point them out. Let us not persist in the imbecile idea—common to most of the well-meaning international organizations of our day—that the world's peoples will get together because 'we have so much teaching in common';

for this implies that if, after all, it should transpire that we do not have so many beliefs in common, we should have to fight each other. Negatively, it would also imply that people who share the same doctrines never fight each other, which is blatant nonsense. The Theravāda Buddhist Burmese invaded the Theravāda Buddhist Siamese and burnt up Ayuthia, the former Siamese capital, breaking up some of the Buddha images to see if there was any gold hidden in them; nor did European Christian countries always live in amity with one another. No, our getting together, or at least our not shooting at each other must rest, not on similar religious views, not on the fictitious 'essential unity' of all religions and 'good' ideologies, but on the simple fact that it is infinitely more pleasant and expedient not to shoot at each other.

We should then study each other's culture with zealous application—and as a test of our successful research, let us criticize each other with all the scholastic and discursive apparatus at our disposal, and let us do so on a level where the use of force or even the emotional rejection of this cultural criticism appear ludicrous anomalies. This will be achieved if the cultural agents learn to dissociate themselves from their commitment through their cradle. No one is born to an ideology; everyone must find his own, be it theistic, atheistic, or no religion at all; everyone must find his own, using whatever his native surroundings may be as a starting place. If he then reverts to the inheritance of his birth-place, that does not show its intrinsic superiority, but only its greater attraction for his psychological makeup.

Cultural criticism may then become the finest tool of cosmopolitan communication and of humanism, for its object is not to change another's culture, but to point out what is possibly wrong or could possibly be wrong with it, thereby opening up fruitful avenues of human discourse. It goes without saying that the Indian will criticize the West and vice versa, not to convert or correct the other, but to show the different light in which things important to the other can appear.

I believe that cultural criticism is the only contribution we can make to cultures not originally our own, or not our own by choice. Instances of this criticism of a cultural environment into which the critic is born but which he never made are on the increase: M. N. Roy's cultural criticism was mainly of India, and my own initial criticism was of a German or a Continental set of thoughts and ideas. The method tends to avoid the disastrous distinction between 'outsiders' and 'insiders', for the fact that one contributes to a culture makes one an 'insider', and if cultural criticism is successful then the critic becomes an 'insider' by virtue of the value of his criticism; or to be more exact, the distinction between 'outsider' and 'insider' becomes irrelevant.

PRONUNCIATION OF INDIAN TERMS

Long and short vowels are phonemic in Indian languages: the length mark (¯) over a vowel indicates its natural length (a short, ā long, etc.); s and ṣ are both pronounced like 'sh'; ṛ sound like 'ri' in Sanskrit terms—in Hindi words, the symbol ṛ stands for a single domal flap of the tongue; s is pronounced like English 's' in 'sing'; there is no voiced 'z' sound (like in 'measles') in Indian languages; the letter 'h' after vowels and consonants has to be pronounced as a distinct aspiration; the dot under ṭ, ṭh, ḍ, ḍh, and ṇ indicates domal (cerebral) pronunciation, which has no phonetic equivalent in any occidental language.

GLOSSARY

S=*Sanskrit;* H=*Hindi*

ācārya S—a scholastic savant and teacher of the religio-philosophical lore; in monastic parlance, the master who ordains the novice as a sannyāsī (q.v.).

adhikārabheda S—lit. 'difference in entitlement'; it is based on the idea that each individual seeker is entitled to a specific approach to religious exercises and to a specific method of meditation, on the basis of his capacity, which again is based on his past saṃskāras (q.v.)

ādiguru S—the first preceptor of a religious order or a tradition, e.g. Śaṃkarācārya of the Advaita school and the Daśanāmī Order.

advaita S—the monistic absolutism in Vedānta (q.v.), systematized by Śaṃkarācārya in the 8th century A.D., who was also the founder of the Daśanāmī Order of monks (q.v.) An 'advaitin' is a person adhering to this philosophy.

ahiṃsa S—non-violence, the abstention from killing and from doing harm to any living being.

anātmavāda S—the teaching which consists in the denial of the ātman (q.v.), i.e. the central teaching of Buddhism which rejects any personality concept.

āratī S—a ritualistic lamp consisting of a handle with five oil-traylets, used for waving lights around the idol or around a saintly person; the act of waving the light.

āsana S—lit. 'seat' 'posture'; any one of a great number of prescribed postures taken during meditation; 'that which is easy and pleasant and by remaining in which the mind remains calm'—is the definition of āsana.

āśram(a) S—a monastery, a solitary place for meditation; also, any one of the four stages of the Hindu's life, i.e. brahmacaryam or celibate studenthood, gṛhastha or the life of a householder and citizen, vānaprastha or the life of a recluse, preparing him for the fourth āśrama, viz. sannyāsa (q.v.).

ātma(n) S—the innermost Self of Brahmin thought. The central personality principle in Vedānta philosophy.

avatāra S—an incarnation of the deity.

bhajan H—a religious song or litany, chanted in groups or individually; any sort of audible worship.

bhakti S H—devotion to a personal deity, a guru, or any divine principle; religious fervour. Hence 'bhakta' a devotee cherishing this intensive emotion.

bhaṇḍāra H—a banquet given to monks and brahmins, where they are fed sumptuously by a wealthy person or by anyone desirous of spiritual merit.

bhikṣā S—alms-food; any food taken by a monk is referred to as bhikṣā; alms in general religious contexts.

bīḍī H—the indigenous Indian cigarette, made of extremely strong, cheap, but pure tobacco.

brahmacārī S H—lit. 'one who walks in the brahman'; a novice, a monastic neophyte; any celibate person.

brahman S—the supreme, absolute spirit; the impersonal, ubiquitous conscious principle. The texts define it as 'sat-cit-ānanda', viz. 'being-consciousness-bliss'. It is the key term of Brahmin philosophy.

cādar H—a long piece of cloth draped around the upper part of the body; the usual orthodox upper garment of Hindu men; the monk's cādar is ochre coloured.

cirañjīvī S—lit. 'long-lived'; some mythological figures who are thought to roam about the earth in their physical body throughout the ages; Hanumān, the monkey warrior of the Rāmāyaṇa, is the most prominent among them.

dāhasarī H—man working on the cremation grounds; they transport and cut wood and prepare fuel and erect the pyres, and make the corpse ready for cremation. They belong to the lowliest caste, as contact with the dead means constant ritualistic pollution.

dakṣiṇā S—the fee given to a priest of a religious teacher for the performance of any ritual or for spiritual instruction and initiation.

dāl H—a variety of pulses, lentils, etc., the staple food of India; it is one of the chief protein sources in the Hindu vegetarian diet.

daṇḍa S—'stick' 'staff'. The distaff carried by some daśanāmī monks (q.v.), covered partly or wholly with ochre cloth; it symbolizes control of body, speech, and mind.

darśan H—lit. 'vision' 'sight'. The act of beholding a saintly, powerful, or any outstanding person, or of a deity in a temple or a dream—in short any actual or imagined vision of a person or object of charismatic value. Having a glimpse at Queen Elizabeth, Pandit Nehru, Agehananda Bharati, Nikita

Khrushev, the God Kṛṣṇa—all these are instances of merit conferring 'darśan'; in a more consummative sense, it is approximately equivalent to the Christian *visio beatifica.*

daśanāmī S—the monastic order founded by Saṃkarācārya (abt. A.D. 720). Its members are the sannyāsīns (q.v.) *par excellence.* They wear the ochre robe, shave their heads completely and lead an anchorite, coenobite, or mendicant life of learning and austerity. The term means 'having ten names', i.e. the order is divided into ten subdivisions (whose origin is disputed). Each daśanāmī monk has the name of his subdivision as his last name, as Giri, Puri, Bhāratī, Sārasvatī, etc. He automatically becomes a member of a particular subdivision on being ordained by a sannyāsī preceptor (ācārya, q.v.) belonging to this subdivision.

dharma S—the religious lore; the totality of duties and observances enjoined by the sacred texts; the Hindu (or Buddhist) religion itself.

dhoti H—loincloth worn by men in northern India. It is a long piece of cloth draped around the waist and tugged between the legs, usually covering the ankles.

dhyāna S—(from which Chinese 'chan' and Japanese 'zen')—non-discursive contemplation, meditation; the meditative stages of yoga (q.v.).

dīkṣā S—initiation of a disciple by the guru; its essence is the imparting of a mantra (q.v.) on the aspirant.

gurdvārā (Panjabi, H)—'the gate of the guru'; the temple of the Sikhs. The sacred book of the Sikhs, the *Guru Granth Sāhib* is placed on the altar in lieu of any other icon.

guru S H—the religious teacher who imparts the mantra (q.v.) to the aspirant and who instructs him on the way to redemption; the most exalted title in the Indian religious tradition.

gurubhāī H—'guru-brother'; any male person initiated by the same preceptor (gurubhaginī or 'guru-sister' being the female counterpart).

haṭha-yoga S—a type of yoga which avails itself of certain physical exercises of a very elaborate order; it gives control over the body and is said to confer occult powers on the successful haṭha-yogī.

iṣṭam S—'desired' 'cherished' 'beloved'; the deity or aspect of the deity chosen by the individual aspirant in accordance with his religious inclinations and talents and his 'adhikāra' (q.v. adhikāra-bheda).

japa(m) S—silent or audible repetition of the name of the iṣṭam (q.v.) or of the mantra (q.v.); one of the most pervasive observances of the Hindu religious life.

javā S—the China Rose. The flower sacred to the Goddess of the Universe (Durgā, Kālī, Śakti, etc.—the spouse of Śiva).

jhāṇam (Pali for Sanskrit 'dhyānam' q.v.).

jilebī H—a North Indian sweetmeat, looking like a miniature pretzel.

jñāna(m) S—the state of wisdom resulting from yoga, the consummation of Hindu spiritual life in general. It is not discursive knowledge, but an incontrovertible, intuitive perception of the total, absolute reality referred to in the sacred texts.

kaivalya S—lit. 'only-ness'; the closest Hindu parallel to the Buddhist nirvāṇa. It is particular type of mukti (q.v.), entailing complete identification with the absolute brahman (q.v.) after total submersion of the ego consciousness in the absolute object. It is the state sought by sannyāsīns and lay advaitins (q.v.).

kāmaśāstra S—the Indian *ars amatoria*; its canonical text is the 'kāmasutra' 'guiding thread of Cupid', ascribed to the Brahmin Vātsyāyana, abt. 3rd century A.D., around which a large quantity of commentative literature has clustered through the ages.

karma-yoga S—the discipline which consists in doing all one's actions and performing one's duties without the desire for their fruits. It is the central teaching of the Bhagavadgītā and has been taken up as the core of Hindu doctrine by Tilak Gandhi, and by most of the protagonists of the Hindu Renaissance.

kaupīna(m) S—the monk's or novice's underwear, which is actually only a sort of chastity belt, tied narrowly around the waist with a string and concealing only the private parts.

khīr H—Sweet milk-rice, flavoured with several condiments. It is the Brahmins' and the sādhūs' classical dainty.

kumbhamela S—the largest assemblies of monks and laymen in an interval of six years, at Hardvar and Allahabad in northern India and at Nasik in Central India. It takes place when Jupiter enters Aquarius.

kūrtā H—of Persian origin, the long-sleeved shirt worn by north Indian men and by Panjabi women; it is worn outside the dhoti (q.v.) or the trousers and reaches down to the knees.

laḍḍū H—a popular northern sweetmeat, of ball shape, with a diameter from 1 inch to 4 inches; it is rich in proteins.

langoṭhī H—loincloth worn by monks and by laymen of certain areas. It is about three yards in length and one yard or slightly more in width and is draped around the waist; it differs from the dhoti (q.v.) in that it is not tucked through the legs, but hangs down loosely to the ankles.

liṅga(m) S—the phallic symbol of Śiva, who can be ritually worshipped only through this symbol. The liṅgam is definitely pre-Aryan in origin; the early Vedic texts rejected its cult, but later canonical texts show that it got completely absorbed in Brahmanical ritual.

mantra S—a sacred, mystical syllable or formula, potent with numinous power. There are meaningful mantras as well as semantically meaningless syllables like krīṃ, hrīṃ, laṃ, etc. The mantra is secret and is imparted to the disciple by the guru; it loses its redeeming force when revealed in any situation other than dīkṣā (q.v.) and in the initiate's meditation. Mantra is somewhat similar to the logos-aspect of the Deity in apocryphal Christian and Neoplatonic thought.

māyā S—a key-word of Brahmin and Vedāntic thought. It is inaccurately rendered 'illusion'; correctly, it means the totality of phenomenal experience and of relative existence, it denotes the qualified universe as opposed to the absolute, the brahman (q.v.). The classical analogy showing the relation of brahman to māyā: a man sees a rope and thinks it is a snake, and he is affected as though it were a snake, unless he realizes its real character: the 'snake' is māyā, the 'rope' is brahman. The scriptural qualification of māyā is 'indescribable'—no proposition about its nature can ever stand unchallenged.

mleccha S—a barbarian, anyone born outside India; the most pejorative term for a foreigner in the Brahmin tradition.

mokṣa S—synonym of mukti; the state of release from bondage, and from the chain of birth, death, and rebirth. It is the most common generic term for spiritual emancipation, and applies to the various types of release described in Hindu, Buddhist, and Jaina doctrine.

mukti S—synonym of mokṣa (q.v.)

Nārāyaṇa S—mythologically, an eptihet of the God Viṣṇu; the personal deity in general. The principle of anthropomorphical hypostasis constantly at work in the Indian tradition: a philosophical principle is partially transmuted into a personalistic image of the deity. The common salute between monks of all orders is 'oṃ namo Nārāyaṇāya', 'praise to Nārāyaṇa'.

navya-nyāya S—the 'new Nyāya'; the reformed school of Brahmin logic. It stands first in the classical enumeration of the orthodox six Brahmanical systems of thought, the others being Vaiśeṣikā (atomistic epistemology), sāṃkhya (a system of spiritual dualism, vd. also nirīśvara), yoga (i.e. Patāñjali's classical school), mimāṃsa (the science of ritual and of the necessary cosmic effects of the ritual), and finally Vedānta (q.v.). Navya-Nyāya set in about A.D. 1600; the classical Nyāya system may be older than Buddhism.

nirīśvara S—lit. 'without deity'—atheistic. The Buddhist doctrine is nirīśvara, and so are several Hindu schools like sāṃkhya, from which the yoga of Patāñjali derived its philosophical framework.

pāṇḍā S H—a temple priest whose function it is to guide pilgrims or temple visitors on their ritualistic routine and to administer the ritual on their behalf; in certain regions, the pāṇḍā keeps a ledger into which he enters the names of the persons and families who have offered worship at his shrine—these ledgers provide an important source for genealogical information.

paṅgat H—a 'line', a 'row'—the commensural arrangement for the monks' meals—they sit either in one row or in several, and food is served on their thālīs (q.v.) or on banana leaves; the meal is spiced by incantations which individual monks chant spontaneously.

pāppaḍam (Tamil)—Hindi 'pappaṛ'; a disk-shaped, highly spiced crisp delicacy made of certain cereals and pulses and baked in oil.

paramahaṃsa S—lit. 'supreme swan'—the epithet of certain highly emancipated monks. The term stems from the mythological notion that this particular bird has the ability to drink the pure milk out of a mixture of milk and water—thus the supremely advanced monk drinks only the pure essence of the absolute, leaving behind māyā (q.v.).

parikrama S—circumambulation of a shrine, a sacred object, or a holy person; the more exact term is pradakṣiṇā, lit. 'walking around to the right', in a clockwise direction.

prāṇāyāma S—an important discipline in the yoga tradition; it means control of the vital forces in one's body. The actual process is a gradual mastery of breath-delayed exhalation, inhalation, and retention of breath constitute the obvious procedure.

prasād(a) S H—food or any other gift ceremonially offered to the deity or to a saintly person; the item is then blessed and redistributed amongst the devotees, and is regarded as having been given by the deity itself. If offered to a sādhū, he usually touches it with his right hand or eats a token piece of it before it is given to the pious.

rasam (Tamil)—'pepper-water', but not just that: a most delicious, hot and pungent concoction of the South Indian cuisine.

roṭī H—wrongly translated as 'bread' in all dictionaries. It is what the British Indian tradition called 'cappātti' with an obsolete term—i.e. the round, flat, unleavened, hot flour-cake which is the staple food of North India together with dāl (q.v.).

sādhanā S—spiritual exercise of any sort. It is a wider term than 'yoga' (q.v.) and denotes every kind of effort toward religious achievement. In its wider sense, every practice, like the artists' etc. is called sādhanā.

sādhū S H—any ascetic, but particularly a monk, a holy man, ordained or lay. The unaffiliated sādhū is called 'svatantra sādhū'; there are anchorite and coenobite sādhūs. The total sādhū—population—if this definition be applied—is estimated between three and five millions.

śākta S—a worshipper of śakti (q.v.).

śakti S—lit. 'ability' 'power'; the cosmic principle of energy, the Greek δύναμις, in Hinduism, apothesized as the supreme goddess, the magna mater, the spouse of Śiva, but often represented as more powerful than the male god. All goddesses, and by extension all female beings are manifestations of śakti. The tantric tradition (q.v.) rests entirely on the worship of śakti as the supreme principle.

śālagrāma S—a natural stone of conic shape, symbolizing the God Viṣṇu. It is the Viṣṇuitic counterpart to Śiva's symbol, the liṅga (q.v.), but has no conscious phallic reference.

samādhi S—lit. 'bringing into one' 'bringing into evenness'. The states of mind in which spiritual equipoise has been reached through yoga and meditation, or through the guru's favour. It is the gateway to redemption from birth, death, and rebirth. As a euphemism, it is used for death when referring to a monk. By extension, it is also the term for the burial mound of a monk or any great man. Thus, Gandhi's 'samādhi' at Rajghat, New-Delhi, is the place where his body was cremated.

saṃskāra S—the rituals and ceremonies of the Vedic tradition, including the daily observances (sāndhyā), marriage, sannyāsa a.o.; the innate tendencies of any living being, which are the direct results of its past accumulated actions and attitudes in previous existences—in this sense, the term comes to mean 'proclivities' 'trends' 'predilections' etc.

sannyāsa S—lit. 'total putting away', viz. complete renunciation of worldly desires and duties, and of the worldly life in general. It is both the state of institutionalized monachism as well as the last of the four successive phases of the Hindu's life, the highest 'āśrama' (q.v.). Sannyāsa is irrevocable.

sannyāsī(n) S—a person who has taken sannyāsa (q.v.).

sastra S—any didactic text, any traditional science, ranging from the art of love to astrology, theology and other subjects of traditional learning.

satsaṅg H—lit. 'assembly of the good'; the most frequent Hindu term for any function where communal worship takes place. Religious sermon, litany, bhajan (q.v.), all these are satsaṅg—programmes. Usually, the assembly is directed by a scholarly and saintly person, monastic or lay. Many hold that satsaṅg is the only spiritual remedy in our corrupt age.

śikhā—the hair-tuft of the upper caste male Hindu and of the monastic novice. It is cut off when a person becomes a monk.

śloka S—the most frequent metre in classical, especially in didactic Sanskrit; a verse composed in this metre, which consists of two himistichs of sixteen syllables each.

śruti S—the canonical texts of the Hindus, thought to be revealed and hence irrefutable, though there is full freedom of interpretation. The Veda, Upaniṣads, and the Brahma Sūtras constitute śruti; it is thought to be self-evident like direct perception and valid syllogistic inference.

swami S H—this is the Anglicized spelling; the correct transliteration of the Sanskrit word is svāmī(n), which means 'master' 'lord', also 'husband', 'lover', etc. As a monastic title prefixed to the monastic name it simply corresponds to 'Reverend' or Hebrew 'Rabbi'—(which also means Master). Any monk who has taken sannyāsa (q.v.) is called 'svāmin'.

tantra (-ic, -ism) S—lit. 'thread'; a category of religious literature, Hindu, Buddhist, and Jain, which centres in a specific mode of yoga (q.v.)—whereas classical yoga eschews the senses and enjoins asceticism as a prerequisite to spiritual success, the tantric tradition enhances the senses, harnessing their force for meditation. The śakti (q.v.) element, which is more or less suppressed in the orthodox Brahmanical schools, gains a pivotal position in tantrism.

tarpanam S—the Brahmin (Vedic) libation of water into water, or any water libation; an important incipient ritual in all Brahmin ceremonies.

ṭhākur H (and Bengali)—'Lord'; an honorific address to any Brahmin including the Brahmin cook; an address to a deity; in the parlance of the Ramakrishna Mission, the term is reserved for Sri Ramakrishna Paramahaṃsa.

thālī H—a circular, pan-like plate, of any metal, with a diameter from 10 inches to as much as 30 inches. It is the Indian dish or plate, and combines the functions of the several plates and dishes of occidental eating in one. It is the most common eating utensil in India, but in the extreme south-west banana leaves are more commonly used.

vākyamidaṃ navīna-yuktiḥ S—'this proposition is a novel argument'.

vedānta S—the most general meaning is 'essence of the Veda', referring to the final portion of the canon, i.e. the Upaniṣads—in this sense it is synonymous with 'Upaniṣad'. In this book, however, V. usually means the systematized theology of Brahmanical India. It is a thoroughly absolutistic Weltanschauung, affirming the existence of a single, impersonal, ubiquitous spiritual principle, the neutral brahman (q.v.), and all other things including the universe have a derived existence, they are manifestations of the brahman. There are three main schools of Vedānta, i.e. radical monism or advaita (q.v.), qualified monism taught by Rāmānuja (11th century) and radical dualism taught by Ānandatīrtha Mādhavacārya (13th century).

vijaya-letter—'vijaya' (S) is the tenth and last day of Durgā Pūjā, the most important Bengali festival, the annual worship of the Goddess Durgā, or Śakti (q.v.) celebrated in September-October. On and around this day, Bengalis write congratulatory letters, notes, and messages in red ink (red being Durgā's own colour) to their friends, relatives, and to all people they care for.

yoga S—controlled meditation on the non-discursive, interiorized theological object. Lit., the word means joining, and is cognate with lat. iugum Gr., ξυγόν, Engl, yoke: the mind is yoked to its object through yogic training.

yogi S H—a person who practices yoga (q.v.).

INDEX